*f*P

ALSO BY STANLEY WEINTRAUB

Aubrey Beardsley: Imp of the Perverse

Whistler

Four Rossettis: A Victorian Biography

Victoria

Disraeli

Uncrowned King: The Life of Prince Albert

Edward the Caresser: The Playboy Prince Who Became Edward VII

Silent Night: The Story of the World War I Christmas Truce

CHARLOTTE
and LIONEL

A Rothschild Love Story

STANLEY WEINTRAUB

The Free Press
New York   London   Toronto
Sydney   Singapore

THE FREE PRESS
A Division of Simon & Schuster. Inc.
1230 Avenue of the Americas
New York, NY 10020

THE FREE PRESS and colophon are trademarks
of Simon & Schuster. Inc.

For information regarding special discounts for bulk purchases,
please contact Simon & Schuster Special Sales at
1-800-456-6798 or business@simonandschuster.com

Designed by Jeanette Olender
Genealogical chart designed by Jeffrey L. Ward

Manufactured in the United States of America

1   3   5   7   9   10   8   6   4   2

Library of Congress Cataloging-in-Publication Data
Weintraub, Stanley.
Charlotte and Lionel : a Rothschild love story / Stanley Weintraub.
p.   cm.
Includes bibliographical references and index.
1. Rothschild, Lionel Nathan de, Baron, 1808–1879.
2. Rothschild, Charlotte de, 1819–1884.
3. Rothschild family. 4. Jewish bankers—Great Britain—Biography.
5. Bankers—Great Britain—Biography. 6. Great Britain—Biography.
I. Title: Charlotte and Lionel. II. Title.
CT788.R64 W45   2003
332.1'092'241—dc21   [B]   2002029994
ISBN 0-7432-2686-0

For Rodelle—my Charlotte

'Tis not for mortals always to be blest.

JOHN ARMSTRONG, Scottish poet and physician

CONTENTS

Mayer Amschel **ROTHSCHILD** (1743–1812)
m. Gutle Schnapper (1753–1849)

Jeannette (1771–1859)
m. Benedikt Moses Worms

Amschel Mayer von [F] (1773–1855)
m. Eva Hannau (1779–1848)

Salomon von [V] (1774–1855)
m. Caroline Stern (1782–1854)

NATHAN Mayer [L] (1777–1836)
m. **HANNAH** B. Cohen (1783–1850)

Isabella von (1781–1861)
m. Bernard Judah Sichel

Babette von (1784–1869)
m. Sigmund Beyfus

Carl Mayer von [N] (1788–1855)
m. Adelheid Herz (1800–1853)

Julie von (1789–1811)

Henrietta von (1791–1866)
m. Abraham Montefiore (1788–1824)

James Mayer de [P] (1792–1868)
m. Betty von [V] (1805–1886)

Descendants of
Mayer Amschel ROTHSCHILD

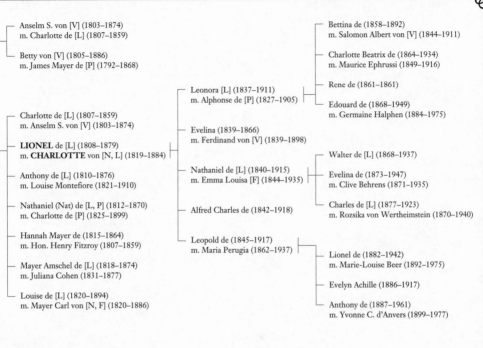

Anselm S. von [V] (1803–1874)
m. Charlotte de [L] (1807–1859)

Betty von [V] (1805–1886)
m. James Mayer de [P] (1792–1868)

Charlotte de [L] (1807–1859)
m. Anselm S. von [V] (1803–1874)

LIONEL de [L] (1808–1879)
m. **CHARLOTTE** von [N, L] (1819–1884)

Anthony de [L] (1810–1876)
m. Louise Montefiore (1821–1910)

Nathaniel (Nat) de [L, P] (1812–1870)
m. Charlotte de [P] (1825–1899)

Hannah Mayer de (1815–1864)
m. Hon. Henry Fitzroy (1807–1859)

Mayer Amschel de [L] (1818–1874)
m. Juliana Cohen (1831–1877)

Louise de [L] (1820–1894)
m. Mayer Carl von [N, F] (1820–1886)

Leonora [L] (1837–1911)
m. Alphonse de [P] (1827–1905)

Evelina (1839–1866)
m. Ferdinand von [V] (1839–1898)

Nathaniel de [L] (1840–1915)
m. Emma Louisa [F] (1844–1935)

Alfred Charles de (1842–1918)

Leopold de (1845–1917)
m. Maria Perugia (1862–1937)

Bettina de (1858–1892)
m. Salomon Albert von [V] (1844–1911)

Charlotte Beatrix de (1864–1934)
m. Maurice Ephrussi (1849–1916)

Rene de (1861–1861)

Edouard de (1868–1949)
m. Germaine Halphen (1884–1975)

Walter de [L] (1868–1937)

Evelina de (1873–1947)
m. Clive Behrens (1871–1935)

Charles de [L] (1877–1923)
m. Rozsika von Wertheimstein (1870–1940)

Lionel de (1882–1942)
m. Marie-Louise Beer (1892–1975)

Evelyn Achille (1886–1917)

Anthony de (1887–1961)
m. Yvonne C. d'Anvers (1899–1977)

CHARLOTTE von [N, L] (1819–1884)
m. **LIONEL** de [L] (1808–1879)

Mayer Carl von [N, F] (1820–1886)
m. Louise de [L] (1820–1894)

Adolph von [N] (1823–1907)

Wilhelm Carl von [N, F] (1828–1901)
m. Mathilde von [V] (1832–1924)

Anselm Alexander von [N, F] (1835–1854)

Charlotte de [P] (1825–1899)
m. Nathaniel (Nat) de [L, P] (1812–1870)

Alphonse de [P] (1827–1905)
m. Leonora de [L] (1837–1911)

Gustave de [P] (1829–1911)
m. Cécile Anspach (1840–1912)

Salomon James de [P] (1835–1864)
m. Adèle Hannah von [F] (1843–1922)

Edmond de [P] (1845–1934)
m. Adelheid von [F] (1853–1935)

Abbreviation	Rothschild House
[F]	Frankfurt
[V]	Vienna
[L]	London
[N]	Naples
[P]	Paris

FOREWORD

"Rothschild" was a household word in Victorian England—even when the house was Windsor Castle. Queen Victoria employed the fabled Rothschild courier service for her most private letters, and Prince Albert borrowed money confidentially from the Rothschild Bank. Lionel de Rothschild initiated Irish relief funding during the famine, helped guarantee the Prince Consort's Great Exhibition at the Crystal Palace, and at Disraeli's request would lend millions to the government on no security whatever to purchase what was in effect a controlling interest in the Suez Canal. To protect the Prince of Wales from drowning in debt, the Rothschild bank, N. M. Rothschild & Sons, discreetly issued a large mortgage on Marlborough House.

Many of Her Majesty's prime ministers prized a place at Charlotte de Rothschild's burgeoning table over dinner invitations to Buckingham Palace. The conversation, the cuisine, and the company were all preferable to the stuffy royal ambience. Yet, sniffing at the *assemblée choisie* of the Prince of Wales, the haughty Earl Spencer as Master of the Household would advise the Queen that her heir "ought only to visit those of undoubted position in society." Charlotte and Lionel de Rothschild were "very worthy people," he conceded, "but they especially hold their position from wealth and perhaps the accidental beauty of the first daughter they brought out." Leonora may have been as ravishing as her mother was at the same age, but she was a Jew.

As Gilbert and Sullivan would put it in song in their *Utopia, Limited*, "a Rothschild" had become a metaphor for ultimate wealth. Admittedly, the family was super-rich. Yet this was a mixed blessing. Even its blessings of relatively aristocratic birth were mixed. For services rendered to the nation, W. E. Gladstone on becoming Prime Minister proposed elevating Lionel to the House of Lords as the head of the great family firm. Lionel and Charlotte were already Baron and Baroness, but the inherited title was Austrian although neither were. In regal third person the Queen expostulated, "She *cannot* consent to a Jew being made a Peer." Then, casting about for an excuse beyond bigotry, she claimed that "however high" Lionel stood "in Public Estimation," what he did in professional life was "a species of gambling . . . on a gigantic scale—& far removed from that legitimate trading wh[ich] she *delights to honour*." Yet had she withdrawn all the peerages she had made of men who actually gambled, or speculated in shares, she would have emptied the Upper House.

Charlotte and Lionel understood that storied birth and fabled wealth could be disadvantages as well as opportunities, and learned the virtues of resilience. It took nearly a dozen frustrating years of election, and reelection, as a Member of Parliament, and of being denied a seat each time on grounds that he would not take the prescribed religious oath, before Lionel could overcome that barrier. "For eleven years," Charlotte wrote in relief, having pressed Lionel to maintain the fight, "we've had the M.P. question screaming in every corner of the house." It was a breakthrough for political democracy.

Perhaps only the marriage of Victoria herself, with Prince Albert of Coburg, had greater implications for England in the nineteenth century than did the marriage of Charlotte von Rothschild to Lionel de Rothschild. Wed in June 1836, a year before Victoria became queen, the Rothschilds, like Victoria and Albert, were betrothed in arranged marriages between English and German first cousins. Both brides were even born in the same year—1819.

While Prince Albert in his short lifetime (he died in 1861, at forty-two) was, effectively, the uncrowned king of England, Baron Lionel was, in practice, uncrowned king of the English financial world, and inevitably the most powerful financier in Europe. They knew and respected each other. Albert dealt with Lionel's firm, and the Baron visited the Palace on business—although seldom socially. And some of the initiatives by which Prince Albert created the reputation he truly earned were sponsored in substantial measure by Lionel.

A second son in a minor dukedom, in a culture of primogeniture, Albert knew that he would inherit almost nothing and that he needed an occupation befitting his birth and class, which at best in his case would be that of royal husband. At his wedding in 1840, the most awkward moment in the ceremony came when he had to profess endowing Victoria with all his worldly goods. No such sweeping offer was part of the marriage liturgy for Lionel, but had it been, there would have been no cause for laughter. In 1836 he was the wealthiest newlywed in Europe.

Both men would struggle against inevitable political disfavor—Albert for being a German, Lionel for being a Jew. Both overcame their disabilities, and in neither case was this easy. They were patient and persistent. Further, they had the staunch support of shrewd, powerful spouses.

Sophisticated connoisseurs of art, each nevertheless acquired an expensive collection he had not seen. Albert's acquisition, worthy of the National Gallery, where many of the pictures are now displayed, came not because he coveted it, but because a hard-up Austrian cousin had persuaded him to cosign for a loan—with Lionel—on which his cousin defaulted. Lionel, whose pictures included major Old Masters, once bought a huge Netherlandish collection, sight unseen, from executors of an estate eager to sell it off. He could afford it: Lionel could afford almost anything. And like Prince Albert, Lionel knew the artists' reputations.

Despite the parallels, their spouses were dramatically different. Never exploiting her position, Charlotte was as private as Victoria was proud. Although recognized as a great beauty, Charlotte posed only twice for a painter, the second time only to showcase her young family. She permitted few photographs. Short and plump, Victoria—although realizing she was no beauty—was one of the most pictured women of her time. Court painters were not paid in golden guineas for scrupulous accuracy, and cameras would expose their bankable discretion.

A great lady in her special domain, Charlotte entertained many of the powers in the kingdom, but never the Queen. Yet Victoria's closest friends in her royal household were often at Charlotte's sought-after salons. A celebrated hostess (who seldom dined out), Charlotte thrived in the company of the politicians, diplomats, writers, and social lions crowding her elegant drawing rooms. And Lionel, whose brother Nat in Paris owned the Château Mouton vineyards, made certain that with every course a vintage wine for the occasion was served. When the Queen dined at great houses, the cost of entertaining her entourage came close to bankrupting her hosts. Many invitees dreaded dreary dinners at Windsor or at Buckingham Palace with the Queen. She downed her meals with gusto and with alacrity, while guests were encouraged to entertain her with talk. Yet when her own dishes were removed, so were all the others, laden with food often frustratingly untasted. No such anxieties occurred at the Rothschilds' Piccadilly House or Gunnersbury Park

At home, Charlotte kept a diary in her native German, but she wrote and spoke English with flair. Victoria spoke perfect German in the privacy of her household, for better rapport with Albert and to confound curious servants, but she almost never wrote in German other than to use a few colorful phrases, which come off less so in translation. Charlotte also disdained jewelry, wearing very little of it although her bank account could sustain any bauble available for sale;

Victoria wore rings on almost every one of her stubby fingers and so coveted jewels that her senior uncle, the King of Hanover, had to sue her to recover gems he had inherited from her royal predecessor, William IV. Both disdained high fashion—Charlotte because after her first years of marriage the matter was of no interest to her; Victoria because she assumed as she aged (and this turned out inadvertently to be good public relations) that dowdy clothes became her better than fashionable garb.

After Charlotte's death (shortly before Victoria's Golden Jubilee on the throne), her eldest son named a block of flats he had built for the poor "Charlotte Buildings," which very likely would have pleased her. Her social conscience motivated much of her life. Since Victoria's teenage days as a princess, a plethora of islands, cities, provinces, bridges, streets, lakes, and waterfalls had been named for her. Charlotte was uninterested in geographical or any other kind of fame. Even the most significant book she wrote was published anonymously, and the unidentified copy in the British Library is shelved with its pages still uncut. If Charlotte lives in memory, it is because of who she really was.

No buildings or bridges or anything else bears Lionel's name. What he accomplished in his time, and how he met his own tests for himself, seemed sufficient for him. Thus the pages that follow evoke a marriage of mixed blessings rather than a financial empire. The book is also about the couple's character. Although Lionel was once tempted to do something utterly unworthy of him, and potentially embarrassing, he drew back in time. Charlotte kept whatever asperity was in her—and there was plenty of cause—within her sparkling private letters. Never entangled in the notorieties of the overprivileged in their orbit, Charlotte and Lionel are a rare exception to Shakespeare's adage that "greatest scandal waits on greatest state."

In working on biographies of Disraeli, Queen Victoria, Prince Albert, and Victoria and Albert's errant son Bertie, the Prince of Wales, I found myself often in the elegantly maintained Rothschild Archive, now housed again, appropriately, in the family bank on St. Swithin's

Lane, its site in the City of London for nearly two centuries. Charlotte and Lionel, I realized, were not confined to the edges of Victorian life, but were integral to it. And there was high drama for both—and for us—as well. They had earned their own story.

Here it is.

Stanley Weintraub

CHAPTER ONE

INVESTING IN A BRIDE

1808–1836

"[I] have to thank you for my fair bride," Lionel Rothschild wrote to his mother, Hannah, from Frankfurt on May 15, 1836. Charlotte was clever, beautiful, and sixteen. Lionel, the eldest of Nathan Mayer's four sons, was already twenty-seven. Although they were first cousins, Charlotte hardly knew him. There weren't many alternatives for the world's wealthiest Jews if they wished to marry within their faith and maintain their status. Lionel might have been surprised by his own reaction, since theirs was an arranged marriage that could easily have failed to please either of the pair.

The betrothal was no surprise to the shrewd and formidable Hannah Cohen Rothschild, wife of the richest man in London. She had arranged it with the elegant, society-focused Adelheid Herz von Rothschild, spouse of Nathan Mayer's brother Carl (or Charles), head of the Naples branch of the banking octopus. Their primary home was in Frankfurt, where Adelheid stylishly entertained many of the prominent non-Jewish families, who seldom if ever reciprocated the invitations.

Adelheid knew a good, even a grand, match when she saw one. Yet she wanted no wedding before her daughter, however precocious, was seventeen. Dark-haired and dark-eyed, dreamy and inexperienced, Charlotte had learned about life largely from books and had been protected from other suitors.

The family had been prominent for just two generations. There were nineteen grandchildren of the founding father, Mayer Amschel Rothschild of Frankfurt. Eight would marry one another. Five others married within the family but across the generations. Two never married. Only four (all daughters) "married out."

The family patriarch, Lionel and Charlotte's grandfather, had begun his startling career as a teenage money changer and coin dealer in the Grand Duchy of Frankfurt, and gone on to create one of history's greatest banking dynasties. Mayer Amschel had died a very rich man in 1812. His venerable wife, Gutle, now in her eighties, exhibited her rejection of every vanity by stubbornly refusing to leave the old Jewish ghetto, the narrow, grimy Frankfurt Judengasse. Much of her life had been spent in the *Stammhaus* "*zum grünen Schild,*" where the family firm had first thrived. The unpretentious house "of the green shield" hints at how the family got its name. In the 1560s a predecessor named Isak lived in a house in the ghetto identified as "*zum roten Schild*" from the symbol on his door. After legal surnames were mandated, the identification survived changes of address in the Judengasse, even new doorway symbols of a *Hinterpfann* (warming pan) and, finally, the green shield. Charlotte's father, the most handsome of Mayer Amschel's sons, had relocated, once anti-Semitic laws eased, to a mansion and a country house befitting his income and style. (He had another home in Naples.)

Four of Mayer's five sons had prefixed to "Rothschild" the posh German *von* or the French *de*, thanks to baronies granted by the Austrian Emperor in 1822. Only Nathan Mayer, in London, ignored the title, taking public pride in being simply "Mr. Rothschild." But in

1825, harboring private second thoughts about the cachet of the barony in class-conscious England, N. M. applied to the Royal College of Arms to register it. Since he had only "denizen" (permanent residence) status and was not a citizen, he was denied use of a foreign honorific. Such technicalities were ignored by Hannah, Nathan's wife, who called herself Baroness de Rothschild although she knew she had no legal basis for it. N. M. made a virtue of being an unpolished but acknowledged gentleman, a condition which money could buy.

With or without the aristocratic prefix, Lionel would inevitably succeed as head of the nearly mythic English branch of the firm at New Court, St. Swithin's Lane, notable for having bankrolled the Duke of Wellington's armies which defeated Napoleon. (Nathan had, perhaps too hastily, turned down a knighthood in August 1815 which recognized his achievements.) Born on November 22, 1808, in rooms above Nathan Mayer's offices at 2 New Court, Lionel was the second oldest of seven children, and the oldest of four boys. The family lived among so much bullion stored in the living area of the building that, according to an obituary decades later, "the family literally walked on gold." According to malicious gossip, Nathan kept pistols under his pillow to secure his person and his fortune. He never did, but it was useful not to deny the rumor. Below their apartments, Nathan, having become a financial magnate, was alleged to have received an unnamed prospective client whose self-importance it was necessary, for business reasons, to diminish. Since the great dispenser of state loans was still busy, he advised, at first kindly, "Take a chair."

"But I am—" interposed the visitor.

"Take two chairs, then," said Rothschild.

Lionel grew up in the years after the Napoleonic wars that had prompted the large state expenditures for which, across Europe, the Rothschild brothers were relied upon for their efficiency and their probity. Yet wealth and status opened no public school doors for Nathan's four sons in England. But for boy cousins in Europe, and his younger brothers at home, Lionel had no companions in London and grew up shy and withdrawn in a household of strong-minded parents. Lionel's and his brother Anthony's first tutor, in 1815, when they were seven and five, was a Pole who strode about their home schoolroom in a tall hat and with a cane stuck into one of his tall boots. When he failed to work out, Nathan replaced him with a mentor named Garcia, apparently a Sephardic Jew, once a book-keeper, who was subsidized to set up an academy at Peckham, where the boys became his first charges.

At home the stocky, balding Nathan Mayer offered himself as an implicit model. Already able to purchase whatever material pleasures life offered, his sons in their early teens needed, Nathan thought, the spur of competition and risk, and the sense of joy in hard work. That was how one maintained success in business and made it grow. "It takes ten times more cunning to preserve a fortune," he preached, "than it does to make it, and the task requires sacrificing body and soul, heart and mind."

Admonishing the young Nathan Mayer for the untidy state of his accounting books, his father in Frankfurt had once warned that "lack of order will turn a millionaire into a beggar." Everything that Nathan now did was brusque and efficient. There was no small talk, even with his four brothers. The Prussian ambassador, Alexander von Humboldt, took sardonic delight "in the combination of bad man-ners, sharp wit and lack of deference which Nathan brought to polite society." N. M. (as he preferred to be known) considered deference as akin to insignificance, and skill in dealing as akin to nerve. Although not as insensitive as he preferred to be characterized, he once told the music master of one of his daughters, as he jangled the coins in his pocket, "That's my music."

In the ruthless mercantile world of the City, where financiers were segregated into interest groups, each was allocated a pillar area on the trading floor of the Royal Exchange. Jews received the remote right-hand corner column. Nathan did not intend to be that obscure. In the bullion crisis of 1825, the Rothschilds maintained the solvency of the Bank of England. Without "old Rothschild," the Duke of Wellington conceded, "the Bank must have stopped payment." Later, in 1835, Nathan made possible the end of slavery in the British West Indies by raising, together with his brother-in-law Moses Montefiore, £15 million. It was a riskily immense sum, one that enabled the government to compensate slave owners for freeing their chattels. Nathan's faith in the stability of the government proved justified when the former slave owners bought government bonds with their payments, and the public's imagination was again fired by the Rothschild house's interest, whatever its profits, in the public good.

While Wellington had long been in Nathan Mayer's debt for services rendered, both civil and military, his friendship had its political limits in an age of open discrimination against Jews. As prime minister, he was urged to follow parliamentary emancipation for Catholics with legislation permitting Jews to sit in the House of Commons. Isaac Lyon Goldsmid, who, with Moses Montefiore, led the Jewish Association for Obtaining Civil Rights and Privileges, tried to persuade Rothschild to join in an appeal to the great duke for alteration of the oath. (To sit in Parliament, one then swore "upon the true faith of a Christian.") When Montefiore reached Rothschild on the road from Stoke Newington on January 29, 1830, N. M. was in a carriage with Lionel and Anthony. Montefiore explained his mission and then changed conveyances with the boys to parley further with Nathan as they clattered on.

Soon after, Rothschild met privately with Wellington, appealing to the Duke, "God has given your Grace power to do good—I would entreat you to do something for the Jews." The Duke, whose prayers had often been answered by Nathan, replied that although God bestowed benefits in moderation, he would at least read over the petition. Finally, Wellington allowed the motion to provide an alternative oath to be presented in the House of Commons that April by Robert Grant, M.P. for Norwich, and to be debated. It narrowly lost. Even had it succeeded, it would have been overwhelmingly defeated in the hidebound Lords. The next year, Montefiore persisted and went with his wife, Judith, Hannah's sister, to visit Nathan for discussion of further strategies. N. M., according to Montefiore's diary, "said he would shortly go to the Lord Chancellor and consult him on the matter. Hannah said that if he did not, she would." Although Lord Brougham would have spurned an audience with a woman, the episode reflected Hannah's activist impulses. The oath was a stumbling block to Jewish acceptance by England's democracy that would become a major challenge for Lionel.

At a meeting of the Board of Deputies of British Jews on April 16, 1829, N. M. appeared by invitation and reported that he had consulted with Wellington and the Lord Chancellor "and other influential persons . . . concerning the [legal] disabilities under which Jews labour, and recommended that a petition praying for relief should be prepared, in readiness to be presented to the House of Lords whenever it may be thought right." But Nathan advised that it would be politic that only English-born Jews should sign, which excluded him. The deputies asked two not of their number to add their signatures, Isaac Lyon Goldsmid and young Lionel, who was barely of age. The appeal would fail, but the episode was an introduction to an issue that would have an impact on Lionel's life for the next three tumultuous decades.

Nathan Mayer's usual brash manner, described as "a licence allowed to his wealth," was often toned down by secretaries to whom he dictated letters, but his impatient exchanges with his brothers in Frankfurt and Vienna remained uncensored. One of his agents, Meyer Davidson, Hannah's brother-in-law, a connection which permitted him some courage, once wrote to Nathan, "I have to confess, dear Mr. Rothschild, that I was embarrassed for your own brother [Salomon], when I found these big insults in your letters. Really, you call your brothers nothing but asses and stupid boys. . . . It makes your brothers quite confused and sad." Nothing would change.

After Garcia's efforts at schooling, N. M. employed an English tutor, John Darby, who remained with Lionel until he was eighteen. In 1827 he took Lionel and Anthony on a tour of central Europe, from

Frankfurt (where their cousin Charlotte was a child) through Prague and Vienna, and home via Baden, Strasbourg, and Hanover. En route they attended lectures at Heidelberg and Göttingen and in Weimar met gaunt old Goethe. Anthony then returned to Strasbourg to study in company with his brother Nat, who was two years younger, while Lionel assumed his hereditary vocation in London. His mother Hannah was already thinking of a proper match for her son. Lionel's older sister, another Charlotte, had recently married Anselm, Salomon von Rothschild's eldest son. Their uncle James, the first to marry within the family, at thirty-two in 1824, had wed his sophisticated nineteen-year-old niece Betty, Salomon's only daughter.

The other family practice, begun with Anselm, was to initiate a son in his home Rothschild bank (in his case, Vienna), send him to apprentice at a brother's branch, and then test him on a foreign mission (Anselm's was Berlin, the Prussian capital) before settling him down in one of the five houses. When Lionel's educational tour ended, he returned to St. Swithin's Lane to take temporary command—"Lieutenant General," quipped Uncle James—when Nathan Mayer left for Frankfurt, to a partnership conclave of the brothers. Possibly the first suggestions for a *shiddach*—Yiddish for "marital match"—between Lionel and Charlotte arose then, although neither party would know of it. Lionel was eighteen; Charlotte only eight. "You are the General now all on your own," James then wrote encouragingly from Paris before departing by carriage himself, "and you will no doubt attend to business very nicely." A few days later he wrote again to persuade Lionel to "make some nice business deals" while his father and mother were away, to validate that he was becoming "a clever and good businessman."

Learning the counting-house routine was insufficient for Lionel's energies. Like his younger brothers, he loved to ride, and in 1828, despite a regulation which made Jews ineligible, Lionel applied to serve in the London and Westminster Light Horse Volunteers. By a considerable majority the regiment voted that August to repeal the Christians-only rule, and Lionel's name appears next to last (probably the order of admission) on the original roll of the Volunteers. Reversing religious bias could be accomplished, he learned, but the next time, the effort would take much longer.

From Frankfurt that August, Hannah wrote to Lionel while "Papa and his brothers with Anselm" were deliberating the renewal of the "perfectly *secret*" partnership contract "in the Tower in the Garden" at Amschel's home. Sending both professional and personal guidance, she announced her satisfaction (and his father's) with Lionel's handling of "the important concerns of the Counting House," but counseled that he was to drive home from the bank "in a close carriage as open ones are very liable at any time to give [one a] cold, particularly so when the atmosphere is wet and changeable." The unwelcome motherly advice was curiously at odds with his expectations to ride—in whatever weather—with the Volunteers.

The London Rothschilds were the chief benefactors of the Jews' Free School in Bell Lane, Spitalfields, near Bishopsgate in the City. At Hannah's instructions, Lionel was to order their supplier ("as usual") to have school uniforms made for the children at her expense before she returned ("I cannot say when we shall"). With her were Anthony and Nat, on leave from their studies. Nat, she reported, was "very much grown and is the exact height of Papa." After both boys accompanied their parents back to London, Anthony would return for an apprenticeship in the Frankfurt firm, something spared Lionel. Hannah went on to talk of tea at the home of his Aunt Adelheid—Lionel's future mother-in-law—and of Adelheid's sister and her daughters, one "a pretty little girl." There was not a word about Adelheid's own Charlotte.

A daughter of the London banker Levi Barent Cohen, Hannah was that rare wife then, even among Rothschilds, who was a savvy financier, however informal her position at New Court. For years she traveled not only with N. M. but on her own for the family firm. Her businesslike letters to her husband were devoid of endearments (although their relationship was devoted and warm). She usually addressed him in such correspondence as if he were a colleague rather than her husband. In a letter from Paris at the time when the troubled Dutch-controlled provinces that became Belgium were to be separated, she wrote, "I suppose in England this fall [in bonds and shares] will cause some alarm but there is no occasion [for apprehension] as it appears more of a financial [matter] than a political one. You must look at it coolly, dear Rothschild." When Lionel, on an apprenticeship to Paris, failed to write his daily update to his father in London, she admonished Nathan Mayer gently while away herself early in July 1830, "My dear Rothschild your letters of today are rather grumpy. Lionel did not write on account of Saturday [being the Sabbath] but I hope you are now quite satisfied that we do not neglect an opportunity [for investment]. . . . Today the reports are of a much brighter cast and the [government] funds also are assuming a better appearance." She advised "more patience" in waiting for higher yields.

In addition to filling in at the efficiently run counting house at de Rothschild Frères, Lionel would undertake missions to Brussels, where the family quickly became the dominant financiers to the new nation, and to other capitals. In London, one of Lionel's sisters wrote, he was already "a complete man of business." Before departure for New Court from 107 Piccadilly he would "pay his respects in the morning and we do not see him again until dinner at 7." His brothers often called Lionel, jovially, "Rabbi"—which had no religious significance but suggested his role as their senior and their exemplar.

New Court had been the family's City residence, above the bank, until N. M. rented 107 Piccadilly in 1825 from banker Thomas Coutts, purchasing the ninety-nine-year lease on March 31, 1831. Despite social prejudice, civil disabilities in England for Jews were comparatively unburdensome. Although a statute barring Jews from purchasing property was not rescinded until 1845, it was no longer enforced. By 1804, when Nathan was granted denization, he had owned property in Manchester and would soon, in London, have not only his establishment at New Court but a suburban eight acres between Stoke Newington and Stamford Hill.

If the evidence of William Armfield's family canvas of 1821 is reasonably genuine, Lionel grew up in a warm home environment. While the apartments in the bank off St. Swithin's Lane were kept for convenience, the spacious house with large garden at Stamford Hill, on the River Lea, which flowed south into the Thames at Blackwall, was an easy commute for N. M. Just above Stoke Newington, north of Islington and Hackney, where prosperous Jewish families had begun to build homes, Stamford Hill, across the river from Walthamstow, offered country air. N. M., no collector of art although Hannah had a favorite by Bartolomé Murillo and would acquire more pictures, displayed in his drawing room the portraits of sovereigns with whom he had done business. Some had gratefully presented him with their likenesses—the kings of Holland, Portugal, and Prussia, and the Tsar and Tsarina of Russia. Possibly originating with such canvases may be the apocryphal story (also imputed to James) that when Rothschild was asked by a journalist whether he would like to become king of the Jews in a restored Palestine, he said, "Oh, no! I would rather be a Jew of the kings than a king of the Jews."

In the Armfield group portrait in the contemporary anecdotal tradition, the family dog is chewing N. M.'s hat—Nathan is bald, but for a fringe—while Mayer (then "Muffy"), only three, tries to pull a letter from his father's hand, possibly symbolic of the banker's seldom leaving business entirely to his hours at the bank. Legs comfortably crossed, he sits in a favorite armchair. To add further narrative, the artist shows Hannah dropping her bonnet at the feet of their eldest daughter, Charlotte. By 1825 there was a third Charlotte, in Paris, the eldest daughter of Uncle James. Names would repeat themselves among the Rothschilds.

Lionel's uncle Amschel had acquired his house beyond the Frankfurt ghetto in 1811, before the Napoleonic liberties were suspended with the Emperor's defeat and exile. Although Jewish civil rights in Germany receded, the commercial importance of Amschel's brother Carl made it possible for him to purchase his own house in Frankfurt in 1818, just before Charlotte was born. Yet Lionel noted in a letter home in 1827 with some bitterness that the Habsburg domains he had visited remained even more rigidly restrictive than the disparate states of the German Confederation. "Jews are very much oppressed, they can hold no situation under [the] Government, nor possess any land property, not even a house in the town . . . and must have permission to hire lodgings." His uncle Salomon, even as a friend of Prince Clemens von Metternich, who ran the regime of Emperor Francis (which borrowed large sums from Salomon's Vienna branch of the firm) needed permission to rent hotel rooms in the Renngasse. Eventually he leased the entire building. Not until 1842 could he buy the hotel, long his home, outright and, for good measure, the adjoining house.

Lionel's education had ended at twenty, when he began writing business letters for his unschooled father and self-schooled uncle James, whose English and French were often harsh and awkward. Lionel was back in London when an improvised and largely placid "bourgeois revolution" unseated the incompetent Charles X of France and his corrupt court. Through the family courier system, Nathan in London and his eldest brother, Amschel, in Frankfurt, learned the news from James in Paris before foreign governments learned of it. As French financial markets struggled to survive, James, as his own sons were only children, sent anxiously to Frankfurt for young Anselm—"as he really has character." Then Baron James asked also for Lionel, writing N. M., "Should you, dear Nathan, not need him you know how much pleasure it would give me to have him work here with us." James was even willing to apprentice one of N. M.'s younger sons, "whom I always treat like one of my own children." Business, he confided, was at a standstill, but he hoped to turn the new "July Monarchy" to his advantage.

To Nathan in London Lionel reported on July 31, 1830, "The streets are crowded with persons, all laughing and as gay as if they had come from some dance." The Garde Nationale had surrendered their arms and marched off to the cheering of Parisians wearing red, white, and blue revolutionary cockades and waving "three-coloured flags." In case troops loyal to the King tried to put down the insurgents, Lionel wrote, "in the Boulevard & streets every hundred yards the fine large trees [were] cut down and the pavement taken up & piled against them & [also] broken doors &c so that nothing can pass." These obstacles, he explained, were "barricades."

Already both a fiscal conservative and a political liberal, Lionel claimed to Nathan that it was a "glorious week for France," as citizens "behaved in a way that will be admired by every person. . . . It will be a good lesson for other governments." Prudently, Uncle James offered his support to the new government and even dressed his son Alphonse, three, in a miniature Guards uniform to show where their loyalties lay. Then luck intervened, and the avowedly liberal temporary regime, needing internal as well as international respectability, offered the post of lieutenant general of the army, and then the crown (in a constitutional monarchy) to Louis-Philippe, duc d'Orléans. Prince Talleyrand, a survivor of ousted regimes, was sent to London as ambassador and proceeded to bank with Nathan.

James managed to ingratiate himself with the new government, although he worried that the "Citizen King" might not last. Financial losses at the rue Laffitte were covered by New Court, but prices kept falling and James worried that the prestige of the firm was falling with its fortunes. "Uncle James is [so] much shaken by the revolution," Lionel wrote to his father on June 18, 1831, "that I assure you he is no more what he was." Although James was "immediately frightened" by events and bought and sold erratically, this was a reaction he never repeated. Confidence was a Rothschild asset.

Until conditions stabilized, the other family houses supported James, with London sending so much silver and gold to Paris to meet obligations at the rue Laffitte that while other financial houses faltered, the French, thanks in part to the de Rothschild Frères connection with the regime, regained some assurance in its stability. While James was dubious that the "Citizen King" could weather further crises, each month became less strained. In France, Lionel (who almost commuted between London and Paris in the early 1830s) received dispatches about Reform Bill turbulence in England with concern that the political unrest he still saw in France would leap the Channel and affect New Court. From Paris in 1831, realizing that the English establishment soon would have to compromise on political change or face something much worse, Lionel told his parents, "I am very pleased to see that this [future] Reform Bill has had a little effect on the aristocracy. It is a good thing, [as] some of these great persons were really insupportable." If the bill passed, he suggested, "it will have the same result as the revolution here"—and he predicted with more optimism than was warranted, on the basis of the French example, that the great gulf between the classes insisted upon by the aristocracy "will soon be done away with, & the society in England will be more like that here, which is by far more agreeable." Yet, thinking also like a financier, he added that if "in England the king gives the people more than their rights," it could have "bad consequences."

As confidence returned to Parisians, life became more agreeable for Lionel and for the rue Laffitte. "The newspapers write so much about the ministers speculating with us," he confided to Nathan and Hannah on August 19, 1834, "that they don't like to receive us [in their offices] every day." Working for Uncle James was an education, but Lionel rejected his forthright and clever uncle as a role model for an Englishman. Never a French citizen, James thought of himself first as a Rothschild and second as a Jew. Although James never lost sight of the traditional religious observances, he was more loyal to Judaic spirit than to the letter of religious requirements. During Passover in 1829, while James kept de Rothschild Frères open to keep business from going elsewhere, Lionel pointedly would not turn up, and when his brother Nat worked at 19 rue Laffitte during Passover in later years, he wrote home that "although we go to *shul*"—synagogue—"and eat *matzot*, in Paris it is impossible to shut up shop." A cosmopolite in France was safer and freer than was a Frenchman, or too overt a Jew.

Lionel had also learned under James that he was in one of the most hazardous of occupations and that it was vital to enjoy its rough-and-tumble, as, having been born to it, he could never escape it. But for the singular episode of fright, James savored every moment.

Following the stormy French years, Lionel was posted to Madrid to watch over Rothschild banking interests there, which soon ranged from loans to the government to the monopoly of mercury extraction in Spain. As merchant—rather than deposit—bankers, the family firm dealt with governments and their rulers, and rarely with a private individual. In chronic financial difficulties, the Spanish government had put its interest in the Almadén mines up for auction, and Lionel, with more authority than the resident Rothschild agents, outbid the competition. The mines were a major world source of "liquid silver," crucial to the refining of precious metals, and the firm often dealt in bars of gold and silver. In the tightest of times nothing kept its worth like the real thing.

For services to Spain, in 1835 Lionel was awarded the Order of Isabella, named for the queen of Columbus's time. (It was Ferdinand and Isabella who had expelled the Jews from Spain in 1492.) He also expanded his education in more earthy directions. For discreet amorous flings, Spain was even more attractive than France, where Uncle James seemed to know everyone and everything. In Madrid he enjoyed his seasoning on his own as a banker, and his extended bachelorhood happily remote from his father. He admired N. M. greatly, but Nathan was also an irascible counting-house autocrat. Distance kept them close.

To Anthony ("Billy"), already the stud of the brothers, Lionel confessed, hoping to delay the betrothal journey to Germany that would end his independence, "I will do whatever my parents and uncles think best about staying or returning. If Uncle Charles [Carl Mayer] is gone to Naples, it will not be necessary for me to go soon to Frankfurt a few months earlier . . . as I have no particular fancy to get married just immediately; a few weeks earlier or later makes no difference without our good parents' wish to go to Frankfurt [for a wedding]." He saw no urgency in sealing a cousinly engagement.

No sensitive foreign assignment for the family firm seemed likely to be as awkward for Lionel as courting an arranged bride. His choices of a spouse were as severely limited as those of any monarch in Europe—perhaps even more so. His alternatives, realistically, had diminished to zero. Lionel's amorous propensities had been easily and anonymously satisfied away from London (as James's letters hint), but he was expected to marry a Rothschild and, accordingly, keep the family's vast multinational operations financially uncomplicated. No other female cousins were Rothschilds of marriageable age.

Now that Lionel's contented bachelor life was ending, he realized with concern that although his mother and his aunt had come to an understanding before their children had done so, the allegedly lovely and accomplished young Charlotte could still withdraw. If Lionel did not suit her, she would soon have other supplicants—even his own brothers and cousins.

Matchmaking at a distance—and distances made communication arduous and slow in 1835—often required, well in advance, the exchange of letters and small portraits. (Photography was a few years away.) Lionel had curly black hair and was passably handsome, but even a contemporary overly boyish likeness suggested that at best he was of middle height. Charlotte was darkly beautiful, as if an authentic child of Naples, and slender and graceful—a portraitist's delight. Lionel was prepared to be an admirer; still, when he saw her, he was smitten. Everything changed. The child he only dimly remembered had flowered into an irresistible beauty. Suddenly, he was ready to relinquish Paris, and even Madrid.

However timid at first, the sheltered Charlotte proved willing. Yet to exchange the known quantity of Rhenish Germany, with a female cousinhood and warm friends at hand, and the sunny warmth and happy vistas of her second home in Italy, which she might never see again, for the legendary fog and chill of England seemed a heavy price for settlement of her future. In gloomy London she could have only what money could buy. Until her seventeenth birthday the next June, Lionel would have to court her beyond mere material things. And that was a problem beyond his experience.

In Frankfurt, a messenger was sent to the Judengasse to inform the venerable Gutle. Determined to survive into the wedding day and beyond, she would live well into the 1840s, and once, memorably, summoned a physician to complain about the inefficacy of his prescriptions. "*Que voulez-vous,*" he commiserated, "unfortunately we cannot make you younger."

"You mistake, doctor," Gutle explained, "I do not ask you to make me younger. It is older I desire to become."

The new Frankfurt senate, of what was now a Free City after Napoleon's fall, had revoked Jewish legal emancipation and restored a demeaning oath for Jews in the law courts. The city fathers had also reinstituted the discriminatory limitation on Jewish marriages, liberalizing the quota from twelve a year to fifteen. Only two of such marriages could be with outsiders. Despite its wealth and influence, the bride's family would have to petition compliantly on behalf of their Charlotte.[1]

With that formality accomplished, Charlotte wrote to a cousin in Berlin on September 16, 1835, to announce her engagement, and from London on September 25, Hannah acknowledged to her future daughter-in-law the "happy conclusion" to the event that she and Nathan Mayer had been anticipating—"that you gave your consent to this union with our good Lionel." She enclosed a pearl necklace "as a token of love." It arrived via the already fabled Rothschild courier service—the most efficient post in Europe, resorted to by crowned heads when they wanted to ensure delivery. Later, Queen Victoria would tell her uncle Leopold I of the Belgians, "My

---

1. The limitation on Jewish marriages within Frankfurt remained in force until 1848.

letters . . . which are of any *real* consequence I always send through
Rothschild which is perfectly *safe* and very quick."

Hannah was the diplomat of the London Rothschilds. Well-
educated and charming, she could have written to her future
daughter-in-law in English, or in German, Italian, French, Spanish,
or *Judendeutsch*—a curious system of writing German in Hebrew
script (akin to Yiddish) often employed by the family for confidentiality. The cosmopolitan Rothschilds needed, and used, them all.
Some of Charlotte's letters to London on Lionel's return could have
been penned in a variety of European languages in which she was
fluent, but for amorous privacy she often employed *Judendeutsch*. On
his return to New Court, Lionel reassured Charlotte awkwardly—
writing letters to young women was outside his experience—that
without her, his life of interminable if unpredictable business would
seem newly tedious. "Here we have seen no young person, not even
of the family—we go home early and go to bed early, and are all day
in the Counting House. Now, Dear Charlotte, let me ask you what
your occupations have been since my departure. Do you go out
walking often? Your family, your aunts of whom I can tell you many
stories? I must now conclude with my very best love and assurance
that I love you more than ever." In another letter he insisted, now
less stiffly, that he had "no amusement nor occupation, but that of
preparing for and thinking of the happy times when I can call you
Dearest Charlotte mine and mine for ever."

Lionel returned to Frankfurt, and Charlotte, in December to plan
their future in London, which only he could do, as she could not visit
England unchaperoned until she became his wife. Then Lionel left
reluctantly for family business in France, writing afterward that the
"long hard" coach-and-horses drive of thirty-six hours in winter,
"hardly without leaving the carriage," would never have been under-
taken "had it not been necessary to make some preparation for the
only person for whom I would make every sacrifice." He explained
that his temporary residence in Paris now seemed too lavish, but that
Uncle James wanted his associates at the firm to demonstrate appro-

priate style. Living ostentatiously implied Rothschild business success.

Except in Paris, Lionel explained to Charlotte, "such an establishment would appear ridiculous. The first floor, the daily habitation, is nearly as splendid [as the sumptuous ground floor], so much gold that for the first few days one is quite dazzled." The rather cynical playboy had vanished.

Charlotte praised Lionel's attempts at elegant German—he was trying desperately to win her regard—and she responded in both her impeccable English and traditional *Judendeutsch*, in the metaphors of fashionable romantic novels accessible to a girl of sixteen. Very likely weaned on Goethe's passionate *The Sorrows of Young Werther* (1774), which every literate German adolescent still read, she also had at hand sentimental epistolary fiction in several languages—Samuel Richardson's seven-volume *Clarissa*, Jean-Jacques Rousseau's *La Nouvelle Héloïse*, even Ugo Foscolo's popular *Ultime lettere di Jacopo Ortis*, all on love and sexual scruples and marriage. Even the heroine's name in *Werther*—Charlotte—was her own, but Goethe's Lotte has two aspirants for her hand, her betrothed Albert and the melancholy, unlucky Werther, who has only a few weeks of happiness with her before taking his own life in despair. The novel-in-letters inspired sensitive yet sheltered teenage girls to take pen to paper and evoke the Charlotte in themselves.

While Lionel wrote "assurances of my most devoted love" and that he was "as sincere as a man can be," she responded, "My heart is palpitating with joyful emotions," though as yet they hardly knew each other and had little that was real to share. Despite her command of languages, words, she conceded on January 8, 1836, "are unavailing to depict the sentiments which pervade my soul"—and she went on to describe the unusual winter sun in Frankfurt glowing over "the still-lifeless trees." He was now her "beloved Lionel," and she confessed, "Oh, how I bewail your having already quitted us!"

On reassignment to Uncle James, where in earlier days he would have felt liberated, he carefully deplored not only the artificial splendor of his lifestyle, but the "most terrible weather" (unlike tedious Frankfurt) and wished he were "already nearer" to his bride. Despite confessing that Paris "never was gayer," he offered Charlotte an epistolary "thousand embraces" and remembered to add, cautiously, "I have not one minute to myself." His most "agreeable occupation" was "writing to [her]," and he had declined "parties of amusement with old friends" because he could not enjoy them without her. Separated from her, he wrote, he wished that he were able to put the right words together to describe his devoted love: "But I cannot; even in endeavouring to do so my pen has fallen from my hand and more than a hour has passed thinking of you, without taking it up." In return she wrote to her "beloved reader"—a novelistic device Charlotte borrowed—that her parents had given a grand ball to celebrate the birthday of King Ferdinand IV of Naples, during which new portraits of the King and Queen were "unwrapped" amid "thousands of flowers." Seizing at further hints from romances, she added, "I did not partake of the amusements of the evening. The possession of a magic mirror would have enabled you to behold in me the melancholy sister of sorrow."

Still struggling for the appropriate romantic language, Lionel confided, "I have so much to say to you and feel so much the want of conversing with you, Dear Charlotte, that my ideas are confused. I begin with the same and end with the same, and then find myself in the same place; if I cannot have the happiness of telling you so verbally within a short time, I shall go mad."

On Saturday evening, January 16, 1836, he sent her "a thousand kisses and the assurance of my for ever devoted attachment and love." The next morning, as his carriages were being packed for his return to London, he wrote that his first priority would be to find a house to let for a year, until she could choose one on her own. Still, sentimental novels intruded into mutual expressions of "attachment," for Charlotte began to question the effect of wicked Paris upon his "constancy." He knew, Lionel conceded from home, "that you have heard many things since my departure but have thought you never could have believed any of them." Then he apologized in another letter early in February for reading reproaches into her lines, but she had already denied everything but affection. "I like to imagine that my letters afford you pleasure, because I always peruse yours with heart-felt joy," she wrote, while her own were only "insignificant, uninteresting epistles." She teased Lionel that she hoped her affection had, in Paris, "enabled you to resist the beautiful Matilda's transcendent loveliness. . . . Love me as I love you, and grant me some moments of happiness in these melancholy days of separation by writing very, very, often to your faithfully devoted Charlotte."

Lionel knew the beautiful, tempestuous grisette of twenty who was called "Mathilde" by her lover, the poet Heinrich Heine, a friend of Uncle James's and frequenter of the rue Laffitte. Heine's liaison with the willful Crescence Eugénie Mirat, who once destroyed his manuscripts in a fit of jealousy,[2] was the talk of Paris, and Charlotte, distant in Frankfurt, knew of it. Even at her age it was difficult to be innocent in the worldly circles of the wealthy, although her own acquaintances were circumscribed by her faith.

Since her primary occupation was imagining her future life with Lionel, her letters were longer and arrived more often than he could write in return. On every day but Saturday—the Sabbath—he put in long hours when back at the London offices in the City. She confessed that her heart had been accusing him of "indifference" when a letter of his arrived, and she contrasted her "agonizing state of incertitude" to his "love and constancy," pledging to love him "as long as I exist." Even when visiting the family counting house in Frankfurt, Charlotte wrote, she indulged in "the agreeable occupation of conversing with you. . . . I only should have reproached you with indifference, for your [too] few lines having caused me to weep for hours,

2. Heine would marry Mathilde, nevertheless, in 1841.

and to philosophize the whole morning on the vicissitudes of human life in general, [and] the inconstancy of your sex in particular." Then his "kind letter . . . again rendered me happy." She was, after all, still sixteen.

Lionel assured her that he could hardly wait to leave England again to prepare for their marriage, scheduled for two days after Charlotte turned seventeen on June 13, 1836. He had already learned of balls celebrating the engagement, given by his future mother-in-law "to amuse the Frankfurt society." Although a Jew's outsider status was fixed and immutable, save by conversion, even the grand *Damen* who never deigned to invite a Jew condescended to come. A Rothschild soiree included the best orchestras, succulent food (even if kosher), and unending champagne, and drew the showiest gowns. Such spectacles were of no interest to Lionel, but he knew that he was likely to be on display himself once he returned to Frankfurt.

In one letter entirely in German, Charlotte assured him of her love *"bis an der Tod"*—even unto death. She knew that she would soon—ceremonially—have to affirm that. In the exchanges through March, in English and in *Judendeutsch*, including reproaches that would not have been out of place in a Jane Austen novel, Lionel hoped that she was no longer dissatisfied with him. He had to confess, however, that the house lease he had negotiated for them had fallen through, but that he was able to close on another, in Hill Street, Mayfair. It was not very large but was, he claimed, "quite neatly and elegantly furnished." The rental was settled just in time. He would return on family business to Paris and then travel to Frankfurt to remain through their wedding.

Charlotte's informal education was winding down. It is unlikely that she had the same tutorials as her three young brothers, Mayer Carl, Adolph, and Wilhelm Carl, which included five science subjects, but she was probably supervised, as were her brothers, by Henri Blanvalet, a French physiologist. He coordinated the tutors and prepared assessments for Carl von Rothschild, who was often away in

Naples, a city Charlotte loved for its lush extravagance. Decades later she recalled her childhood home in Italy as "a paradise on earth," with a garden that was "by far the most wonderful in the world." The diary of her uncle Sir Moses Montefiore records visiting Naples from Malta in January 1828, where he was greeted by the Rothschild family, including Charlotte, then eight. As she grew older, her father wanted her educated in Frankfurt. She spent little but holidays in Italy, which made Naples even more her city of dreams.

Carl's children (at least his young sons) wrote weekly reports for their tutors, while he was less demanding of Charlotte, who would be only a spouse. Still, all Rothschild girls, wherever located and educated, were encouraged "to be useful" to their future husbands. They were even supposed to learn enough about the family enterprises to understand, as Carl explained to Charlotte, how to run a bank. But to be female meant being taught the traditional upper-class subjects of drawing, painting, and music, all of which, like mastery of languages, came easily to her. She read Goethe and Schiller, and very likely Bettina von Arnim's just-published and partly imagined *Correspondence between Goethe and a Child*, having no idea that her future husband had met the great Goethe, or that Heine and Ludwig Börne, whom she also enjoyed, were practically dependents of her uncle James. (In their writings, Heine and Börne brazenly satirized James, who was amused.)

The family planned to gather in Frankfurt not only for Charlotte's marriage to Lionel, but for another conclave of the brothers, to formulate a new configuration of the partnership to accommodate the next generation of sons. A later, scurrilous, article would claim that the real reason for the meeting was that "Nathan [had] conceived the idea of perpetuating the name and power of the house by such consanguineous connections. . . . With this view he called in 1836 a congress . . . at Frankfurt to consider the momentous question. They all favored it, and as an introduction to the settled connubial policy, Nathan's eldest son, Lionel, was united to his cousin Charlotte.

Nathan was overjoyed at the adoption of his matrimonial system."
Nothing in the allegation was true.

The Rothschild brothers would arrive with their families, except
for those essential to keep the five houses going. Though few came
by rail, the new transportation system would soon revolutionize
travel, and the firm's sponsorship of and investments in it would be
profound. Eighteen railway companies had been organized in England in 1836 alone, and a mania for railway stock was beginning, although as yet Nathan Mayer was no more interested than most other
London financiers in what seemed risky investments. At first only
James among the brothers was exploring the phenomenon of the
chemin de fer.

For a traveling companion, Lionel turned to plump, amiable
Gioacchino Rossini, who had become a good friend. Long a Parisian,
Rossini, now forty-four, banked with James—a rare compliment to
an individual from the Rothschild houses. It had been seven years
since the last Rossini opera, the popular *Guillaume Tell.* That April he
was being importuned to accept a commission for a new opera, which
the impresario of the Théâtre-Italien assured him would be his usual
masterwork and create "an ecstasy of joy." Rossini now preferred
composing less demanding music and was planning a holiday trip to
Bologna when the invitation to Lionel's marriage arrived. Only one
other non–family member would be coming, Mayer's German tutor,
Dr. Schlemmer, who was preparing N. M.'s youngest son for Cambridge, which would admit, but not award a degree to, a Jew.

Rossini was delighted to be a wedding guest. James casually sup-
plied the composer's expense account. On the journey out, Rossini
and Lionel went by carriage and by rail from Paris through Belgium
and the Rhineland, through Antwerp, Brussels, Aix-la-Chapelle,
Cologne, Coblenz, and Mainz. Rossini was excited by the luxuriant
banks of the Rhine, the impressive cathedrals they passed, and the
galleries at which they stopped with pictures by Rubens and Van-
dyke. He did not enumerate them, he wrote to his friend Emilio

Loup, "as I should want to have twenty pages. . . . I am truly satisfied with this little trip, the entire purpose of which was to attend at Frankfurt the marriage of Lionel Rotschildt, my very dear friend."

Rossini was anxious about the Antwerp-to-Brussels railway segment. He had heard that boilers sometimes blew, and track beds sometimes collapsed. Nothing happened, but he was so unnerved by the experience that he composed a satiric piano piece afterwards, *Un petit train de plaisir (comique-imitatif)*, which mimicked the clatter of a railway journey and which concludes with a "terrible *déraillement du convoi*," the deaths of two passengers, and the flight of their souls to heaven and hell. At the close, the music turns sardonically happy as the heirs of the victims celebrate their legacies.

More relevant to the occasion was an ode by a local poet, S. Messeritsch, in parallel Hebrew and German texts, on the marriage of Lionel and Charlotte. The lines prophesied the blessings of children and long years of happiness, and invited the citizens of Frankfurt to feel pride in the union of the shoots of a great tree. Another, equally apt, symbol was the family coat of arms; the bride's family had ordered an ornate silver service for the young couple with the family's Austrian arms at the center, surmounted by the entwined monogram "C.L.R." While Rossini mingled with local musicians like Felix Mendelssohn (distantly related to Charlotte through her mother), Lionel prepared for the wedding and his father and uncles began to gather for their negotiations.

The wedding would be solemnized under a canopy in the town residence of the bride, at 33 Neue Mainzer Strasse, an upper-class address on a courtyard once out of bounds to Jewish families. Its greatest moment was to be the materialization, however brief, of the legendary matriarch, the venerable Gutle.

In London the stout pillar at the Royal Exchange at which the bulbous profile of Nathan Mayer was often visible was unexpectedly bare. In Paris at the rue Laffitte the financial courtiers of James Mayer were nowhere to be found. Both brothers were en route to Frankfurt. In temporary charge of the Paris house was Anthony; presiding at New Court was young Nat. Just in case, because of their youth, two of Hannah's brothers, Benjamin and Isaac, now with their late father's banking firm, were tendered power of attorney for Nathan's London house. Everything seemed arranged with proverbial Rothschild organization and efficiency; yet in the suddenly frantic and even incoherent messages from Frankfurt to both young Rothschild brothers the wedding would begin to appear less celebration than catastrophe.

CHAPTER TWO

A WEDDING IN THE COUSINHOOD

1836

Unknown to any of the family, even himself, Nathan Mayer was dying. N. M. was not the eldest Rothschild brother, but his dramatic successes in London had made him the most powerful of the partners. Even James, the youngest and possibly the shrewdest of the five, deferred to him. As the clan began gathering to revamp its working agreement, Nathan expected to preside, yet unless some unanticipated matter arose, every clause had already been negotiated. Fraternal disagreements always faded. The brothers and the new partners to be made of their adult sons understood how absolutely crucial were familial unity and loyalty.

Wedding receptions enlivened every evening early that June at either Carl's or Amschel's mansion, and even at the grandiose residence of Lionel's brother-in-law Anselm. At each, with champagne goblets in hand, guests flowed out into gardens then surfeit in June luxuriance. There Rossini, wit, sage, and bon vivant, flourished in a mélange of languages, while at his hotel at other times he received local musicians who came, in homage, to call on him. Mendelssohn, twenty-seven, and too famous himself to concede any awe, reported to a friend, Heinrich Schleinitz, Rossinian embraces and kisses: "We swore eternal friendship (à la Parisienne)." Rossini "says that he is [so] enthusiastic about Germany," Mendelssohn wrote to his mother and sister Rebecka, "that if in the evening he finds himself on the Rhine and the wine list is given to him, the waiter has to accompany him [back] to his room, as otherwise he'd never find it again. . . . He tells the funniest and most amusing things." Lionel expected Rossini to be the life of the wedding party.

Young Mendelssohn—a child of expedient converts from Judaism—added between galas that he was also charmed by the Rothschilds. "Their splendor and luxury, and the way they compel the philistines to regard them with the utmost respect (though these would gladly give them a sound thrashing if they were let loose!), is a source of exultation to me, because they owe this to their own industry, good fortune, and abilities."

Lionel found the pervasive *Gemütlichkeit* tedious and forced. He was eager to hurry Charlotte back with him. Rather undiplomatically he confided to his eldest uncle, Amschel, at a "diplomatic" dinner, that he would be "most heartily glad" to quit "beautiful Frankfurt" for London. Yet the bridegroom's own family was late in arriving. Those who could be spared from New Court were still crossing to Calais, seasick in rough Channel waters. At Brussels they were met by James, who had left Paris on June 4 with Betty and their brood. At eleven their Charlotte was the eldest. Her three brothers were Alphonse, Gustave, and Salomon—who, at one, was the baby of the cousins.

With Nathan, James paid an afternoon courtesy call on Queen Victoria's favorite uncle, King Leopold of the Belgians, an old friend and a client. Declining his invitation for dinner, as they had their families with them, the brothers planned to continue on early the next day. At court Nathan had struggled to conceal his discomfort. His travel was now complicated by an "old companion, a most disagreeable boil," as Hannah wrote to Anthony from Frankfurt. "The movement of the carriage inflamed it." Nathan was susceptible to painful carbuncles (a staph infection treatable then only by lancing and draining), which the jolting journey from Calais to Brussels had aggravated into an abscess on his buttocks. Then James had to delay his own departure. Chicken pox had broken out among the children. It was an unpropitious prelude to what was expected to be the most joyous event in the history of the already celebrated family.

As Charlotte and Lionel awaited their nuptials, they sat for portraits by Moritz Daniel Oppenheim, then thirty-six, a professor at Weimar (although a Jew) and one of Frankfurt's leading painters. He had studied at Munich and Paris, and at twenty-one had met Charlotte's father in Naples—a connection that led to family commissions. In 1828 he had painted a small dual portrait of Anthony and Lionel when the Londoners were in Frankfurt for a partnership conclave, making the brothers look even younger than their years, and he continued to advise the family on purchases of Old Masters. For the wedding canvases he painted a sideburned, youngish Lionel against an imagined English landscape complete with romantic ruined castle tower; and, to recall Naples, Charlotte was posed pensively against a dreamy background of a smoldering Vesuvius. Behind both are symbolic trees—an orange tree already in fruit and a broad English oak. The romantic climate of the time required a faint air of melancholy, and in retrospect that aura proved insufficiently prophetic.

Conducting business between festivities, Lionel wrote to Nat at New Court, describing the fraternal arrangements of the older generation to be ratified by all five brothers. Their conclave promised to be amicable. "Papa proposes that we should have half the profits of the London House and that he should have only half the profits the others make [at their branches]; everything was agreed to immediately and not a word said [against]. I was not in the room but this morning"—it was June 12—"[I] have heard so. . . . They are all pleased with each other and there have not been any disputes. . . . They are all very satisfied with the cash accounts and did not expect to have seen the Houses so flourishing."

Although the brothers (and Anselm of the next generation) had acquired lavish homes in Frankfurt once ghetto restrictions lifted, the Londoners had been booked for privacy into the Römisch Kaiser; the Parisians were put up at the Russisch Hof; and the Montefiores at the Englisch Hof. Nearly forty of the family would be at the wedding. Assigned to oversee the Paris and London offices, Anthony and Nat complained to each other of their dull lives. "Am not in good spirits," Anthony declared, perhaps to deflect suspicions of Parisian womanizing. ("Billy" suggested his goatish predilections, and soon Mayer would be dubbed "Tup"—a ram.)[1] "Nothing is so disagreeable than to remain alone. . . . How do you amuse yourself quite alone? You are better off than I am for here they have all gone and shut up the house, so I dine every day at a Cabaret."

Nat was less bored, for he was badgered by letters from his father and mother, and instructed as well to prod Anthony into visible activity at the rue Laffitte. Nat also had forty clerks to oversee at New Court, some of them distant cousins, others young men related by cousinly marriages. Family connections helped to get some started in business; several remained comfortably at St. Swithin's Lane all their lives. "Pray let the Clerks have a good dinner," Lionel advised breezily to Nat on June 9, "and get all drunk or if they like . . . I think they might make a party to Greenwich; if some are too proud, let them make two parties and take their better halves with [them]." Greenwich was a popular holiday haunt, known for its restaurant, The Ship. It had become accessible on the London-Greenwich Railway, opened that February, which speeded daring passengers by

---

1. The City Tup, on Gresham Street, a short walk from the Rothschild bank, displays a ram on its pub sign.

steam locomotive at a headlong thirty miles an hour. (Although his father thought it was imprudent, Lionel would invest in railways, as his uncle James was already doing.)

Despite his discomfort, Nathan reminded both sons (through Nat) on June 12 to buy Spanish bonds if on offer, and added, "You must always put Anthony in the way of selling, as he belongs to the Bull party and does not like to sell until you have made some few purchases; therefore when the prices are low you can buy a little and encourage Billy to do business. . . . I have written to him, that every day he must do something[,] whatever may be the price. . . ." On the reverse side, Hannah added, "Papa's disagreeable swelling. Somewhat better today. . . . Papa has spoken about the partnership and half the [New Court] profits to the younger 'Branches' of the London house—believes it will be agreed upon." Lionel wrote to apologize for sending no instructions the day before "as our uncles do not like to see us write on Saturdays." To James it would have made little difference, but Amschel of Frankfurt and Salomon of Vienna were strictly observant. More realistically than his mother, Lionel confided that Papa's boil "persists."

Travel between the branches had become more onerous as the brothers aged. The multinational partnership was also mutating both in management and in nature. Salomon's son Anselm had long been admitted as a partner; now other elder sons, like Lionel, were moving up. As the new politics and the newer technology intruded, the banking houses' transactions had become complex. There were new nations in which the firms were financially involved, like Belgium, and new forms of transportation, like steamships and railways, in which to invest and to encourage. There were questions about sending agents out to the Americas and to Russia. There were recurrent crises in banking centers, the Rothschilds proving more adaptable in emergencies than most of their rivals. But now there was an appalling new crisis, more dire than the family first realized. Nathan—the dynamo of the partnership since the founding father died in 1812—was not going to recover.

No one admitted as much. The brothers now "pass their time," Lionel wrote to Nat, in Papa's bedroom at their sister Charlotte's residence. When Nathan Mayer was more comfortable, they met at the Frankfurt counting house or in one of the other Rothschild homes to dine or chat "en famille"—"dreadful tedious long dinners," complained N. M.'s rebellious daughter Hannah Mayer, who found Judaism itself tedious, rejected every suitor from, or close to, the *mischpocheh* (the family), and would be the first in the family to defect. Although the older women enlivened some of their hours in matchmaking scenarios among the cousins, the girls were discreetly left to reading and to recurrent rounds of embroidery, gossip, and German lessons. Occasionally, they were amused by an unconventional music exercise from Rossini. All the younger women played the piano, some very well indeed. But boredom always threatened.

At first Hannah dismissed her husband's affliction as only a "disagreeable" inconvenience "particularly in sitting down." Nathan had suffered such distresses before. A Frankfurt doctor, reputedly among the finest in the profession, was called in to lance the boil, now a suppurating abscess in an age before antisepsis; and he claimed, complacently, even as the persistent swellings recurred, that (so Hannah wrote to Anthony) there was "no danger." But N. M. remained in obvious danger, and a specialist was summoned. The next day, June 13, Lionel reported to London that the renowned Professor Maximilian Joseph Chelius of Heidelberg, surgeon and *Prorektor* of the *Medizinische Facultät*, had rushed north through Mannheim and Darmstadt, and attended their father. Reassuringly, Chelius declared that "both wounds"—there were now two open infections—were "in a much more forward state than he had imagined." "In fact," Lionel wrote, "he is quite satisfied with the way they are going on and assures us that only time is requisite to see Papa quite restored."

Gritting his teeth, Nathan insisted that the wedding proceed on schedule, and that the grand ball that Charlotte's parents had planned that evening to mark the bride's seventeenth birthday go on, but he was too ill, and the bride too agitated, to attend. Even the signing of the revised partnership papers was put off. Dr. Chelius, who had been an army surgeon during the Napoleonic wars, and whose current and quite irrelevant specialty was ophthalmology, hovered about with his scalpel and furnished what Hannah described confidently to London as "incessant attention." In the grand home of Carl and Adelheid, where a *chuppah*, the traditional wedding canopy, was being erected, final arrangements for the ceremony on the fifteenth[2] overwhelmed everything else, but for concern whether the father of the groom would be able to stand under the *chuppah* with the bridal party.

On the day before the wedding, the marriage contract (in Hebrew, *ketubah*), three pages with nine articles, in German, notarized with a large seal in red wax, was ceremonially signed at the home of Baron Carl Mayer. It spelled out the groom's financial and personal obligations to the bride. Lionel and Charlotte signed first, followed by Hannah and young Mayer, standing in for his ailing father. Adelheid and Carl Mayer signed next, followed by ten others, four of them Rothschilds. One enthusiastic signature, boldly under the large wax seal, was, inappropriately, "G. Rossini." It was a gesture which, when Benjamin Disraeli learned of it later, seemed to have convinced him that Rossini was a Jew.[3] Converted conveniently to the Anglican Church as a boy by Isaac D'Israeli, Ben's father, to open professional doors to him, Disraeli—four years older than Lionel—had dropped only the apostrophe from his name and made no effort to conceal his background or his ethnic loyalties. Anti-Semitism had thwarted sev-

2. June 15, 1836, was a Wednesday, the customary day then for a Jewish wedding, as the next day, Thursday, was the day when rabbinical courts met. Had there been a dispute following the wedding night about the bride's virginity, it would be settled immediately. The marriage of a widow was usually solemnized on a Friday as no such problem was envisaged.

3. In Disraeli's novel *Coningsby* (1844), the mysterious banker and visionary Sidonia explains sweepingly to young Harry Coningsby that many movers and shakers of Europe, as well as its culture heroes, are secret Jews, including several of Napoleon's marshals, and composers like Rossini.

eral tries at a seat in the House of Commons, but he was contemplating yet another attempt. Meanwhile, he supported a flamboyant lifestyle by writing novels.

Before dawn on the wedding day, the "obstinate" Nathan Mayer awakened early, Hannah wrote, "and took courage at 6 o'clock in the morning to get up and walk from their hotel to Charlotte's, which he effected tolerably and afterwards dressed. . . ." (Grüneburg was close to Carl's residence on the Neue Mainzer Strasse.) Then, Hannah added to her son Nat in London, his father was able to walk further "to be present at the celebration of the ceremony." Only N. M.'s stoicism saw him through. "Everything passed off perfectly well," Lionel wrote hurriedly and rather innocently to his absent brothers late that afternoon. "Papa was well enough to come . . . and as his complaint is only one that gives pain, it required but a little resolution, of which you know Papa has enough." The day-long preliminaries, however, were harrowing for him.

How the beautiful and elegant Charlotte appeared as a bride is suggested by the Oppenheim portrait, in which she wears a pale lavender, off-the-shoulder gown with fitted bodice and full, sheer sleeves. A jeweled bracelet adorns her left wrist, and from a hexagonal brooch fall five strands of pearls. Three strands of smaller pearls round her tightly bound hair are anchored by gems on both sides. Lionel is garbed in a formal black suit with waistcoat and bow tie, wearing one glove, with the other clutched in his right hand. Thanks to the tactful Oppenheim, neither shows any sign of the family's anxieties as the actual wedding day approached.

Wedding guests were too distracted by the ongoing and unconcealed drama of N. M.'s struggle to participate in the ceremony to give much thought to the young people to be united in marriage. Disraeli, who saw Charlotte not long after in London, was struck by the dark-eyed Murillo madonna on Lionel's arm. Disraeli seems to have recreated her in his novel *Tancred* (1847) as the Oriental beauty Eva Besso, "young, even for the East," who—like Charlotte—is about to be married to her cousin as the novel opens. Her eyes were like "the starry vaults of Araby," and her "perfection," to Disraeli, was "such as it existed in Eden, . . . and such as it might have been found abundantly and for ever, had not the folly and malignity of man been equal to the wisdom and beneficence of Jehovah."

Although food and drink for wedding guests were served throughout the day, the bride and groom customarily fasted until they shared from the nuptial cup. The ceremony under what Lionel described as "a small temple" (the four-cornered canopy, with posts, of the *chuppah*) ritually began with a brief prayer service, during which the rabbi recited the Psalm of Thanksgiving (Psalm 100: "Make a joyful noise unto the Lord . . .") and read the marriage contract aloud. The bride's veil—a symbol adapted from Genesis, in which Rebekah veiled herself modestly on first seeing Isaac, and later Rachel's veiled sister Leah falsely replaced her[4] as Jacob's bride—was lifted by Lionel, and a goblet of wine was raised by the rabbi for the bride and groom to sip.

Closing, the rabbi shared with bride and groom the ancient formula of marriage from the apocryphal Book of Tobit. As the groom slips the plain gold ring onto the right forefinger of the bride's hand (in Hebrew tradition), he declares, "With this ring you are sanctified to me according to the laws of Moses and of Israel." Following, the rabbi raises a second goblet of wine and chants the Seven Nuptial Blessings, closing with, "Blessed are you, O Lord, who makes the groom rejoice with the bride!" The couple sip again, after which the groom shatters the goblet underfoot to general rejoicing—a ritual symbolizing the transience of life and the imminent breaching of the bride's virginity. (The breaking of the glass had already acquired the

---

4. Jacob, having been required to work for seven years to earn Rachel as his bride, was deceived when the veiled Leah, the less attractive elder sister, was ordered by her father to replace Rachel. Jacob had to labor an additional seven years to earn Rachel—thus the custom of unveiling a veiled bride to ensure her identity.

alternative and more prudish symbolism of recalling the destruction of the Temple in Jerusalem.) The wedding feast would follow before the couple could escape.

What aspects of the ritual were abbreviated to spare the ailing Nathan Mayer further distress are unrecorded. "The ceremony lasted but half an hour and was very solemn," Lionel reported to Anthony and Nat. "[It] went off uncommonly well as Papa was there and our family circle complete." Yet N. M.'s effort merely to stand was an agony. During the ceremony, the tottering Nathan had made light of his difficulties, Lionel wrote, "with jokes of every kind . . . to shorten the speech of the worthy Rabbi and to cheer up those present." But with the solemnities concluded, N. M. was "seized with the excessive pain which usually comes on about 2 o'clock and lasts for six hours." Too ill to remain and blight the celebration, or even to be helped to his hotel, he was assisted after the ceremony to the home of his daughter and Anselm, and put to bed.

At Neue Mainzer Strasse "by candlelight afterwards, a small [and very late] breakfast for religious gents" was served; "and now," Lionel continued, "the ladies are preparing for the dinner which is to take place at 6 o'clock." Despite the seemingly matter-of-fact report, it was a long and terrible day for the dismayed bridal pair. Another urgent summons brought Dr. Chelius and his knife, and in an age when anesthesia was still unknown, Nathan grimly bore further surgery "without a murmur."

Shaken, Charlotte and Lionel hurried off by carriage after dark to the spa hotel at Wilhelmsbad, thirty miles to the east, for their wedding night, arriving at eleven to fulfil the prophecy of the broken goblet. They returned dispiritedly the next evening.

The following morning there were no secrets. "It appears," James reported rather brutally to Anthony at the rue Laffitte the next day, "that the red King would not permit him to spit roast the bird despite the fact that he had caught it in his net." More tactfully, Lionel ("now an old married man") explained to Anthony and Nat, "Till now there is not much to relate as you well know that the fright has generally such an effect upon the young ladies that they are immediately troubled with some thing that pays them very often a visit. I can only say that she is a most beautiful person in every respect." Yet anxieties about consummation probably had less to do with prematurely bringing on Charlotte's menses than the looming presence of the Angel of Death at her wedding.[5]

No one spoke of Nathan Mayer as a dying man, yet in an age when infection often led to septicemia, he was under a death sentence. Implacably, he kept up appearances, dictating instructions for London and parleying with his partners over the draft agreement. Lionel and a lawyer were also present—the son, now, in case the father faltered. The shreds of Lionel and Charlotte's honeymoon were spent gloomily at the Russisch Hof nearby. When he went to the sickroom two residences distant, Charlotte visited with her mother as if she had never left home. For Amschel's Charlotte the torment was far worse. The dying man was her father, and she was early in pregnancy. Soon Hannah moved in to help her distraught daughter, attributing her gratefully received intrusion to the "noise" at the hotel.

As if all were well, Nathan Mayer ordered gold bullion shipped from New Court to Paris, then a further "100,000 sovereigns . . . as money is scarce there." Nat was also "to purchase 200 Danube shares, to sell Exchequer bills even at 7/6; [and] to sell a couple of hundred thousand consols"—interest-bearing government annuity stock. The letter was written by Hannah at N. M.'s direction, but the activity was to suggest that Nathan remained actively in charge, should disquieting rumors arise in the City. Most day-to-day instructions were now from Lionel.

As July came, Nathan was weaker and in great agony. Professor Chelius again returned with his scalpel, Lionel reported to Anthony and Nat, and "Papa underwent the operation with the greatest possi-

---

5. The period of *niddah* traditionally followed—separation during menstruation and for seven days after cessation of the menses when a woman was considered impure and constrained from sexual contact.

ble courage and all the time made jokes. The wound must have been larger than the first as the boil must have been terribly deep and must have been terribly painful." Five days later, on July 14, Lionel wrote to London, "Papa wants 100 bottles of soda water, 20 of lavender water, and a chest of good oranges immediately." Briefly, N. M. seemed his former brash self, but he also asked that his good friend Benjamin Travers, a physician at St. Thomas's Hospital and an official of the Royal College of Surgeons, hurry over. Travers had practiced at No. 4 New Court when Nathan Mayer had taken his lease at No. 2 in 1809. They had been friends since. Travers had already been asked about "poultices," which he advised Hannah frankly were "unsuccessful" as remedies. In 1844 he would publish a monograph, "The Physiology of Inflammation and the Healing Process," and possibly his experience with his erstwhile neighbor was invoked, but in Nathan's case there would be no healing.

On July 21, Lionel hoped desperately to Nat that Travers would soon arrive. Three days later the new bridegroom was summoned by their father. The "uneasy" Lionel told Nat that N. M. now appeared "in danger" and had a "violent fever." Yet their Papa professed confidence "in the Almighty, who has always protected me." He wanted to project a business-as-usual image in the City, as he knew that concerns about New Court could not only damage the family enterprises but affect the European financial world. "He wishes you," Lionel explained anxiously before a courier rushed off with his message to St. Swithin's Lane on July 25, "to go on selling English Securities and Exchequer Bills, as well as £20,000 India Stock more. You are also to send an account of the different Stocks on hand. I do not know if I misunderstood him, but I did not like to ask for an explanation." The bewildered Nat, in his early twenties, was also to sell "the securities that the Portuguese Government has given for the money they owe us, not minding [a loss of] one or two per cent."

The likely costs to the London house would be considerable. Lionel's gloss on N. M.'s instructions made it obvious that he felt their father was too feverish to make sense, but had to be indulged as he lay dying.

Anthony as well as Nat began preparing to leave for Frankfurt. Agents for the firm—in London, two of Hannah's brothers, both bankers—held powers of attorney in the event that no Rothschild was available. The family began gathering round the bedside.

The revised and updated partnership papers, Salomon von Rothschild later told the Austrian chancellor, Prince Metternich, with whom his relations were close, had already been drafted. "Embodying every point," they only awaited signatures, "for we still believed that our late brother would, with God's help, recover. However, this was not to be, fate had decided otherwise." Without altering a word, the brothers loyally signed off on minor amendments to their agreement.

Aware that he was close to death, Nathan Mayer summoned Salomon and told him "all his thoughts and wishes with regard to the will which he then drew up, and which I then had written out in accordance with his intentions." N. M. did have a will on deposit in Frankfurt, but wanted to review his thoughts about it. "Drew up" meant dictated, and he began, formulaically, to Salomon and a notary, "Inasmuch as it has pleased all-gracious God, in His inscrutable disposition, to visit me with sickness at this place, of which indeed through Him, the Almighty, I hope to recover, still, as the lives of all mankind stand in His hand and as I cannot know in what manner it will be His will to call me from this world, so have I thought it proper, now, while I possess my full mental faculties, to make, after due consideration, my testament and therein state what my will is."

Largely coherent, although feverish and in pain, N. M. was firm in his confidence about the family and its future. Much as his revered father before him, he hoped for "harmony, constant love and firm unity." He enjoined his sons to "carry on in harmony and peace the banking house founded by me under my name in London." They were to work in consultation with their mother, soon his widow, whose business sense was acute. "My dear wife Hannah . . . is to co-operate with my sons on all important occasions and to have a vote. . . . It is my express desire that they shall not embark on any transaction of importance without having previously demanded her motherly advice, and that all my children, sons and daughters [alike,] are to treat her with true love, kind affection and every possible re-spect, which she deserves in the highest degree, having shared with me joy and sorrow during so great a number of years, as a fond, true and affectionate wife." He also offered his "earnest wish" that the present association between the London branch and the "other Houses, which my four dear brothers direct, shall be allowed to con-tinue," and that his sons "always willingly . . . follow the advice and recommendation of my brothers."

Although *The Times* on July 27 claimed to its readers that N. M. Rothschild's condition was "not all dangerous," the markets slumped. A week later *The Times* reported, under "Money Market and City In-telligence," that the "dangerous state in which Mr. Rothschild re-mained, by the accounts from Frankfort, has again had its effect upon Spanish and Portuguese securities. . . . [I]t seems generally accepted that the firm would call in all the loans advanced upon those securi-ties by Mr. Rothschild, and hence the anxiety of the borrowers to dis-pose of their stock, so as to be in a position to meet the demands upon them. The sales today were extensive."

Neither Nathan Mayer nor Lionel nor young Mayer knew, in Frankfurt, anything of the precarious financial situation in the City, and in any case, N. M. always thought in the long term. He was al-ready assured that his brothers would renew the London bank's con-tract, in his name, with his sons, for a minimum of five years. "The firm of N. M. Rothschild," Salomon would explain afterwards to Metternich, "remains unaltered, the sons together acting as a unit with one vote in the partnership. The whole trading capital . . . can-not be touched for the next five years, and nobody can draw anything out of the working capital, while we have reduced the interest that we draw individually from four to three per cent, so that the partnership as a whole will, with God's help, still further improve its position."

Further updating his intentions, which remained, essentially, business equality for his sons, he confirmed compensatory legacies of £100,000 each for his daughters. With his two middle sons rushing vainly to Frankfurt, and unavailable for his parting words, N. M., fading, "charged his eldest son, and through him all those who were not present," Salomon wrote, "always to apply all their efforts to keep the business property intact and not to participate in any risky adventures." He urged them to avoid "evil company" and keep in the path of "true virtue, religion and righteousness." They were to be wary of being exploited, and of being jealous of each other. "Whether any son had £50,000 more or less, was a matter of indifference to him. All that mattered was that they should hold together in unity."

At the end, on July 28, 1836—ten minutes before Nathan Mayer died, according to Salomon—as he received "the last consolations of religion that are customary with us," he was offered the text of the Judaic confessional by an attending rabbi. Reading from the prayer book in Hebrew, N. M. began, "I acknowledge unto Thee, O Lord my God and God of my fathers, that my cure and my death are in thy hands. May it be thy will . . ." He paused, then put the *siddur* down. "It is not necessary," he concluded, "that I should pray so much, for, believe me, according to my convictions I have not sinned."

In tears at his side was his eldest niece, the beautiful and much admired Betty—Salomon's daughter and James's wife. Turning to her, Nathan Mayer said, simply, from his pillow, "Good night for ever." His eyes closed. N. M. was fifty-eight.

Pigeon post was a crucial means of communication for the firm. His son Nat once explained, as messages sent that way had to be brief, "A B in our pigeon dispatches means: buy stock, the news is good; C D . . . means sell stock, the news is bad." It took five days before a courier on horseback could reach the Channel at Boulogne, affix a laconic message to the leg of a Rothschild carrier pigeon, and send it off to London. The three words were "Il est mort."

Burial traditionally was within twenty-four hours of death. Yet N. M. had instructed Lionel that he wanted to be interred in England. A simple wooden coffin alone, with pegs rather than nails, according to Jewish "dust to dust" tradition, would have been impossible, given the time necessary to return him to the country he revered as his. Under the circumstances, the family used a lead-lined inner coffin encased in another of oak, rather than the customary plain pine boards which symbolized that in death all humans were equal. (In any case, N. M. was clearly more equal than most others.) A breastplate of oak was affixed to the outer coffin, on which was carved the family coat of arms granted in Vienna in 1816—a lion grasping five arrows in its right forepaw. (The ennoblement patents had omitted Nathan at his request, and the Austrian arms actually displayed four arrows rather than five.)

Once the grim preparations in Frankfurt were accomplished, the linen-shrouded body of the stocky financier, who had been one of the most powerful men in Europe, was lifted, in a long, weighty double coffin, aboard a Rhine paddle wheeler to Rotterdam. From Holland much of the family that had gathered for the marriage in Frankfurt embarked on a chartered North Sea steamer on August 3 for the funeral in London. It was hardly the wedding journey that Charlotte had envisioned.

The Rothschilds had barely disembarked at the Thames dock where N. M.'s remains were transferred to a sturdy carriage when, on August 6, a commemorative lithograph appeared for sale in the City. In a vast and otherwise empty Stock Exchange, the silhouetted and easily recognized stout, top-hatted profile of Nathan Mayer appeared before his pillar, sunlight casting a long shadow behind him. At his back he clutched four keys, possibly representing the succession of his four sons. The caption in block capitals read "THE SHADOW OF A GREAT MAN."

The knowledgeable obituarist of *The Times* the same day described Rothschild's death as "one of the most important events for the city and perhaps for Europe, which has occurred for a long time. . . . No operations, comparable to his, have existed." It was no exaggeration. "All the brothers of Mr. Rothschild are men of great capacity and knowledge of business," *The Times* added, "but it is generally admitted that they deferred to his judgement in all their undertakings, and that he was the moving principle of the great mass of capital they represented." N. M. had never accepted his baronial title, it closed, "and was more justly proud of that name under which he had acquired a distinction which no title could convey."

In a separate column the editor observed, "We have only to add, in a few words, the impression which we have received from minor personal acquaintance with the deceased. Though he had never acquired a correct knowledge of the English language, and consequently expressed himself in a strange sort of diction, yet it was impossible to be with him for ten minutes not to perceive that his understanding was eminently sagacious, clear, and sound. Though his manners were somewhat uncouth, and devoid of conventional courtesies, it could not escape even a careless observer that his nature was good, cordial, and friendly."

That Saturday evening, August 6, once the Sabbath had ended, N. M.'s son Nathaniel went to New Court to consult with the family elders who had accompanied the body to London, and with officials of the City, about arrangements for the funeral, to be held on Monday afternoon at one o'clock. In deference to Lionel's newlywed circumstances, he was excused from the conference, to be with the distraught Charlotte.

Temporary market instability on the day of the burial, and beyond, appeared inevitable, but a banking rival, Alexander Baring, coldly dismissed the fuss about N. M.'s death as an "emancipation" and a "benefit," although "the sudden cessation of a despotic rule is apt to exhibit such symptoms." Others paid their respects in the bank foyer at New Court, where the body lay in its closed oak coffin, upon which, observed *The Times*, "not a joint is to be seen."

According to strict tradition, the mourning women, including both Charlottes, daughter and daughter-in-law, remained in N. M.'s darkened mansion at 107 Piccadilly. As the cortège began moving from New Court, it was led by rows of uniformed police four abreast and gowned City officials who preceded the horse-drawn hearse. Before the coffin, also, marched a delegation of children from the Jews' Free School. N. M.'s sons and other family members, including many related by marriage, followed in carriages. Behind them came thirty-five further carriages, headed by the Lord Mayor and the first Jewish Sheriff of London, David Salomons,[6] after which proceeded dozens of coaches of ambassadors and nobility.

As the column passed through Cornhill, crowds pressed against shop windows boarded up to protect them from shattering. Hawkers sold broadsides of *The Shadow of a Great Man* and printed silk commemorative handkerchiefs picturing *A Pillar of the Exchange*, copied from an 1829 caricature in which Thomas Jones adapted an 1817 etching by Richard Dighton, *A View from the Royal Exchange*. Soon on sale would be a printed mourning scarf with a tribute in the four languages of the Rothschild houses, including a list of N. M.'s best known transactions with governments and rulers, and an estimate of his personal wealth at £5 million. Mourning rings, mourning brooches, and commemorative medals with N. M.'s balding head looking much like a laureled Roman one would follow, as well as elegiac verses and obituaries in the foreign press that made much of him as a power in European affairs.

At the Great Synagogue in Duke's Place, Aldgate, more than a century old, where Nathan Mayer had been named a *parnass*, or war-

---

6. Elected that year, he was prevented from taking office because the oath was a Christian one, but Lord John Russell pushed through Parliament a Declaration Act for sheriffs that removed the religious barrier.

den, in 1818, the aged rabbi Solomon Hirschell preached an elegiac sermon, after which the coffin was lowered into a plot at the northwest corner of the Jewish burial ground in Whitechapel Road, which continued Aldgate High Street eastward. On a slab of Yorkshire stone would be carved the simple words he wanted that said nothing of his improbable career:

Nathan Mayer Rothschild:
born at Frankfurt on the Main 7th September 5537[7]
third son of Mayer Amschel Rothschild, a man known
and venerated throughout Europe, whose virtuous
example he followed.

For eleven months thereafter, seven members of the synagogue would join with N. M.'s sons at New Court each evening except the Sabbath for the required minyan of ten to recite the *Kaddish*, the prayer for the dead. (Repeated in honor rather than in memory of the deceased for more than two thousand years, the Aramaic prayer makes no mention of death, declaring only the glory of God.) Every eight weeks each participating elder would receive four guineas from the family in token of services volunteered.

The week of the funeral was Charlotte's first in London—a traumatic beginning for a lifetime in marital exile. With her dowry and her husband's inheritance and instant authority, she may have been one of the richest women in England, but her melancholy was profound and her sense of isolation in a strange new land extreme. The Hill Street lease secured for her would at first be of little use, as Lionel had to be with his mother in mourning, and wherever Hannah resided was a house of sorrow.

With his three brothers, Lionel shared equally in his father's in-

7. The year in the Jewish calendar for A.D. 1777 combined with the month and day in the Gregorian calendar.

heritance. Much of the capital could not be touched, yet he was now the head of the London house, the fulcrum of the multinational family bank. His father had very likely been the wealthiest businessman in the world, and effectively Lionel had replaced him. With shifting and inflationary money values since, Nathan Mayer's actual net worth, excluding property, remains difficult to measure; however, at a time when the Prime Minister's annual salary was £5,000 a year, then an enormous sum, N. M., utterly without debt to apply negatively against his income, may have controlled sums more than a thousand times as large. Baron James was outspokenly now the leader of the surviving brothers, while Hannah held ostensible testamentary veto over decisions of N. M.'s sons. Still, the authority of the flagship London house remained unimpaired, and Lionel at twenty-eight suddenly held its reins. That reality, and the likely labor involved in not losing it, were new shadows on a marriage solemnized in the shadow of death.

On August 9, 1836, barely a day after N. M.'s burial, a black-bordered circular was sent to clients and business associates announcing the continuation of the firm under a new name carrying on Nathan Mayer's identity:

> In announcing to you, which we do with feelings of the deepest sorrow, the death of our lamented Father, Mr. N. M. ROTHSCHILD, we beg to inform you, that the Business carried on by him will be continued by us, under the firm of N. M. ROTHSCHILD & SONS, IN EVERY RESPECT AS HERETOFORE, in connexion with the Establishments at Frankfort, Vienna, Paris and Naples.
>
> We request your attention to our respective Signatures at foot.
> We are,
> Your obedient servants,
> N. M. Rothschild & Sons
> *London, 9 August* 1836

Beneath, the three sons of age, Mayer (at eighteen) excluded, each signed—as

> Lionel Nathan de Rothschild
> Anthony Nathan de Rothschild
> Nathaniel Nathan de Rothschild

Their father had eschewed, of necessity, the baronial style, yet in the brothers' first official act they had (without license) adopted it. In their youth and inexperience they may have felt the need for its cachet. Charlotte was now the loneliest baroness in England.

CHAPTER THREE

CHARLOTTE IN EXILE

1836–1839

At first London seemed a place of exile for Charlotte. Looking back later on her beginnings in England, she recalled the pervasive gloom "in the land and city of fogs."

> I missed the bright skies of other climes, the . . . exhilarating air of other countries, because I allowed the dense atmosphere of the metropolis to weigh down my spirits, which had been buoyant, because I was far away from my parents, brothers & friends, because I knew no one in this large town save those who were too much engrossed by their own painful feelings & [who] neglect[ed] to bestow indulgent thoughts on the stranger who in the transient brightest hour of her youth had left beloved and adoring parents & affectionate playfellows and brothers, the pleasures of her childhood, the occupations of adolescence, the friends of both aspects of

life, a happy home endeared by thousands of associations, . . . to seek a new country, a new love, a home quite silently uninterested.

Her first days were spent in the curtained family mansion at 107 Piccadilly, where the Rothschilds were "sitting *shivah*"—observing the traditional seven days' mourning for the dead. (There was remission of mourning, however, on the Sabbath.) The practice required discarding shoes for slippers and reclining on stools or low benches —both symbolic demonstrations of grief replacing the requirements to rend clothes[1] and sit on the floor. Meals were to be simple and were often brought in by visitors comforting the mourners. *Kaddish* prayers for the person mourned—a father-in-law (and uncle) she hardly knew—were repeated twice daily. For visitors unfamiliar with *shivah*, the most striking phenomenon was the covering of mirrors— possibly a relic of the early folk belief that the image of one's soul could be reflected, and had to be guarded from being snatched by death, which pervaded a house in mourning. Similarly, portraits were covered or turned to the wall, and clocks were stopped and shrouded to indicate that for the dead, time had stopped.

The close of *shivah* might have meant, gratefully, a flight to the countryside, as would have been possible in Frankfurt, but Nathan Mayer's recently purchased country manor, Gunnersbury Park, had not become Lionel's inheritance. The seventy-six acres between Acton and Richmond remained the property of Charlotte's mother-in-law, who would gradually increase her holdings by a further thirty-three acres. Renovations ordered by Nathan on its purchase late in 1835 remained ongoing, and it was accessible only for afternoon visits to look over the progress of Sydney Smirke's architectural alterations.

Soon Charlotte would be trapped there stylishly, in a grand residence not her own. Her husband saw no reason to acquire an alterna-

---

1. A symbolic tear was usually cut into a garment worn by a sitting mourner; later a black mourning ribbon was cut or torn.

tive retreat simply because his mother was overseeing the improvements to the family property. Besides, Gunnersbury was indeed "country": the London suburbs had not yet sprawled that far westward. Still, it was an easy carriage ride via the Great West Road to the City. One could leave early for St. Swithin's Lane and return for a late dinner.

Until 1786 the home of the long-forgotten Princess Amelia, a daughter of George II, Old Gunnersbury House had a spacious park of cedar and elm, and a substantial lake. (Horace Walpole, once her guest, was commanded to write verses on the setting and produced a mediocre poem about "Gunnersbury's charm." If the lines were poor, he explained, "Consider I am sixty-nine, was half asleep and made them by command.") After Amelia the unused acreage went through several hands before a prosperous builder, Alexander Copland, acquired the site, demolished the house, and built a more lavish residence, employing Sydney Smirke early in the 1830s to add wings, an entrance hall, a saloon and dining room, and a library. When Copland died in 1834, his executors, one of whom was young Smirke, advertised it for sale as "a most enviable property, . . . which, from its superior arrangement, and proximity to the metropolis, is well adapted for the residence of a nobleman, minister of state, or family of the first description." Nathan Mayer, who by wealth rather than position fit the third category, bought Gunnersbury for £13,000 but never lived in it. Still, his confidence in Smirke, then only thirty-five, was not misplaced. Twenty years later, among other major commissions, he created the great Round Reading Room for the British Museum, topped by a dome larger than St. Peter's and St. Paul's in Rome. It was one of the great accomplishments of mid-nineteenth-century architecture.

While his workmen improved the kitchens ordered by Nathan Mayer and enlarged the stables, glaziers erected a conservatory and orangery (which would be reputed for its pineapples), both also at Nathan's direction. In the Long Gallery, Edmund Parris had executed a French-inspired neoclassical ceiling painting, *The Four Sea-*

sons, for Parris was then, by appointment, Historical Painter to Queen Adelaide, which gave him sufficient cachet for Nathan; however, Lionel and Charlotte—and Hannah—may have been chagrined a few years later when Parris won a prize, in a competition to decorate the new Houses of Parliament under construction, for his painting *Joseph of Arimathea Converting the Jews*.

In practice Gunnersbury would be Lionel and Charlotte's country home, ready to use just in time. The house in Hill Street, off Berkeley Square, which Lionel had rented temporarily early in 1836, was already vacated, as the couple had purchased 148 Piccadilly when it came up for sale, a grand residence on the north side adjacent to the Duke of Wellington's Apsley House. Once known as "No. 1, London" (afterwards 149 Piccadilly) the Duke's mansion was the first residence east of Knightsbridge, the road to rural Kensington. But for the Rothschild property, Wellington was surrounded by parkland. Often the Duke could be seen strolling in Green Park, walking stick in hand. Westward was the long, tree-lined avenue of Sloane Street, which ended at Knightsbridge. It ran south to the Thames at Chelsea, a village then known for old J. M. W. Turner's eccentric waterscapes—but that was too remote from urban London for anyone who dwelled there, however genteel, to be eligible for inclusion in the *Court Guide*.

As workmen were completing their renovations at Gunnersbury and vans came and went bringing Hannah's furniture and rugs and pictures, a similar scene was occurring while Charlotte supervised her move from Hill Street to what the Rothschilds eventually called Piccadilly House. Bills to Charlotte for purchases beginning in late 1836 show her becoming her own mistress at 148 Piccadilly.

Hannah was devoted to French cabinetry and French art, and had encouraged Lionel to follow her practice. There was already much to move. As early as 1831, still learning about what to buy, Lionel had written to his mother from Paris, where he was assisting Uncle James, "Be so good as to let me know if you would like some old inlaid furniture, a secretaire or commode made in the time of Louis

XIVth. Here these things are quite the rage; or if you would prefer some old Sèvres china." And from Madrid in 1834 he wrote to Hannah, perhaps deflecting suspicions about his interest in local señoritas, "All my leisure time I pass in running about after pictures which are in very great numbers but few good ones."[2] The same year Lionel bought Jean-Baptiste Greuze's *La vertu chancelante* (Fickle Virtue), the first of his five canvases by Greuze. The French painter, who had died in 1805, produced anecdotal, rather than religious, scenes, making him accessible to the still-unsophisticated Lionel. Later he would buy, with Charlotte's encouragement, as she was better educated in art than her practical husband, Old Masters and German art. As early as 1836 they bought the Gerard Terborch *Young Lady with Her Page*.

Charlotte at seventeen began life in London by losing herself in reading. She was rescued from loneliness by books, she recalled, and regretted not having exploited them more. "Lionel was never with me between the hours of tea in the morning & 6 in the evening. Oh! Why did I waste those hours in warm regrets, in tears? Why did I not then, ardently and assiduously, apply [myself] to study? Possibly, that would have dried my tears and made my thoughts play into pleasant and profitable channels. I could have accomplished much in those days. . . . I also had few cares and domestic duties to fulfil. I also endured much bodily pain, but why dwell so long upon my own sufferings?" As a very young wife, not accepted in society and far from home, it was a strangely oppressive plight to be a Rothschild.

The physical pain remains a mystery. She complained of headaches all her life. Whether they were neurotic ailments at first, a product of displacement and solitude, is unknown. For a time the aches fled. She became too busy to indulge them.

Lionel was immersed in business during Charlotte's early months in London. Plunged into taking control at New Court, he had no

---

2. A clue may be a later letter from Nat to Lionel that he could not buy art for his brother because "pictures are something like ladies; everyone must please himself and select according to his taste."

idea how much Charlotte felt abandoned. The months after N. M.'s death were, at St. Swithin's Lane, a frightening descent into red ink. Nathan Mayer's feverish orders from his sickbed in Frankfurt had been erratic if insistent. His sons, with deliberate absence of drama, had to restore confidence in the firm. N. M.'s brothers across the Channel contributed to the problems in London. On September 15, barely two months after Nathan's funeral, James rushed in (by letter) with avuncular advice for Lionel, suggesting that the Paris branch was now the power within the family and that the young partners at New Court needed his advice. The derangement in the market caused by the sudden slump in Rothschild activity in London had to be righted, James urged, elaborating the obvious, before rivals filled any perceptible vacuum.

Lionel struggled to be diplomatic in handling his uncle, for strategies effective in Paris often were not useful in London, which James seldom visited and did not know. "I would ask you kindly, my dear nephews," he reminded the brothers on October 25, 1836, as if they were children rather than reliable deputies who sometimes oversaw his affairs at de Rothschild Frères, "to pay a little more attention to my letters, because quite frankly I was very cross today, for I would very much have wished to continue working with London in the same way that I have done in the past with your late father, and not have to write argumentative letters, for a business can only be managed well if one pays as much attention to the smaller business transactions as one does to the larger ones."

To the uncles, the crucial strategy in their nephews' taking hold at New Court was to appear as active and as confident as possible, even if that meant forgoing earnings. There was plenty of capital upon which to fall back. "When you are buying or selling rentes," James further reminded N. M.'s sons on November 15, 1836, about French government bonds, "try not to look at making a profit, but rather your aim should be to get the brokers used to the idea that they need to come to you. . . . [O]ne initially has to make some sacrifices so that the people then get used to the idea to come to you, my dear

nephews, and as such one has to first spread the sugar about in order
to catch the birds later on."

The London house would suffer significant losses in 1836—about
4 percent of its very large capital. As senior partner among three
young men handling huge amounts of money, Lionel had to balance
prudence and risk, making it clear that New Court was functioning
efficiently. (He understood the Rothschild maxim that only fools
seek the highest returns.) Lionel also had to forestall any perception
that Hannah or his uncles were running the affairs of the most
powerful and authoritative of the Rothschild houses—and he had to
become, and would be, a caring spouse to a lonely and frightened
seventeen-year-old wife.

Some of the physical distress Charlotte remembered was yet to
come, as a welcome yet worrisome pregnancy. Lionel's prying family
awaited the event eagerly. On October 11, with the Rothschilds
hardly out of mourning, his sister Louise wrote to Mayer, who had
just arrived at Magdalen College, Cambridge, "Charlotte is not yet
confined, and we are getting impatient." The town house in Hill
Street that was to provide some serenity for the young couple was
furnishing not nearly enough of it, as the difficult Hannah, more ex-
acting as mourning widow, expected Charlotte to comfort her on demand at 107 Piccadilly, even more so after the couple's move to
nearby 148. Her mother-in-law had no idea that Charlotte was lost
in depression, or that she needed more of Lionel's presence than he
could provide in a period of critical strains—which meant long
hours—at the firm.

A house that Charlotte could call her own, and that needed a great
deal of attention to make liveable, helped to transform her outlook.
Young and resilient, she had found a challenge. That November,
Hannah, who had perceived none of the early tension to which she
had contributed, reported to Mayer that "la Belle" and her "caro
sposo" appeared very much in love: "There is many a fond look and
kiss from dimpled lips and brilliant eye."

In December 1836 Charlotte became pregnant. The family was

delighted. Despite a retinue of servants, she had a difficult time of it; and once spring came, Charlotte longed for the expected country peace of Gunnersbury Park. On May 27, 1837, the invitation came. Hannah wrote, opening access to their Eden in what seemed more an order than an invitation: "I suppose we shall go to Gunnersbury, which is nearly finished." It would never be completely finished for Hannah, who had arranged with Smirke to have Copland's library turned into a spacious salon, and a larger library built off the entrance hall and Grand Staircase. Princess Amelia's eighteenth-century temple by the round pond was renovated and enlarged to be a small synagogue for use on holy days when the family worshiped at home. Hannah also had plans for a guest residence drawn up that February, and the North Lodge continued the new construction.

Little of it then concerned Charlotte. Although she would learn quickly from observation, she was far from ready to be a grand hostess at Gunnersbury, or Piccadilly, cultivating financiers and politicians on Lionel's behalf. Yet what she wrote years later must have been equally relevant then. "Without exaggeration," she wrote one September day, "Gunnersbury looks like a paradise, trees, shrubs, flowers and greensward, smiling from daybreak till dusk in the unveiling, golden light of glowing sunshine." She began spending weekends, and some weeks, there.

To the east, along Lionel's daily carriage route to the City from Gunnersbury, the world that Charlotte could not see was swiftly renewing itself—almost like another new birth. What she knew, if only from *The Times* and the myriad other papers Lionel brought home, and from gossip around her table, was the imminence of change at Buckingham House (not yet "Palace"), across the park from Piccadilly. In May 1837, William IV, the bluff Sailor-King who had succeeded his corpulent brother, George IV, in 1830, was seventy-two and failing. William's niece, Princess Alexandrina Victoria, the presumptive heiress of the childless king, was a girl only three weeks older than Charlotte.

On May 24 the Princess, at eighteen, became eligible to reign without the requirement of a regent. Bedridden in his last illness, King William was fading away at Windsor Castle. At her mother's apartments at Kensington Palace, Victoria waited out her accession.

Impatient for the birth of her baby, Charlotte could no longer go out publicly in Piccadilly. Custom precluded a woman big with child, however many her petticoats, from abetting such indecency. But into her broad windows on the morning of Tuesday, June 20, the Church of St. James, Piccadilly, tolled the news of William's passing. The streets burgeoned with people wondering whether to mourn or to celebrate, and placards quickly proclaimed that "the High and Mighty Princess Alexandrina Victoria is now, by the death of our late Sovereign William the Fourth, of happy memory, become our only lawful and rightful liege Lady Alexandrina Victoria I, Queen of Great Britain and Ireland."[3]

Leonora was born on August 25, 1837. Lionel grumbled tactlessly that he was not furnished a male heir. Girls would not do. It was unhelpful that one of the senior clerks in James's Paris house congratulated him about the birth of a Rothschild girl as prelude to the arrival of a child of the other gender: "I actually compliment you that it is a daughter which our dear lady has given you"—language that suggested how employees of the firm felt like extended family. "You may have wished for a son," Monsieur Haas went on with confidence, "but he will come—in two years you will announce him."

However disappointing to Lionel, the event, Charlotte recalled nine years later, brought her "happiness so exquisite, felicity so perfect, bliss so unexpectedly great." She was transformed by having, at eighteen, something of her own to be responsible for, and the arrival of his first child brought, to his surprise after the initial letdown, a new sensitivity to Lionel, who was drawn more than he had expected

3. Victoria quickly ruled out "Alexandrina," which was her unused baptismal name derived from her godfather-in-absentia, the Russian Tsar. Six years earlier her royal uncle, the King, tried unsuccessfully to foist on the future queen a new name— "Charlotte." She resisted it.

to be from such cares at New Court as could be assumed by others, especially Anthony. The first days of Leonora's life "were the purest, the best, the most completely enchanting I ever experienced," Charlotte remembered. "I could scarcely credit my eyes, and believe that Laury was my child. I thought she may be my sister sent to me by my kind mother to enliven my solitary house. . . . I learned her tiny features, I felt the happiest and grandest of human beings."

Spurning the reliance of wealthy and well-born women upon hired wet nurses, who abandoned their own suckling, often unwanted, infants to make use of an easily renewable source of income, Charlotte insisted on breast-feeding the baby herself. Between such sessions of jealously guarded personal time with Leonora, Charlotte hosted aunts and cousins who fawned over the child, and the socially connected wives and daughters of Lionel's business associates. Lionel hovered about when he could, and to warn him against becoming overly distracted from the counting house, his uncle Salomon wrote patronizingly to his "dear children" at New Court: "We have to push the business. . . . This is what your late father always said. Whenever he saw that others wanted to push us out of a business deal, he always wrote, 'My dear brother, we have to push it through.' It is all the same whether we make a loss or a profit, whether we earn something or suffer a loss, we must not . . . let anyone grow over our heads, or we will be simply pushed aside." James's letters would sometimes hint that his insufficiently single-minded nephews may have been off riding or hunting, pastimes they loved, but Lionel now had a more meaningful excuse for arriving late at St. Swithin's Lane, or leaving early.

The London house was again prospering, and not long after, Anthony would explode to his elder brother in exasperation about avuncular intrusions, however well meant, into their operations. Of the rather mild uncle who was Charlotte's father, "Billy" complained, "I assure you that although Uncle Charles is your father in law, that the less one has to do with this gentleman, the better."

Lionel also had to confront a cousinhood problem that seemed likely to arise again and again in a family so closely interrelated. Joseph Montefiore, who was the son of his Rothschild aunt, Henrietta, and an aspiring banker, had asked to be taken into New Court as a prospective partner. Lionel would not hear of it, whatever funds cousin Joseph proposed to bring into the business. "He was averse to this," Montefiore disappointedly explained to his uncle (and Lionel's), Moses, "alleging that there were already too many [partners] and that it would be a bad precedent." Since Lionel assumed that N. M.'s brothers would also disapprove, he suggested that Joseph ask for advice from their uncles, and also consider changing his surname to Rothschild. Then Montefiore proposed, with no more success, to marry Lionel's waspish sister Hannah Mayer—although he had not asked her, and she would have refused—in order to join the London firm by that route.

A well-to-do cousin, Henrietta Worms, whose family owned a tea plantation in Ceylon christened "Rothschild," was one of the first to visit Charlotte and Laury, as Leonora was already called. "Mrs Worms," Charlotte remembered, "said the baby had an ugly nose and her sister-in-law thought it looked like a frog or [a] toad! It was the first cloud that came upon the abundance of my happiness, and it caused . . . tears." But, she conceded, "I was only eighteen years old." At the end of the month, released by her doctors from the lengthy customary lying-in, often then four weeks or more, she and the child went with the family in a procession of carriages to the Great Synagogue in Aldgate, where she "gratefully and reverently returned thanks to Almighty God for the blessings he had vouchsafed me and my heart and home." There Leonora was formally named, with Charlotte (as a woman) having no role in the ceremony. Lionel, as the father, brought the child before the ark containing the Torah scrolls, where the appropriate blessings were intoned, while Leonora's mother sat upstairs with her London family in the area set aside for female congregants in the male society that was Orthodox Jewry. Then

Charlotte went to the city "registering office" and "wrote my darling's name in the book." In civil society she had gained a role.

Soon Charlotte realized, as Laury failed to flourish at her breast, that she "had not strength and ability enough for the task. . . . When out of her mother's arms she grew and thrived." Traditional aristocratic distance from the physical side of infant care asserted itself. Charlotte had a plethora of maids, and soon Laury, with wet nurse in attendance, was "admired, petted and spoilt" not only at Piccadilly House, but in Gunnersbury and at the seaside in Brighton, where Hannah liked to spend her holidays, including Passover in the spring and the High Holy Days of Rosh Hashanah and Yom Kippur in the autumn. Since Hannah had a vast suite and tipped lavishly, the hotel management indulged her utterly, and her own servants laid out kosher cuisine sent down from London at each mealtime.

By early 1838, assisted by the best local dressmakers money could buy, who came to her boudoir with silks and laces and patterns for fittings, Charlotte was deep into the London social scene. It was already clear that since Baron Lionel had become a major factor in the City, the Baroness could not be ignored. Now an M.P., and on guest lists himself, Disraeli, in a letter to his sister, Sarah, recorded seeing the young Baroness at a chamber concert in mid-February 1838 at the home of the Mayfair socialite Robert Parnther, "where I found all the *élite* of town,"—including "the Duke"—only Wellington was referred to that way—and where jewelry glittered as extravagantly as Diz's language. "There were," he gushed, "indeed as many stars as in an Arabian story." After citing for Sarah a litany of nobility, he added, "But the most picturesque group was the Rothschilds, the widow still in mourning, two sons, some sisters, and above all, the young bride, or rather wife, from Frankfort, universally admired, tall, graceful, dark, and clear, picturesquely dressed, a robe of yellow silk, a hat and feathers, with a sort of *Sévigné* [4] beneath of magnifi-

4. Very likely here a jeweled hair band.

cent pearls; quite a Murillo." A connoisseur of beautiful and inter-esting women, Disraeli would get to know her better.

Charlotte learned how to entertain—and how not to entertain—from Hannah's lavish style. As Charlotte understood Lionel would want, she was almost always at her mother-in-law's side when festivi-ties on behalf of the bank occurred. Lionel wanted no misunder-standing that his mother ran the firm; yet Gunnersbury Park was her estate, and determined to make Rothschild clients content, and to make those less favored aspire to be fiscal wards of New Court, or at least to harbor good feeling, Hannah laid on a bounty of food and drink and music about which guests literally wrote home. Sallie Stevenson, the young wife of the U.S. Minister (the United States wasn't sufficiently important to qualify an ambassador), wrote to her sisters in Virginia about a "breakfast" at Gunnersbury on July 18, 1838, that began at three in the afternoon. When she, in white silk, and her husband Andrew arrived, a fashionable hour late, at the main carriage entrance, with its four white Doric columns on either side, the "thrilling notes" of the soprano Giulia Grisi, star of Bellini's op-eras, could be heard from Smirke's Grand Salon, while from the ter-races came the "distant strains" of Italian nightingales. Later, guests strolled about the blossoms and greenery and, surfeited with cham-pagne, shed "much of their constitutional reserve." At six-thirty a bell summoned everyone to "a magnificent tent on the lawn where tables had been set for 4 or 500 guests and every luxury provided." There were "hot & cold meats, delicious viands of all sorts with the most costly fruits & wines."

Following the feasting, guests returned to the lawns, on which car-pets had been laid and chairs set, and "the young people waltzed to the music of two bands who played alternately throughout the day & night" from two marquees. As evening shadows began replacing the sunlight, the "brilliant glowworms" of Chinese lanterns appeared be-neath "every bush & shrub & tree," and Andrew Stevenson went off in the radiance to chat with the Queen's uncles, the Duke of Sussex and the Duke of Cambridge. At a "temple" near the lake, where guests floated in "pleasure boats," coffee was served, while back at Gunnersbury House "we found a refreshment table delightful to our eyes in one of the large & splendid salons where ices, lemonade and orangeade &c was served and disappeared as snow in sunshine & at one end of the table that never failing accessory to English comfort, a tea urn."

On the terrace, where Lady Jersey and Lady Londonderry, "two of the brightest stars in the world of Fashion," were chatting with the Duke of Wellington and Prince Esterházy (a major New Court client), Lady Jersey exclaimed, "Prince, I am fainting with fatigue. Do get me a chair!" When the Austrian ambassador, unused to effort, "after some little flourish pronounced it impossible," Stevenson jumped from the terrace to the lawn and plucked two chairs. Gunnersbury was that kind of locale, and it promoted the burgeoning of Rothschild business.

Gossiping afterwards to the American Minister, the Duke of Sussex, an inveterate party-goer (and scholar of Hebrew[5]) but no party-giver, estimated to Stevenson that the Rothschild fête "must have cost 2000 pounds—$10,000"—twice the annual salary, he understood, of President Martin Van Buren.

Even smaller, family-focused, occasions at Gunnersbury were often grand. Sir Moses Montefiore, knighted by Queen Victoria, and a guest at the fête, was back for a typical Sabbath weekend on September 15, a Saturday. "We all assembled in the Library," he wrote in his diary, "where Louise de Rothschild read the Sabbath morning service aloud extremely well." (At seventeen the youngest of Lionel's sisters and brothers, Louise had just rejected her persistent cousin Joseph Montefiore; she would later marry Charlotte's brother Mayer

---

5. Victoria's uncle possessed at his death a library of four thousand volumes of Judaica, many of them in Hebrew. Before they could be dispersed at auction in 1860, Lionel would purchase the entire collection and present it to the Jews' College, 10 Finsbury Square, to be available to the public.

Carl, another cousin and a Rothschild.) "At three o'clock we lunched, and then walked in the garden, after which we re-entered the house and recited the afternoon prayer." At sundown, dinner was served to twenty-four, "and guests did not leave till after eleven. Wester on the guitar and Benedict on the piano, amused the company at the conclusion of dinner and Louise sang one song beautifully." Julius Benedict, born in Stuttgart, had been a conductor and composer in Naples, where he was known to Charlotte's parents, and had moved to London in 1835 to conduct and perform at the Lyceum.

Throughout the century, aristocratic entertaining required chamber music. Composers were therefore a special breed guaranteed personal attention by the firm, as the family was also devoted to music. Rossini and Mendelssohn had been at the Rothschild wedding festivities in Frankfurt. In 1838, Johann Strauss the elder wrote to Lionel asking for an extension on a bill of exchange arranged by Salomon in Vienna so that he could prolong his stay in England. Franz Liszt later invested funds raised by his Continental tours with James's house. Flush from virtuoso appearances as a violinist, the already legendary Paganini, after hearing a performance of *Harold in Italy* in November 1838, wrote effusively to the chronically impecunious composer Hector Berlioz, "My dear friend, Beethoven being dead, only Berlioz remains to make him live again; and I who have relished your divine compositions, worthy of the genius that you are, think it my duty to ask you to accept, in token of my homage, 20,000 francs, which Baron de Rothschild will pay over when you present him the enclosed. Believe me, I am ever your most affectionate friend, Niccolò Paganini."

Having learned from Hannah and from James, Lionel and Charlotte were ready to make their own way in the worlds of entertainment, music, and art, and to do so—usually—with less ostentation. With the family firm thriving, Lionel, presumably with Charlotte approving his taste, now seriously collected art, but one early purchase was an ego-related commission validating, also, the brothers' passion for hunting and racing. In 1838 he arranged for a portrait of himself by Alfred de Dreux, notable for his animal painting. Lionel is at the reins of a gig, accompanied by a groom dressed in the Rothschild colors. The groom wears a blue coat with gold buttons, while the gig and the harness are decorated in blue and gold, with the family crests emblazoned on the horses' blinkers.

Charlotte would not be painted until she could show her family on canvas, but she and Lionel bought Dutch and Flemish art, largely, one might assume, because the serene domestic interiors usually had little or no religious content. It was a severe limitation for collectors of Old Masters, an impediment long ignored by Hannah. Two by Philips Wouwermans came from the duchesse de Berry sale of 1837 and would be added to by Netherlandish interiors, townscapes, and landscapes. Eventually, their galleries and staircases displayed Rothschild connoisseurship to the appreciative, and their open pockets to the envious.

The Rothschild social world was intimately connected to the business of the bank. More and more—although pregnancies would limit her social activity—Charlotte became the focus of a salon in London, an occupation encouraged by her father, who thought that she and Lionel should do more to further his business interests beyond the offices at New Court. The key to successful investment was privileged information, which often emerged over teacups, champagne glasses, or dinner. In March 1839 Carl Mayer explained to his daughter. "Business or just being busy—tell your husband he should assiduously visit diplomats in order to hear the news. . . . You should try to find out what is happening in London, and can go visiting every Sunday in London." Soon it was Charlotte, more so than Hannah, who was efficiently entertaining diplomats, Cabinet ministers, princes, and peers. Her guests evidenced her pragmatism. Charlotte knew she did not even have to like them.

Evelina was born on August 25, 1839, and Charlotte pointedly recalled that Lionel was not present at the birth. (Her labor had been unexpected and brief, and Lionel's carriage from New Court arrived too late.) More unhappily, he could not conceal his disappointment that the male child he still awaited had not materialized. It did not help, too, that the baby suffered intensely from convulsions, or that Leonora disliked her new sister so much that she had to be kept away from the infant. Then Leonora, at Gunnersbury, was taken ill with measles, and on summoning Dr. William Herbert urgently to prescribe for her, Charlotte discovered that despite his apparent prestige and his knighthood, he was immured in debtors' prison after a bankruptcy plea. Shocked, but her confidence in him unaffected, she employed her prestige as a Rothschild and a baroness, and got him released. Charlotte was learning how to take charge. He came to Laury's sickbed directly from his cell.

On November 8, 1840, Lionel finally achieved his hope for a male heir with Nathaniel Mayer. For years, Charlotte quietly but actively disliked the child. "He was a thin ugly baby but that did not signify. He was a boy and as such was most welcome to his father and the whole family. I never could prefer him to his sisters." Probably to dramatize her distaste for the family fuss, she inconvenienced herself while ostensibly demonstrating her caring maternity. "I nursed him but not so well as he ought to have been nursed for he was a sickly child and I was not a robust mother."

On his eighth day, Nathaniel, as a male child, was circumcised and given his Hebrew name at the traditional Brith Milah, held at home using the *kiseh Eliyahu* (Elijah's chair) sent to the home of the infant for the ceremony from the Great Synagogue. More than the ten adult men required to make up the minyan, but no women, were present. As it was still a lying-in time for the mother, one of the men, the *sandik*, or proxy, fetched the firstborn son and brought him to the room where the rite was to be performed. Dexterously, using a tiny protective shield, the *mohel* who performed the minor surgery made the single, circular cut. Two small cups of wine were at hand. The *mohel* used one cup for rinsing his mouth before draining what drops of blood, if any, oozed from the tiny wound—a primitive form of antisepsis—and to dip in a finger as needed and offer it to the child to

suck, to quiet its crying. The other cup was for the ceremonial blessing for the boy's long life. Further prayers followed; then the infant
was returned to what was now a room full of women, dominated by
Hannah, where wine, tea, and coffee, and sweet cakes were tucked
into. It was the only part of the ritual in which the mother had any
role.

Soon Charlotte referred to her third child as "constitutionally in-
dolent." Natty—"Nathaniel" to his mother—had many early failings
to outgrow, few of which Lionel noticed. Natty was listless and lazy
as a child, and became a poor student. But it was crucial for the London house to have a male successor, and Lionel intended to ensure
that Natty would be up to the mark. The stability of New Court had
been Lionel's chief focus before Natty's arrival, and the fact of a son
created new impetus to assure its continuing centrality in London financial life and among the family firms. The pressure to produce a
male heir was as strong on Lionel and Charlotte as for any of Europe's monarchs. Charlotte had resented it, yet she had seen it in operation within the family on the Continent. She was a firstborn, and
a daughter. Their uncle Amschel in Frankfurt had no children and
had to informally adopt a nephew. Their uncle James lived with the
problems of unstable France and still lacked a son old enough to second him at rue Laffitte, while Lionel had three mature younger
brothers at New Court, one of whom, the financially shrewd Nat, at
Baron James's plea, would move to Paris in 1840 to assist his uncle.
Soon, conveniently, he would marry James's artistically and musically
talented daughter, another Charlotte, in the garden of the Rothschild château at Boulogne. James often leaned on the young men at
New Court. Now he had one of them.[6]

In London in the year of Nathaniel's birth, the solid status of the
financial house was evident from the complaint of the architect

---

6. In the same year, 1840, Anthony ("Billy") would marry his cousin Louise Montefiore and settle at 2 Grosvenor Gate. They would have two daughters. Mayer would
later marry his cousin Juliana Cohen and have one daughter. Charlotte and Lionel
had the London firm's sons.

Welby (A. W. N.) Pugin to his patron, the Earl of Shrewsbury, about a pair of fashionable Soho antique dealers. "It is quite impossible for me to drive any bargain with Storr and Mortimer. I might as well attempt it with Ro[th]schild himself." One didn't drive a bargain with Lionel and his brothers. One accepted Rothschild terms. Their family name had been a byword since N. M.'s time. It was also, formally now, aristocratic. Only in 1838, two years after the brothers first employed the "de" prefix, did Lionel formally apply for and receive (that June 16) a royal license for himself and his brothers to bear the inherited Austrian title and arms. There were no complications: They were English-born.

CHAPTER FOUR

THE WORLD INTRUDES

1839–1846

As the other children of Nathan Mayer and Hannah found spouses, one daughter remained obstinately unwilling. Turning aside all arranged suitors, Lionel's sister Hannah Mayer shattered the unwritten marital code and wed not only outside the extended family, but outside the faith. Suddenly the world outside intruded.

Not only an internal family matter, it became a public one, an embarrassment reported in *The Times*. On May 18, 1839, three weeks after the marriage, the paper reported that the condition "imposed upon Miss Rothschild on her marrying the Hon. Mr. Fitzroy was that she should embrace the Christian religion. This is the first instance of a member of the Rothschild family abandoning the faith of their fathers, . . . as they had hitherto distinguished themselves by their adherence to the Jewish creed. It is said that the bride's uncles are by no means pleased with a match which renders a change of religion necessary."

In Paris in her father's lifetime, Prince Edmond de Clary had proposed to her, but Nathan Mayer disapproved. Hannah Mayer's legacy of £100,000 was half outright with the remainder to be part of her dowry. Marrying out of the faith eliminated the dowry, but she had already been given additional wealth, in effect replacing her losses, on attaining her majority. In the case of the handsome Henry Fitzroy, who appeared likely to inherit his childless elder brother's estate, and had, at thirty-two, promising further political prospects, the socially ambitious younger Hannah was willing to take her chances. She chafed at the confines of Judaism, and Fitzroy was already what her legally constrained Jewish admirers could not be—a graduate of Oxford and of Cambridge, M.P. for Lewes, and Deputy Lieutenant for Northamptonshire. Hannah Mayer was ready to forgo a traditional wedding under the *chuppah* in the garden at Gunnersbury.

Lionel and Charlotte regretted her decision, and Lionel had delayed the marriage in hopes that he could persuade Fitzroy that he would see little of Hannah Mayer's money. He was also trying to inhibit further defections among the surplus of well-to-do Rothschild daughters. Each would be an additional family humiliation. Undismayed, Fitzroy observed that although he had been only three when his father had died and that no provision was made for him in his father's will, he had an allowance from the 3rd Baron Southampton and was likely to succeed him. He returned contentedly to his flat in South Street to dine on a large beefsteak—at which Nat found him. Nathaniel was his sister's only supporter in the family. Although he would be making his own endogamous marriage in a few years, he saw no reason why women in the family, excluded from partnerships in the firm, could not wed as they wished.

Uncle James, who would become Nat's father-in-law in 1842, was furious when he learned of the betrothal from Lionel. "Nothing could be more disastrous for our family, for our continued well-being, for our good name and for our honour," he charged. It was renouncing "the religion which, thank God, made us great." In his will, N. M. had asked that all marriages in his brood be approved by his widow and her sons, who would have the last word in any disagreement. But accord was irrelevant if Hannah Mayer forwent any future Rothschild funds. Deploring her "independent character," James wrote again to Lionel and Nat, this time from Charlotte's former home in Naples, where he was sharing the unhappy news with her parents. He suggested unhopefully that mother and aberrant daughter visit him in Switzerland, where he was going to convalesce further after an illness.

Next it was the imperious Lady Southampton, Fitzroy's sister-in-law, who tried to break the betrothal. Since Fitzroy, she told her husband, was marrying into the wealthiest family in Europe, why continue his allowance? On receiving word that he was losing what he assumed was his birthright, Henry Fitzroy rushed to Lord Southampton at Whittlebury, quarreled heatedly, and departed. It would be nineteen years before he saw his brother again.

Since the betrothed couple could live splendidly on the money that Hannah Mayer already had, they set a wedding date. Risking nothing, Henry turned his charm on his future mother-in-law, who agreed to escort her daughter only to the church door. Of the brothers, only Nat offered to attend. None of the Rothschild women would come. On April 29, 1839, a Monday, Lionel had his usual breakfast tea with Charlotte and went off to New Court. Nat took a carriage to St. George's, Hanover Square, to be there when both Hannahs, mother and daughter, arrived. Fitzroy left his flat with his friend Lord Castlereagh, who would be best man in the absence of Lord Southampton.

Hannah called for an ordinary four-wheeler cab, as she did not want a carriage with the Rothschild coat-of-arms seen at a church, and the two ladies clattered off to Hanover Square. There she kissed her daughter and left her to Nat and Fitzroy. The curate in his surplice came up to ask if the entire party—fewer than a dozen—were present. There were no bridesmaids. In fashionable but nearly empty St. George's, Hannah Mayer, "for better for worse, for richer for poorer, in sickness and in health," became Mrs. Fitzroy.

Taking a Channel steamer, Nat departed to preside at de Rothschild Frères while James was still taking his cure. A letter from Heinrichsbad awaited in Paris. The marriage made him even more ill than he had been, Baron James grumbled in *Judendeutsch*. It "robbed our whole family of its pride. . . . We shall therefore wipe her from our memory and never again during my lifetime will I or any other member of our family see or receive her. We now want to wish her all the best and banish her from our memory as if she had never existed." James pontificated as if he were titular head of the family; and though he considered himself as such, Lionel and his brothers often quietly put down his attempts to exercise undue avuncular authority. James needed London, and both uncle and nephews knew it.

Wearily, Hannah tried to have it both ways. She wrote to Nat in realization that he would remain close to his sister, for whom life would not be easy. Although Hannah Mayer, whom she declined to name, had "separated herself from me," her mother would be "most happy," she confided to Nat, "to receive daily bulletins of domestic as well as all other concerns . . . if there should be any news from an Individual who still so much interests me." Unwilling to toady to his uncle, Nat responded to James's outrage by observing casually that all Hannah Mayer had done was to marry "a Christian in a Christian country." In time Charlotte, who saw no virtue in vindictiveness, would resume low-key but open contacts with her husband's outcast sister. Lionel would follow. Although James remained passionately hostile, his wife, Betty, made her peace, as she put it, with "HM" ten years after.

Increasingly to James, religious unity went well beyond the family, and in that spirit he paralleled initiatives already taken in Britain by his brother-in-law Moses Montefiore. Since Lionel's primary business was in raising large loans for foreign governments, his chief interest in foreign affairs had been international stability. In February 1840, however, Egypt, long a dependency of the Ottoman regime in Constantinople, was reaching out to absorb adjacent Turkish provinces like Syria, which included Lebanon and Palestine. In Damascus, when a Capuchin friar, Father Tommaso, and his servant, disappeared, the gruesome, eleventh-century "blood libel" resurfaced. Allegedly—and imaginatively—the two had been killed in the Jewish quarter so that their blood could be used ritually in making matzoh (unleavened bread) for Passover. The blood libel was a much repeated canard during medieval times. The Egyptian governor ordered a number of Jews, including three rabbis, arrested and subjected to torture, under which one hostage, a barber, fearfully and inventively admitted having witnessed the murders. Soon others confessed under the lash, and seventy further Jews were jailed, including children baffled by the wild charges against them.

Eagerly assisting in the witch hunt, the French consul exploited endemic anti-Semitism in the mostly French Catholic population. When one of the imprisoned Jews turned out to be an Austrian subject, the merchant Isaac de Picciotto, the Jewish community in Constantinople appealed to Lionel in London, and to his uncles Salomon and Carl. Baron Lionel, whose title was Austrian, had also inherited from his father the honorary Austrian consul general post in London. The Austrian consul general in Cairo appealed to his Paris counterpart, who happened to be Baron James. In Paris, James consulted Adolphe Crémieux, vice president of the Consistory of French Jews, an accomplished journalist, who got the matter into the papers.

For Lionel it was the first of what would be many situations where he had to consider risking business advantages for his ideals and his faith. In London, he discussed the affair with the Board of Deputies of British Jews and joined a delegation that, on April 30, 1840, saw Viscount Palmerston, the foreign minister. From Paris, Nat proposed that Lionel "get up a good subscription to pay the expenses of sending Crémieux there fast." Although Lionel could fund the mission himself, it seemed more politic to suggest wide support, and the Rothschilds became treasurers of the Damascus Jews Fund. Even at that, the family contributed at least £2,500—and also sponsored Sir

Moses Montefiore, who sailed with Crémieux in part because Lionel felt uneasy about him and wanted someone along to moderate the indiscreet Frenchman's passions.

At Naples, Charlotte's father provisioned the rescue ship for the voyage to Alexandria, and fruitlessly pressed the Vatican to remove the anti-Semitic allegation of ritual murder from Father Tommaso's gravestone. The calumny was repeated by the French premier, Louis-Adolphe Thiers, who declared that if Christian blood were required in the making of matzoh—which he believed to be true—the patriotism of French Jews was in question. Baron James despised the premier; and Thiers in turn called the Rothschilds "more powerful in the world than they pretend to be."

Pressure from England was stepped up as the mission arrived in Egypt to see Mehmet Ali, the Turkish viceroy. On August 19, they presented him with an ultimatum backed by Britain and Austria. Lionel asked Leopold, the King of the Belgians, who was a good friend and whose Queen was a daughter of the French King, to use his good offices to undo the slander.

A British naval expedition sailed for Alexandria to turn up the pressure. Ali's viceroy, however, remained dominated by the local French, now wobbling, who recommended only that the purported religious motive for the killings be dropped, the Jews who had already died in prison be declared the murderers, and the other hostages released. When Montefiore refused the phony compromise and warned of military force to expel the Egyptians from Syria, Ali gave way and put his seal to a *firman*, an edict by the sultan, denying the existence of ritual murder in Jewish rites and assuring the freedom, and safe return, of all Damascene Jews. With the exception of French Consul General Cochelet, all the European representatives in Alexandria signed a démarche in agreement. On September 5, 1840, all surviving prisoners were "honorably discharged."

While the mission wrangled with French agents and Egyptian proconsuls, France—happily to James—wallowed in financial and political difficulty. French bonds fell on the Paris bourse, but the

Rothschilds had prudently rid themselves of rentes. François Guizot, then ambassador in London, asked the gossipy Princess Dorothea Lieven ruefully after a talk with Lionel, "Do you think he is praying to God for the safety of his money?" Obviously, this was unnecessary. To conduct business a Rothschild did not rely on prayer.

From Hanover, King Ernest Augustus, Victoria's uncle who had merely been Duke of Cumberland until Salic Law prevented the Queen (as a female) from inheriting the German state, would growl to his friend, Viscount Strangford, "I suppose we shall see ere long Rothschild created Duke of Jerusalem, and sitting in the House of Lords, and who knows if a Moses, Solomon, or Montefiore may not be created a Lord Chancellor and keeper of the conscience of Her Majesty Queen Victoria."

With French credibility slipping, eroded further by Louis-Napoleon Bonaparte's failed attempt to seize the shaky throne, the Paris government had difficulty borrowing money. James denied any political involvement in the plots of the late emperor's nephew. A Rothschild never encouraged opposition to a regime, he explained. As a banker, he, like Lionel, preferred continuity to chaos. "Financiers," added James, "have the opportunity of rendering services to the country under any circumstances, and I think that in this respect I have never been slow to respond." (In the circumstances, his services to France were to encourage the departure of Thiers.) On October 20, 1840, the premier resigned, and a new government was formed by Marshal Nicolas Soult with Guizot as his foreign minister. The Rothschilds had indirectly exacted payment for Damascus.

Sir Moses returned to England in triumph, but anti-Semitic outrages in the Middle East and in Eastern Europe were far from over, and the Rothschilds would be drawn in each time. Talk grew that the family had an obligation to restore the Holy Land to dispossessed and persecuted Jews, but the Rothschilds, particularly from France, would work at ameliorating conditions where possible, avoiding politics. According to Nat, whose emotional temperature was being raised by Baron James, Lionel preferred to operate differently, in excessively low key. Stability was good for business, and peace was good for people. Others, largely Christian evangelicals, talked of reclaiming the Holy Land for the Jews.

Exposure to politics of every sort was opening up Charlotte's world. Little more than twenty, and with three small children, she might easily have turned more inward. Life in London for her, however, had changed. More and more, Gunnersbury was her domain, as her mother-in-law, unhappy about Hannah Mayer's marriage and her own perceived embarrassment, had taken energetically to traveling, visiting other Rothschild houses for long stays. Baroness Hannah also traveled across England and Scotland on family business. Charming and sophisticated, she was received everywhere as the great lady who was cofounder of the London firm. A letter survives from "Grandmama" to Leonora, then four, written from Glasgow on October 24, 1841, responding to a note from "Lee" on the back of which were pencil drawings, possibly meant to be of her father. "It is some time since I have seen you all," Hannah wrote, "and [I] often think how happy we shall be, please God, to meet [again] all well and happy."

Charlotte had taken the children to Brighton, and Grandmama, now returned, wrote of their enjoying the sea and running about the Esplanade. Traveling further with her children and a suite of servants, Charlotte visited Frankfurt en route to Naples. Carl had bought the Villa Pignatelli, which his daughter recalled as having a breathtaking view of Vesuvius above and the bay below, overlooking "the most animated [local] street and the Villa Reale, the Neapolitan Kensington Gardens." Until then, Carl had rented an attractive villa nearby, in which Charlotte had lived as a child, as the laws forbade property ownership by Jews. Officials now ignored such restrictions when the head of the Rothschild counting house opened his checkbook. Even the Pope continued to borrow money from Carl.

Acquiring property in England was no problem for the brothers at New Court, but as with all their investments, they looked at land not only for its price at the time and its likely earnings, but for predicted

rise in value. They examined property also for its political benefits, should they became major proprietors in a jurisdiction, and—not least of all—for what economists since might call its psychic income, its emotional worth to four young men who loved to ride and race and hunt. A picture was commissioned by them from Francis Grant (as Sir Francis, later the president of the Royal Academy) in 1841, showing the pink-coated brothers, topped by black hats, ecstatically riding to hounds on an autumn morning in the Vale of Aylesbury. The year before, Grant's portrait of Queen Victoria and Viscount Melbourne riding in Windsor Park had made him the most fashionable painter of the day.

Lionel had chosen the soft, rolling hills of Buckinghamshire as the most desirable for leasing kennels and stables, as he did at Tring Park, and soon the Rothschilds would purchase further tracts for riding and shooting. Later, Lionel's severe rheumatoid arthritis, which can be triggered by a major physical disturbance, was attributed by physicians, very likely erroneously, to his having continued to wear wet leather breeches after a hard day's hunting. In 1842, Mayer (who lived with his mother at 107 Piccadilly and would inherit it) would purchase several adjacent farms in the Bucks parishes of Wing and Mentmore, and become Master of the local hunt.

In 1844, while on business in Frankfurt, Lionel wrote to Anthony and Mayer about parcels in Bucks that might be put together and earn income while they decided on estate building. (Only in the early 1850s would Anthony, who also loved the hunt, buy a country seat nearby at Aston Clinton.) Close to London, especially as railways were extended, and even closer to Gunnersbury, purchases in Bucks created regional political clout while making access to Piccadilly and to St. Swithin's Lane relatively easy. For the brothers, shooting in Scotland had proved unattractive. The highlands and moors were too remote from New Court; the weather was often harsh; and, Lionel explained to Charlotte from Melrose, in Walter Scott country, "it is rather difficult to find the game." Stalking the stag proved a bore. The Vale of Aylesbury would become Rothschild country. Using the Gunnersbury postal address, Acton, Lionel would even race horses as "Mr. Acton."

On March 21, 1841, Lionel's brother-in-law Anselm had written from Frankfurt that since the brothers were now firmly established, he hoped "in a year or two to be able to congratulate one of you on a seat in Parliament & to admire your eloquent speeches." An Austrian Rothschild, he should have been aware of the legal barriers to Jews in England, but these seemed to be coming down. Their uncle Moses had been knighted by Victoria in 1837, and in 1841, when Isaac Lyon Goldsmid, a stubborn fighter for Jewish emancipation, became the first Jewish baronet—not quite an elevation to the House of Lords[1] —Anthony wrote to Lionel from Paris that he would have liked it "much better" had the honor gone to his brother, who "ought to have tried" for it. Subtly, Lionel may have been seeking a family political entitlement of some sort by insinuating the Rothschilds into Buckinghamshire, yet gaining acceptance into Parliament would become a long ordeal occupying years of his life.

Recognizing the banker's political clout in the City, Tom O'Brien, acting for the Irish radical Daniel O'Connell, M.P. for Cork, asked Lionel to a public meeting to discuss "the political position of the Jews." The Irish members seated after Catholic emancipation in 1829 recognized that with implacable Tory hostility in the Lords, if what seemed to be the last oaths question were settled and Jews were also emancipated, they would be voting from the same side of the aisle.

At a sophisticated twenty-two and as her father had recommended long before she was ready, Charlotte was now entertaining ladies and gentlemen of position in the city and in the country. Having overcome her shyness, she was fully Lionel's partner, and agreed—even conspired—with Hannah to persuade Lionel that he was the Roth-

---

1. A barony brought with it a seat in the Lords, but a Jew would have been barred from taking it because of the Christian oath. A baronetcy earned no entitlement to a parliamentary seat.

schild to make an issue of the parliamentary oath. A new friend who would take their side, Charlotte was sure, was her admirer Benjamin Disraeli, although as an ambitious Tory he would have to vote against the party which, if in power, he hoped would give him Cabinet office. Public life for Charlotte, however, came to a stop, if only briefly, for another pregnancy. Alfred Charles was born on July 20, 1842. "I nursed him only six weeks," she remembered; "then he fell dangerously ill & to save his life I engaged a [wet] nurse. He recovered slowly."

For Charlotte, Alfred's infancy was only a temporary respite. It meant that she could not attend the wedding of Lionel's brother Nat to James's daughter Charlotte. (All three Rothschild girls named Charlotte married at seventeen.) Lionel went alone, traveling to Paris for the first time since the weeks before his own wedding six years earlier and then going on to James and Betty's château de Boulogne, on the Seine beyond Passy, where on August 17 the marriage took place in the garden under the *chuppah*. It was very hot, Lionel wrote to Charlotte amid endearments in *Judendeutsch*. She consoled him that he was "glücklich" to be in Paris again. He promised to bring back French dolls for Laury and Evy.

Soon Charlotte was receiving visitors to admire Alfred—most of her guests now from outside the tight-knit Jewish community—and continuing her beginnings of a salon. She also began traveling again, with her daughters, and a spirited letter to Lionel survives in which she announces, apparently from Frankfurt, "Our stay at Vienna will not probably be of very long duration as I should wish to be back before the arrival of our good Parents." (Her mother and father were apparently in Naples.) "I propose taking Julia[2] with us, and shall leave Natty and baby to keep you company."

On her return, radiant in a black velvet gown trimmed with lace above deep décolletage, Charlotte sat, surrounded by her four chil-

---

2. Possibly Juliana Cohen, a cousin, then eleven. She would marry Mayer de Rothschild eight years later.

dren, for a portrait by Christina Robertson. Natty is as ringleted in the contemporary fashion as are his sisters to Charlotte's right, and Alfred is asleep in a hooded bassinet. Behind them are a marble mantlepiece, a large painting, and statuary. Charlotte was exploiting the setting to take pride not only in her family but in her Piccadilly residence—her own.

Charlotte was also learning more about the family business. Even before Lionel began talking politics and banking with her, Hannah had intervened, intending to sway Lionel to her priorities through his wife. They discussed railway investment ("good for all classes," Hannah wrote to Charlotte from Brighton), the visit of the Tsar and Russian anti-Semitism ("May his understanding at least improve by his travels," Hannah hoped), and directions for Rothschild philanthropies, which already went beyond Anglo-Jewry. From the humble tailor in Whitechapel and the impoverished cobbler in Hoxton to the moneyed Rothschilds of Gunnersbury, there were not many more than thirty thousand Jews in all of England—hardly more than the population of a modest Anglican parish.

Since her charities already extended widely—with the likely exception of the London Society for Promoting Christianity among the Jews—Charlotte was already used to callers soliciting funds, some of them interested also in her social cachet. Charles Dickens visited about a charitable theatrical evening, the play to be Ben Jonson's *Every Man in His Humour*; and Charlotte visited Sir Moses at Park Lane to present him with a silver gilt cup from the Jewish community at Frankfurt to recognize his unceasing efforts on behalf of their brethren. On the great night at the St. James's Theatre, Dickens, wearing enormous boots and spurs, played Captain Bobadill. In the celebrity-studded audience were Prince Albert, the Duke of Wellington, Prince George of Cambridge, Lord Melbourne—and Baron and Baroness de Rothschild.

Charlotte's most imaginative early social coup occurred when, as 1844 began, Phineas T. Barnum, the American showman, came to London to line his pockets. His star attraction was a thirty-seven-inch entertainer, Charles Stratton, whom he had renamed "General" Tom Thumb. The U.S. Minister to Great Britain, Edward Everett, offered to promote an audience at Buckingham Palace, as the royal imprimatur would assure them full houses. Barnum leased the stridently exotic Egyptian Hall, on the south side of Piccadilly at the foot of Old Bond Street, and posted placards which trimmed a foot from Tom's actual height. Then he awaited responses.

The first offer came from Charlotte de Rothschild. She sent a phaeton to the furnished house he had leased in stylish Grafton Street. "Her mansion," Barnum wrote, "is a noble structure in Piccadilly, surrounded by a high wall, through the gate of which our carriage was driven, and brought up to the front of the main entrance. Here we were received by half a dozen servants, and were ushered up the broad stairs to the drawing-room, where we met the Baroness and a party of twenty or more ladies and gentlemen." He must have also met the Rothschild children, as it is inconceivable that they were not at the top of the stairs, giddy with excitement, yet Barnum's memoirs do not mention them. But with his bent for exaggeration he described "the glare of magnificence" radiating from the "immense chandeliers, [and] candelabras" in which he and his remarkable midget basked.

"The Baroness was seated on a gorgeous couch covered with rich figured silk damask (there were several similar couches in the room) and several lords and ladies were seated in chairs elegantly carved and covered with gold, . . . except the bottoms, which were of rich velvet." Very likely Tom Thumb put on his well-rehearsed act, singing "Yankee Doodle" in a treble voice, dancing a hornpipe, and closing with a repertoire of imitations, including one of Napoleon. "In this sumptuous mansion of the richest banker in the world," Barnum boasted, "we spent about two hours, and when we took our leave a well-filled purse[3] was quietly slipped into my hand. . . . That it was no

3. The customary payment to a singer or instrumentalist for a concert was then £20, but at some great houses remuneration for a star turn went as high as £150.

dream was manifest from the fact that, very shortly afterwards, a visit to the mansion of Mr. [Henry] Drummond, another eminent banker, came to the same golden conclusion." Barnum's success was assured, and Charlotte's reputation as salonnière soared.

It was no surprise to Barnum that the Queen became eager to have Tom Thumb visit Buckingham Palace. "The Prince [of Wales, then two] is taller than I am," Tom confessed in her Yellow Drawing Room, "but I *feel* as big as anybody." He was invited back twice and collected purses that made up for closing the Egyptian Hall for three evenings.

Another success some weeks later also put the Rothschilds on the social map. This time, it was Disraeli's doing. In his ornate fashion he had chatted happily with Lionel and Charlotte at a garden party at Gunnersbury, which he told his sister, Sarah, was "worthy of an Italian Prince, though decorated with a taste and splendor which a French financier in the olden times could alone have rivalled." In Paris he had dinner with Anthony and Louise, and learned more Rothschild history and legend. Soon he had visited 148 Piccadilly on enough occasions to refer breezily to "the Lionels." Imaginatively, with the incorporation, also, of some creative autobiography, he wrote Lionel (Charlotte would come later) into the first volume of his "Young England" trilogy of novels, *Coningsby*, which appeared to press acclaim early in May 1844.

Disraeli's Sidonia (he has no other name in the novel) was the most striking character he ever created. Although the worldly, philosophical financier was more myth than reality, the reading public, which took eagerly to the book, associated the superrich, mysterious, aloof banker—the most influential in Europe, and beyond political frontiers despite his domicile in England—with Baron Lionel. As for aloofness, it was known that Lionel never cast his shadow on the Rothschild pillar at the Exchange once tenanted by his father. Outside the counting house he was, like Sidonia, a committed horseman. Unlike many other public men in London, Sidonia, like Lionel, had utterly no taint of indiscretions with women. Also like Sidonia, he was an intellectual who handled power with grace and subtlety. In Disraeli's vision, the impossible but intriguing Sidonia was a Spinoza figure born into the Rothschild inheritance, wealthy beyond avarice and passionate about his people.

Suggesting the unannounced Rothschild interest in a parliamentary seat still barred by religion, Sidonia's Judaism "walled him out from the pursuits of a citizen." Foreclosed from many elite professions, his ancestors turned their intelligence to banking. "Shut out from universities and schools," young Sidonia himself studied mathematics and philosophy in England with a Sephardic tutor and then learned his profession through residence with uncles—again suggesting the Rothschilds—in Naples and Frankfurt. When he came of age, he "made arrangements with the heads of the houses that bore his name" about the management of his assets, unconcerned about public approbation, which was "worthless to him."

Viscount Palmerston, the foreign minister, sent his brother a copy with a list of alleged identifications, notably and unavoidably including Baron Lionel. Disraeli's political understudy Lord John Manners, later 7th Duke of Rutland, was "full of mild rapture." Another disciple, George Smythe, the future 7th Viscount Strangford, wrote to Disraeli that he was "dazzled, bewildered, tipsy with admiration." As reviews emerged, Baroness Hannah told Charlotte that Disraeli had been "rather adept in dwelling upon the good qualities of Sidonia's race. In raising many arguments for their emancipation he cleverly introduced many circumstances one might recognise." She had written to him "expressing our admiration." Lionel made no known comment, public or private, but *Coningsby* propelled him further into public life.

Another of many readers "enchanted" by *Coningsby* was Disraeli's colleague in the Commons, John Ponsonby, Viscount Duncannon, M.P. for Galway. He wanted an opportunity, he wrote to Charlotte, already known for bringing interesting people together, to talk with the author. The Baroness duly invited Benjamin and his eccentric wife Mary Anne, and John Ponsonby, to dinner on Sunday, May 19. Within days of publication, the novelist would be dining with his Sidonia. Thereafter, the Rothschilds were seldom out of Disraeli's mind, and he and Mary Anne were seldom out of the Rothschild orbit. On June 14, the Disraelis gave a large political dinner at Grosvenor Gate, at which Charlotte and Lionel mixed with political bigwigs, and with iron baron Sir Josiah Guest and his literary wife, Lady Charlotte. Dinner was followed by a reception for two hundred additional invitees. (Charlotte and Lionel were not rigid about observing the Jewish dietary laws except when with more traditional members of their own family.) Two days later came an entertainment at the Rothschilds that Sir John Cam Hobhouse, a minister in many Cabinets and a Radical leader, thought was intended by Baron Lionel to bring Disraeli together with influential Whigs.

Disraeli's novel in progress, *Sybil, or The Two Nations*, tried to straddle both parties, but the striking and memorable suggestion of the subtitle, that there were two nations in England, the Rich and the Poor, was remote from the Tory mainstream. Less obvious to readers of *Sybil* in 1845 than was the portrait of Lionel to readers of *Coningsby* in 1844, was Charlotte's first imaginative appearance in Disraeli's fiction. The title character, a radiant young woman who enchants the idealistic Lord Egremont, the aspiring politician of the novel, seems Disraeli's first fictional idealization of Charlotte—but for her "long fair hair," apparently devised to deflect identification. At the close, when the couple marry and honeymoon at Naples, the knowledgeable reader's guess may seem confirmed.

Lionel and the London house would be linked, soon, to the Queen, who was planning, with Albert, to make a sentimental journey to his birthplace in Coburg in the summer of 1845. Already the confidential courier of Victoria's letters to Germany, the London firm through Baron Stockmar proposed "that the honour be accorded to it to be allowed to act as bankers in Germany to supply any need for money which Her Majesty might have on this journey." Since she did not use letters of credit, Stockmar suggested that "if Your Highness before your departure would allow Lionel von Rothschild"—the Baron used the German form—"to be called, the simplest and best way might be arranged for the necessities of the journey. Nor will this involve any bad reflection. People like to say the Queen is associated with them, and the advantages of her relationship can't be achieved without notice."

Lionel became, as needed, banker to the Queen and soon, more quietly, banker to Prince Albert. Already financier for many influential diplomats and foreign ministers, he acquired in such fashion inimitable sources of information. Among the envoys was the American writer Washington Irving, who drew on a London account set up by the Secretary of State in Washington while Irving was Minister to Spain. Later, even the novelist Herman Melville used his Rothschild letter of credit at the Frankfurt and Naples houses, pleased with the guarantee of confidentiality—"no scrutiny as in other places."

Charlotte was again pregnant in the summer of 1845—it would be her last pregnancy. She wanted to spend the summer months in Gunnersbury, but in June Disraeli urged her to "bring the beauteous children" to Grosvenor Gate for a view of the Queen's parade in Hyde Park in honor of the visit of Victoria's uncle (and Lionel's client), King Leopold of the Belgians. And Disraeli would urge that whenever Charlotte wanted to observe a debate in the House of Commons—which she was no longer in condition to do—"You have only to ask for Mrs. Disraeli's place." Mary Anne had been using her privileges to observe the debates over the Jews' Oaths of Abjuration bill, and when it passed its second reading in the Commons, she wrote to Charlotte herself to express happiness at "the glorious end to the debate." The bill removed all municipal—but not parliamentary—disabilities as they affected Jews and seemed to foreshadow the end of all legal barriers. When David Salomons won a City election for the aldermanry of Portsoken but refused to take the required oath "on the true faith of a Christian," the Court of Aldermen had voided the election. Sir Robert Peel, the prime minister, who considered all such oaths outdated, then asked the skillful old Lord Chancellor, Baron Lyndhurst, to draft appropriate parliamentary legislation. Lyndhurst and his young second wife, Georgiana, daughter of the late Lewis Goldsmith, a Jewish political journalist in France, were Charlotte's friends.

One of the great legal minds of the age, Lyndhurst voted his conscience and cherished his relationship with the Rothschilds. On one occasion when Charlotte gave a dinner in his and Lady Lyndhurst's honor, two of the guests were Martha Babcock Amory, his niece from America,[4] and her daughter. Charlotte, Mrs. Amory recalled, "almost reverenced the powerful advocate of their rights. . . . Nothing could exceed the splendour of the banquet. Silver and gold plate shone on the table and buffets; exquisite flowers delighted the eye; while the retinue of servants, in full dress, so well trained that not a foot-fall told of their presence, and the ease and repose which prevailed, . . . were forgotten in the distinction of the company. . . . Thus we were fully launched on the broad current of English society, in the rush of the season,—the talisman of a name, like a modern sesamé, throwing open every door in London."

Peel's bill was enacted on July 31, 1845, and the event emboldened Nat to write from Paris, "I shall be glad to see [you] Ld M[ayor] of London & M.P. for the city. You ought to be canvassing [also] for the E[ast] Ind[ia Company] direction, my dear Lionel." Hannah added her own prodding and also found a willing listener in Charlotte. Peel's government was tottering, and its fall would bring new parliamentary elections—and opportunities. They would open the most significant symbolic battle of Lionel's life.

In late August, after looking in regularly on the ill Hannah Mayer

---

4. Ennobled as Baron Lyndhurst, John Singleton Copley was the son of the American expatriate portraitist from Boston (to whom Washington once sat), after whom he was named.

Fitzroy, who in Disraeli's opinion was "nearly given over," Charlotte left for the country, to wait out her pregnancy. Mary Anne had invited Charlotte and Lionel to Grosvenor Gate before the Disraelis, with parliamentary sessions over, departed for a long holiday in France and the Low Countries. Happily expecting to evade Mary Anne's dinner, Charlotte began a letter with "These are farewell lines, . . . for I begin to fear that we shall not meet again ere you leave the dusty and deserted metropolis." Because of the children's chicken pox, she explained, she had decided not to return from Gunnersbury with Lionel. "Pray tell Mr. Disraeli," she added, "how grateful I am to him for all the beautiful things he so brilliantly & eloquently said during his long & interesting religious discussion with Ch. Cooper.[5] My only regret is that you did not hear them, and that I could not trust myself to repeat them. I wish the orator had a more numerous audience; more enthusiastic listeners he could never & nowhere have found." As he was then writing *Tancred*, the third of his political trilogy, which Disraeli would nearly complete on holiday, he may have been trying out some of his ideas about race and religion in the novel on Cooper and on Charlotte.

Preparing 2 Grosvenor Gate for a long closure, the Disraelis planned to leave on September 9. When Charlotte's letter arrived, Dizzy hastily invited Lionel, who would be alone, to dine the next day, September 3, "sans façon in our dismantled house. We cannot console you for the absence of your agreeable wife, but we will sympathise with you—& it will be a good occasion to try some claret, wh: I have always kept for your palate."

Charlotte would return unexpectedly. Hannah Fitzroy seemed to be fulfilling Disraeli's dismal prognosis. Always unaware of her good-hearted absurdities, Mary Anne, learning of the Baroness's homecoming, hurried from Grosvenor Gate and pulled hard on the bell at 148 Piccadilly. She fell "into my reluctant arms," Charlotte

5. Charles Purton Cooper, a Q.C. (Queen's counsel) at Lincoln's Inn, was an authority on legal history and an activist for law reforms.

wrote wryly to Anthony's wife, Louisa, quoting their "excellent and eccentric friend." It was six on Friday, September 5, and Charlotte had just returned, in time for Sabbath eve, from Hannah Mayer's sickbed:

> "I am quite out of breath, my dear, I have been running so fast, we have no horses, no carriage, no servants, we are going abroad, I have been so busy correcting proof-sheets, the publishers are so tiresome, we ought to have been gone a month ago; I should have called upon you long ere now, I have been so nervous, so excited, so agitated, poor Dis' has been sitting up the whole night writing; I want to speak to you on business, pray send the darling children away" &c., &c., for it would, without any exaggeration, take more than ten pages to put down conscientiously all the lady's words, not noting exclamations and gestures and tears. You know, dear Louisa, that I am easily terrified and almost speechless. I had never seen her in such a state of excitement before, and all I could do was to gasp out—"Has anything happened?"
>
> Mrs. Disraeli heaved a deep sigh and said: "This is a farewell visit, I may never see you again—life is so uncertain. . . . Disi and I may be blown up on the railroad or in the steamer, there is not a human body that loves me in this world, and besides my adored husband I care for no one on earth, but I love your glorious race, I am rich, I am prosperous, I think it right to entertain serious thought, to look calmly upon one's end. . . ."
>
> Mrs. Disraeli's conversation is not exactly remarkable for clearness of thought, precision of language, or for a proper concatenation of images, ideas, and phrases, nevertheless, I had always been able to comprehend and to reply, but on that memorable Friday, I was quite at a loss to understand her meaning. . . . I tried to calm and quiet my visitor who, after having enumerated her goods and chattels to me, took a paper out of her pocket saying: "This is my Will and you must read it, show it to the dear Baron, and take care of it for me." I answered that she must be aware of my feelings, that

I should ever be truly grateful for such a proof of confidence, but could not accept such a great responsibility.

At that point, Charlotte may have been grateful that the children were gone, for the strangely dressed and wild-eyed Mary Anne had no intention of stopping. Also, logic was not her strongest asset. She could never remember, Disraeli once joked, who came first, the Greeks or the Romans.

"But you must listen," replied the inexorable lady: she opened the paper and read aloud:

"In the event of my beloved Husband preceding me to the grave, I leave and bequeath to Evelina de Rothschild all my personal property."

I leave you to picture to yourself my amazement and embarrassment. Mrs. Disraeli rose and would hear no answer, no objection.

"I love the Jews—I have attached myself to your children and she—she shall, she must, wear the butterfly."

Away rushed the testatrix, leaving the testament in my unworthy hands. I passed a miserable night, witnessing all the horrors of boilers bursting on the railroad and steamboats being blown up, and seeing myself as chief mourner at our poor friend's funeral. Then there was a ball at the French Embassy; I was an old Mamma and Evy looked overpowered by the weight of the emerald tiara, and the diamond butterfly was fluttering round her shoulders. The next morning I breakfasted in a hurry, walked to the abode of genius and his wife, to whom I returned the Will. There was a scene, a very disagreeable one, and then all was over—*the dream and the reality.*

Written on September 10, just after the Disraelis crossed the Channel to Boulogne, Charlotte's letter evokes a remarkable talent, in English, for a young woman brought up on German and French and Italian, and reveals a wry wit she would often employ.

Leopold was born to Charlotte on November 22, 1845, and named for the King of the Belgians. Her final accouchement was her easiest. Since names of Jewish children customarily honored family members, the gesture was unusual, evidencing his parents' increasing worldliness—and honoring a major New Court client. Hannah Fitzroy had endured a difficult birth the year before. As Charlotte realized, her outcast sister-in-law had been mentally and physically ill since. HM's daughter, Blanche (a second child), was unkindly referred to by Henry Fitzroy, now a junior minister in the Admiralty, as resembling a young lobster. Alarm about Nathaniel, who was pale and sickly and thin, Charlotte recalled, "distressed my thoughts," especially after he suffered briefly from what was feared to be "inflammation of the brain"—a frightening diagnosis hidden from her until the imagined danger had passed.

Gloomy premonitions about her pregnancy had obsessed Charlotte. Although no one knew of Charlotte's hidden hysteria, she engaged Sir Charles Locock, the Queen's accoucheur, to ensure that she had the priciest, if not the best, medical attention possible. (Wags called him "deliverer of the nation.") "I had been morally, mentally & bodily ill," Charlotte wrote later. She recalled "feelings of great apprehension" and "could not believe it possible that I could not escape unhurt." She "dreaded to find bodily weakness or incapacity" in her child, and "when Dr. Locock informed me that the new born was what is termed perfect, . . . my profound gratitude vented itself in a flood of tears." Leopold was always very special to her afterwards.

In Paris, Disraeli read the news of Leopold's birth. The family now *was* news, whatever it did. On December 3 he wrote to the Baron from the Hôtel de l'Europe, "I hope he will prove worthy of his pure and sacred race, and of his beautiful brothers and sisters. We are anxious to hear that Madame Lionel is as well as we all could wish, and that you are happy." Having just had an audience with King Louis-Philippe, Disraeli then reported on his conversation—the kind of privileged information which Lionel, always au courant, appreciated. (Such intelligence gave the Baron clout with the government, as emerges from a letter from the Foreign Secretary's wife, Emily, to a confidant, about the Spanish succession: "Lionel Rothschild's correspondent says the Spaniards will *not* intervene, and he thinks the French are so sick of all the bother they have brought on themselves by the [duc de] Montpensier marriage that they will try now to keep quiet.") In May 1846 Lionel's cousin Anselm informed him from Frankfurt of conversations with Prince Albert's éminence grise, Baron Stockmar, who did business with the Rothschilds: "He is still as friendly for our House as he ever was and promised me solemnly that as soon as he will know something about the American and Corn Bill question, you my dear Lionel, will be the first person to be informed.")

Following his diplomatic confidences, Disraeli let it be known that he was seeking investment advice, although New Court knew he owed staggering sums to creditors. With Rothschild acumen behind his book income—*Sybil* had just been published—he thought he could turn a profit on railways. He already had Lionel (who did so as a favor) manage a modest 150 shares of Paris & Strasbourg stock. Lionel himself had just helped organize the Compagnie du Chemin de Fer du Nord, to build and operate a railway connecting Paris and Valenciennes, with a branch to Lille and Calais. A quarter of the stock was held by the London and Paris houses; and Lionel, Nat, and James were on the board of directors. (Each held an *administrateur* card guaranteeing free travel on the line.) "I feel half inclined to purchase Foreign Railway shares in spite of the surrounding gloom and terror [about accidents]," Disraeli offered, trying to downplay his enthusiasm. "Do you think we have seen the worst? And what do you recommend?"

English politics was different from the lax French variety, and Lionel was very wary of being perceived as financially involved with any London politician, even a friend. He kept the Disraeli account prudently small and token.[6]

---

6. By January 28, 1846, Disraeli feared that his Strasbourg speculation had "turned out indifferently" and asked Lionel to dispose of the shares. He hoped that the Nord stock "which you so kindly gave me" would do better.

When the Disraelis returned, Mary Anne hurried to 148 Picca-dilly to see Charlotte's child. She had acquired a confusion of Judeo-Christian ideas from her Dizzy in her inimitable fashion, and she gushed over Leopold, "My dear, that beautiful baby may be the future Messiah whom we are led to expect—who knows? And you will [then] be the most favoured of women!" Louisa's daughter Constance re-called that Leopold, afterward, throughout his childhood, was re-ferred to in the family as "Little Messiah."

CHAPTER FIVE

"THE JEW BILL"

1846-1850

Under Gunnersbury Park's festive tents at the Baroness de Roth-schild's crowded fête champêtre on Wednesday, June 24, 1846, the chatter focused upon the vote in the Commons the next day on free trade. Disraeli's defection with his protectionist faction would upset Peel's Tory government and return power to the Whigs. The pros-pect of rain, Disraeli wrote to his sister, Sarah, "is a pity, as it is really the only great fête we have in this country." But the rain deferred to Charlotte.

At Piccadilly or Gunnersbury, her receptions and lower-key salons were opportunities where news was exchanged, and often made. A key factor—he was almost a daily presence, often without a prior in-vitation—was the new editor of *The Times*, John Delane, for whom Lionel had interceded with the proprietor, John Walter, to get the young journalist the post. (Earlier, Lionel had arbitrated a dispute between Walter and Delane's father, who had been financial manager of the paper.) A bachelor who lived at Serjeants' Inn, below Temple Bar, John Delane might be at Piccadilly House for breakfast, once he saw the paper through the press, or materialize at any other time. Charlotte cosseted him whether or not Lionel was about.

At social gatherings, at exclusive clubs, and in the press, railways were a focus of gossip in the 1840s, and the mania for speculation in rail shares was intense. Other Rothschild partners often had to rein in the enthusiasm in Paris for railway investment, James casually bribing French politicians (as everyone did) with stocks. Although the Rothschilds were at a remove from actual operations, rail accidents led to anti-Semitic attacks, including a scurrilous pamphlet libeling James, *The History of Rothschild I, King of the Jews*. After a crash led to losses in patronage, Anthony, troubleshooting in Paris, told Lionel, "I don't care much [about the drop in revenue] as it will give time to our employees to learn their business."

That summer at the spa in Wildbad, in Germany, Mayer, steadfastly optimistic, discussed with James joint investing in improvements to the harbor at Dover to make railway links between London and Paris more efficient. London anchored the family houses, Mayer boasted to Lionel and Anthony: "There is no place like our old New Court. Where would the rubbishy French shares be, if we did not support them? I think we may give ourselves a few airs and be as great men as others." Lionel was above posturing, or upstaging Uncle James. He employed his prestige where he thought it counted, as when he secured a letter of introduction from Sir Robert Peel to Count Nesselrode, the Tsar's foreign minister, before the tireless Moses Montefiore went to Russia on behalf of the Board of Deputies of British Jews to appeal for modification of abuses against Jews. To enhance his pre-travel prestige, the Queen raised Sir Moses to a baronetcy, only the second (after Isaac Goldsmid in 1841) granted to a Jew.

Peel's tenure at Downing Street had been extended briefly by factionalism in the Opposition, but Anthony used the elevation of his uncle Moses as an excuse to goad Lionel into hoping that "perhaps when the Whigs come in . . . they will think they ought to give something to your honour." The pragmatic Nat proposed instead that his brother stand for the City when a seat opened in the Commons. Chances of amending the Christian oath were better there than in the Lords.

Quietly, at home, Charlotte pushed Lionel into thinking more about public life. In effect he spoke and acted for Anglo-Jewry, whether or not he sought it. As the managing partner of a powerful banking house, he had long been in public life via the vast loans he floated for governments. That had seemed sufficiently public for him. Yet when the Whigs settled their disarray and took office, Lord John Russell, who held a seat for the City and was the new prime minister, succeeding Peel, recommended to the Queen that Lionel be made a baronet to recognize his commanding presence in the City. On November 14, 1846, Victoria consented, but no one had asked Baron Lionel, who weighed pride against pragmatism, whether he would welcome the honor of being less than a baron.

Had it been up to Charlotte, the offer would have been accepted with grace. An empty British rank was more significant than an empty, if higher, Austrian one. But Lionel wrote to his mother, then visiting Frankfurt, that he expected to turn the baronetcy down. She saw that as poor politics. "I don't think it good taste," Hannah answered bluntly, "to refuse it, as your little friend"—the bantam Russell—"remarks what she can bestow." The Queen, Hannah realized, could not grant a barony, which would impose Lionel upon the unwilling House of Lords. The Upper House would refuse to seat him. "The Peerage cannot be bestowed at present without taking the Oath and that I suppose that you would not do. A Personal Compliment from the Highest Personage should be esteemed and may lead to other advantages but to repudiate it might create anger—and in accepting it you do not do away with your original Title. . . . The previous granting . . . I think has nothing to do with yours—and decidedly does not reduce the Compliment. This is my opinion—excuse my candour."

Anselm, in Frankfurt—Lionel's brother in-law—agreed, while misunderstanding the difference in degree between baron and baronet: "As an Englishman it becomes you much better to be an English baronet than a foreign one."

Lionel wanted a breakthrough into the Upper House. However bigoted and stuffy, the Lords, he thought, might be sufficiently intimidated by the Queen's nomination to concede to an oath a Rothschild could take. (Seeking that distinction, Lionel apparently asked Prince Albert frankly, "[Y]ou have nothing better to offer me?") But Victoria would not risk a losing confrontation with the Lords, and Lionel realized that spurning the baronetcy would impel him to campaign for the Commons and force the issue into the open in the other chamber. Anthony, Mayer, and Nat all urged acceptance. "Follow my advice and take it," proposed Billy, "and if you don't like it for yourself, accept it for one of us; these things are always better to be had when one can, and don't refuse it." Nat suggested, "Old Billy thinks Sir Anthony would sound very well," and as alternative proposed "Sir Mayer of Mentmore." Baron James added, wryly, that it was "a lot of luck that your nice Queen has, thank God, taken such a liking to you. Do be very careful that your Prince Albert does not become jealous of you." James, too, felt that "one should never let such an opportunity pass by."

In declining the baronetcy, Lionel asked that it be conferred instead upon his brother Anthony, with right of succession to his and Charlotte's eldest son if Anthony had no male heirs. The family compromise avoided further bickering. Sir Anthony it was—and his two children were daughters.

Exactly when Lionel approached Prince Albert on the baronetcy issue is unknown, but he did know the Prince personally and saw him on business matters. Given royal protocol, this meant that although Albert might want to borrow money, he could hardly go to New Court. Lionel would visit Buckingham Palace, as he did on May 13, 1847, when a spendthrift Coburger cousin, Prince Ludwig Kraft Ernst von Oettingen-Wallerstein, asked Albert to cosign a Rothschild note for £3,000 at 5 percent interest on the security of Ludwig's pictures. Lionel explained Albert's liability—that he might get to own the collection. Indeed, Albert did. His perennially hard-up cousin defaulted.

As Lionel's rejection of the baronetcy rippled through family politics, the country was facing a catastrophe that made the matter of policy on which Lionel's decision had turned fade in urgency. Ireland, an island dependency only a few hours away but dealt with by the myopic establishment as if a distant colony of subhumans, was starving. Nearly nine million Irish, mostly Roman Catholics and with minimal education, existed largely on small plots owned by absentee Protestant landlords. Without any skills other than subsistence farming, and mostly poor beyond the imaginations of indifferent Englishmen, the Irish were enduring a blackening blight on the only crop raised for their own food—the potato. As Nicholas Cummins, a Cork magistrate, observed on a visit to Skibbereen, there was nothing for them to eat but rotting root crops. Not only could the victims ill afford alternative edibles, as the Irish exported everything else to pay rent and stave off evictions, most grain imports were banned by the Protectionist Corn Laws intended to keep the squirearchy's farm prices artificially high.

The government had spent millions to emancipate black slaves in the West Indies, much of it raised by the Rothschilds, but was unwilling to allot more than £50,000 in relief funds to stave off the deaths of hundreds of thousands of desperate Irish. On December 22 Cummins wrote a passionate letter to the Irish-born Duke of Wellington, sending a copy to *The Times*. The "spectres" he saw were "frightful," Cummins explained. "My heart sickens at the recital, but I must go on." Delane published the letter the day before Christmas. Lionel read it and determined to do something. Although not passionately religious, he had grown up with the Bible. Proverbs prescribed, "Honor the Lord with thy substance."

On New Year's Day 1847 a hastily convened meeting was held in the Rothschild offices at New Court, and the "British Association for

the relief of extreme distress in the remote parishes of Ireland and
Scotland"—to widen the political net, Scotland was added—was
formed. Among the founder-members were Lionel de Rothschild
and his banker friend John Abel Smith, of Smith, Payne and Smith,
and the Whig (Liberal) M.P. for Chichester. The financier Samuel
Jones-Loyd, later Lord Overstreet, was elected chairman. Symbolically, the first subscriber was "H. M. The Queen," at £2,000. Second
was "Rothschild, £1,000." (Lionel had actually opened the subscription.) Much farther down, at £200, was Charles Wood (the future
Viscount Halifax), Chancellor of the Exchequer. Relief committees
were quickly set up to establish soup kitchens and to distribute food.
Soon £470,000 was raised, and the total would go higher, but for
many thousands in Ireland it was too late. Famished survivors saw
the blight persist.

On February 25, 1847, Disraeli, always financially strapped, wrote
to Lionel enclosing his small check for Irish relief. Candidly, he explained, "Now that the 'large ordnance' have ceased to roar, the still
small voice of this pistol shot may pass muster." For Lionel, who did
not live in his wife's house, or on loans, like Disraeli, help for the Irish
was not token. Once his subcommittee, with Thomas Baring and
Thomas Hankey, had established depots on the Irish coast, and in
the interior, Lionel made good with substance, reshipping cargoes of
wheat, originally intended as Rothschild investments, without charge
to Ireland. On one occasion as he learned that a ship had arrived in
the Thames with a cargo of grain for New Court, he ordered it to sail
immediately for Cork.

Parliament had reassembled on January 19, 1847, just as Mary
Anne Disraeli was writing to Charlotte, "The first proofs of 'Tancred' are now on the table. How much I hope you will be here when
he is presented to the public, for I am sure you will sympathise with
me in my child's fate." Mary Anne was childless. Dizzy's books were
her vicarious offspring.

Tancred, the third volume of Disraeli's "Young England" trilogy,
emerged in March. Its clever and beautiful Eva Besso, daughter of a

Jewish agent of the international banker Sidonia, was the author's idealization of Charlotte. Her witty exchanges on religion and morality with callow young Tancred, Lord Montacute, who travels to the Holy Land to find himself and falls impossibly in love with Eva, suggest Charlotte's rejoinders as Disraeli sparkled at her dinner table and flourished in her salons. Disraeli even borrowed books from Charlotte, who had an account at Hatchards, afterwards discussing with her such authors as Thomas Babington Macaulay, whose ornate style was confessedly too much even for the florid author of *Tancred*.

Sidonia reappears in Disraeli's novel, in flashback at twenty and in the present at forty, many times a millionaire with managers handling his financial affairs across Europe. (Lionel, perhaps by no coincidence, was in his fortieth year in 1847.) Among the many overt allusions to Lionel is Sidonia's imposing bank at "Sequin Court," and his lavish London home, which could be 148 Piccadilly. Eva's religious retorts suggest the outspoken Charlotte, as when she observes to young Tancred, whose Anglicanism is Sunday-schoolish, "Half of Christendom worships a Jewess, and the other half a Jew." And Charlotte's family pride emerges spiritedly when she asks,

"Which is the greatest city in Europe?"

"Without doubt, the capital of my country, London."

". . . How rich the most honoured man must be there! Tell me, is he a Christian?"

"I believe he is one of your race and faith."

"And in Paris; who is the richest man in Paris?"

"The brother, I believe, of the richest man in London."

"I know all about Vienna," said the lady. . . . "Caesar makes my countrymen barons of the empire, and rightly, for it would fall to pieces in a week without their support."

Religion in England, contends the shrewd and engaging Emir Fakredeen, an Arab admirer of Eva, is entirely a creation of Parliament. "The English are really neither Jews nor Christians, but follow a sort of religion of their own, which is made every year by their bishops . . . in what they call a parliament, a college of muftis." The nature of that body, Lionel and Charlotte knew, made his taking a seat in either house impossible. The three oaths of Allegiance, Supremacy, and Abjuration were to insure the monarchy and government against disloyalty, the last oath requiring swearing, on the New Testament, "upon the true faith of a Christian." Its adherents insisted that however free nonbelievers were to conduct their daily business in Britain, they were nevertheless living in a Christian society and had no right to make laws for it. England, Thomas Carlyle insisted to the historian J. A. Froude, as they once stood outside 148 Piccadilly, had "a Gentile legislature." "How can any real Jew," Carlyle wrote crankily to Richard Monckton Milnes, an M.P., ". . . try to be a Senator, or even Citizen, of any country, except his own wretched Palestine, whither all his thoughts and steps and efforts tend?" The future 7th Earl of Shaftesbury, Lord Ashley, despite his philanthropic and Sabbatarian zeal (symbolized by his ring, on which was engraved "Oh, pray for the peace of Jerusalem!"), insisted upon a Christian legislature. Altering the oath, he charged in the Commons, would be "a practical denial of the faith."

Lionel intended nevertheless to contest a seat. More than pride was involved. The religious excuses of opponents rang in his ears as a mockery of conscience, a word he would emphasize in his campaign. The family firm was resilient enough to withstand the brickbats of bigotry. His season for purposeful action had come. ("To everything there is a season," according to Ecclesiastes, "and a time to every purpose under the heaven.") Yet there were "difficulties," as Nat put it, probably echoing his brother. Lord John Russell, while encouraging Lionel, wrote unhelpfully on April 28, 1847, that "the state of public business" would not allow a measure to end Jewish disabilities to be introduced in the "present session, but it will be brought forward in the next session of Parliament." If Lionel were elected, he would have to wait, perhaps indefinitely, for the enabling legislation.

Since a Member did not have to be a resident of his constituency, he also considered standing from safely Liberal seaside Hythe but was persuaded by Russell, who had a City seat, to contest, for its symbolism, one of the four the financial district was allotted. Mayer, who was building a vast country house at Mentmore, had been made High Sheriff of Buckinghamshire in March, yet he opted to try for the Hythe seat. To Lionel, lawful election costs were no problem, yet to overspend (as Mayer proposed) could become an embarrassment. If he won, even more money might be necessary to secure enough M.P. votes, always for sale, to amend the Abjuration oath.

Lionel was adopted as a candidate by Liberals in the City on June 29, 1847. Running for its four seats were four Liberals, one Peelite, three Protectionists (Disraeli's Conservative faction), and an independent. The formal nomination of candidates took place on the day of balloting, which meant that aspirants had already conducted their campaigns. Each was expected to issue a platform. "Sat up late," Delane of *The Times* had noted in his diary for June 26, "and went to Rothschild's house in Piccadilly to assist him in preparing his address. Saw there Sir Anthony and the Baroness [Charlotte]." Prudently, Delane suggested that Lord John Russell see the text, and after he did, the editor returned on the 28th to review Russell's suggested changes.

Lionel began with a declaration for "liberty of conscience"—the cause that had put him into the race. Taking cautious if liberal stances, reflecting his personal views if not those of the propertied City electorate, he meant to represent more than his constituency, and far more than the small numbers of Anglo-Jewry. He proposed lowering the duties on coffee and tea, while balancing revenues by a property tax, which his voters could afford but would not want. His key position, repeated from his stump speeches, remained his trust that electors in the City would attest by their ballots that they were "in favour of civil and religious liberty." They would be demonstrating "to the civilized world generally a great and important example."

Anticipating challenges that Londoners were wasting their ballots if he could not be seated, he declared, "My opponents say I cannot

take my seat. That is rather my affair rather than theirs. . . . I feel assured that, as your representative, as the representative of the most
wealthy, the most important, the most intelligent constituency in the
world, I shall not be refused admission to Parliament on account of
any form of words whatever." City electors placed him third, with
6,792 votes. Russell was first with 7,117. Three Liberals headed the
poll, and the fourth lost to a Tory by only 3 votes. "I saw the Baroness afterwards," Delane noted in his diary, "[who was] in a state of
almost frenzied delight and gratitude."

From Paris, Nat called the result a victory for the "Family." Yet
there was no practical victory unless Lionel could be seated, and the
tally remained only a statistic while legislation on the oath stalled.
When Parliament returned, and the Tory leader in the Commons,
Lord George Bentinck, declared that he would vote, like Disraeli, for
a revised oath, King Ernest Augustus carped to Lord Strangford
from Hanover, "What can have induced George Bentinck to take the
Jews under his protection can only be explained by his former haunts
on the turf, and thus his connection with the Hebrews. . . . According to his principle, Turks, Mussulmans, Hindoos, etc., should all be
placed on one and the same footing." From Woburn Abbey, where
she was visiting the Duke and Duchess of Bedford, Hannah wrote to
Lionel on December 14, 1847, that another guest, the Earl of Or-
ford, had told her that he was "against the question . . . but you will
gain."

With *Tancred*, and Lionel's battle with the Christian parliamentary
oath, being talked about, conversations among the Rothschilds
seemed to end, if not begin, on both issues. "Yesterday," Louisa
wrote that November, "the Disis, [and] Charlotte and Lionel dined
with us. Mrs. Disi was looking remarkably well and as usual an odd
mixture of *good sense* and *nonsense*, of amusing humour and gaiety and
of no less amusing absurdity, but I must like her, for she is, I am sure,
really true. Disi was extremely affected with the children but . . . not
too grand to be amiable. He spoke of the Jews' life in his strange Tan-
credian strain, saying we must ask for our rights and privileges, not

for concessions and liberty of conscience. I wonder if he will have the courage to speak to the House in the same manner." In the Commons, playing to his Tory benches, he would defend both sides of the issue, supporting Lionel as legitimately elected but deploring that his friend believed "only in the first part of the Jewish religion"—a claim that the New Testament was its continuation. Charlotte and Louisa were outraged, as would have been Eva in Disraeli's own *Tancred*. Lionel stood by quietly. Disraeli the politician could not afford a public conscience.

On December 19, with Parliament back in session, Charlotte and Louisa were in the Commons gallery for the first reading of "the Jew Bill," which passed by a majority of sixty-seven. Eighteen Peelites, including the future Duke of Newcastle, voted affirmatively, the Earl of Lincoln (as he then was)[1] telling the ambivalent W. E. Gladstone that he did so "careless of the anger of Constituents or other parties." Monckton Milnes had rushed back from Madrid to vote and found a letter awaiting him from his father, Lord Houghton, confiding that he was "not sorry you are missing this session" as "Mr. Rothschild's dinners" should not be "set off" against the "strong tho' silly prejudice" with which he nevertheless agreed. Ignoring him, Milnes voted for the bill.

The Rothschild women spent, Louisa wrote in her diary, "eight interesting but fatiguing hours":

> The debate was but indifferent and the only time any great enthusiasm was shown was when our opponents screamed out their "noes." Charlotte was dreadfully excited; I cannot say that I was, nor had the violence or ill nature of a few of the enemies of the Bill much effect. . . . On the whole we were very courteously treated and we could not expect all prejudice, bigotry and dislike to be silent.

1. Although an earl, he was M.P. for Falkirk and did not move to the Lords until he succeeded his father as duke.

On December 23, Nat wrote from Paris cautioning Lionel to es-chew "certain means to secure some votes in the House of Lords, which are not peculiarly commendable." He was weighing covert forms of bribery, such as offering loans to legislators and even to Prince Albert, who had influential friends in both houses. From the standpoint of the family, Nat conceded, having consulted their un-cles, "whatever you do is for the best and . . . you may put down the *sum* to the house. Of course you will not cash up until the bill passes the Lords." Bribes, even ostensibly lawful ones, were risky. Lionel might jeopardize the integrity of the firm. It was not only on Nat's warning that he drew back. The issue had become highly emotional for him, almost beyond reason, and John Russell had to add his warning about surreptitiously sweetening the "court party" in the Lords. Perhaps no one had so admonished Baron Lionel since he had apprenticed with his father. "You have such an abominable habit of assigning to anything a money value that you seem to think that even principles may be purchased. . . . The parties hostile to your Bill are [a] great section of the High Church Party and the Low Church Party to a man. Now get one of their organs to fight your battle if you can, for their opposition is a conscientious one." If support could be purchased, Russell was implying, despite his reference to con-science, it was in the press.

Whatever the year, after the first introduction of the "Jew Bill," it loomed before Parliament like the prodigal son even when diverted into legislative limbo. In the Commons on its first readings, Russell's supporters of what he called Lionel's bill remained steady, if reluc-tant, with the fluctuations in the count largely due to absentees. On its third reading, a majority of sixty-seven was tallied. Yet before it could be aired in the Lords, an explosive distraction erupted across the Channel. Widespread unemployment and misery had long been mishandled by reactionary post-Waterloo governments fearing "the spectre of communism," yet not pragmatic enough to liberalize their societies. Radicals took their frustrations into the streets.

On February 13, 1848, Louisa's diary noted from No. 2 Grosvenor

Place House, newly built and occupied less than a year, "Poor Anthony, nervous and unhappy, dreading the worst. But after all, what is the worst in this case in comparison with so many other misfortunes which might befall one? The loss of eyesight; the loss or even the fear of the loss of a child. I feel that I could bear up very well with a change of fortune, but Anthony's distress takes away all my courage." Three days later she confided, "A restless, anxious night. . . . If our house can weather the storm I shall be quite content and shall not care for any losses, however severe. Paid Charlotte a visit. Tired and unwell in the evening." Charlotte had been equally distraught, and the women found no consolation in each other.

With news from the rue Laffitte of barricades in the streets within weeks of the Rothschild firm's underwriting of a 250-million-franc bond issue for the unstable French regime, anxieties were great. "Mamma, C[harlotte] and Lionel dined here," Louisa wrote about Sabbath dinner on February 17, "a melancholy party." As the violence in Paris worsened, both James and Nat prepared to bundle their families off to the safety of England. From Hanover, Ernest Augustus charged inventively that Jews had encouraged the "disturbances," and that "Jewish women have been seen giving handfuls of money to the proletariat working on the barricades. . . . This is a positive fact."

In the House of Commons, Disraeli warned that Radicals were opposed in principle to peaceful settlements, even when they espoused religious ideals. All Europe was professedly Christian, but that had not ended fighting, or armaments, or armies. Charlotte wrote to Mary Anne Disraeli of her husband's "glorious success"—as his argument embodied her views. "Lord Palmerston told me," she added, "he had never heard a more magnificent speech." The Foreign Minister, her neighbor at 97 Piccadilly, was a frequent visitor. He disagreed with his Tory rival on protective tariffs, and on policies toward France, but neither wanted violent solutions.

On February 23, 1848, the day that Nat sourly vowed to his brothers in London that he would "not hold much French stock in future," the *Garde* killed fifty protesters outside the Foreign Ministry in Paris, and injured hundreds of others. James and Nat had not yet heard of it, but Louis-Philippe prepared to flee. The next day he signed an abdication document and slipped away in disguise toward the Channel. As street fighting expanded, a provisional government of opposition parties took over. The Tuileries Palace was stormed, and Rothschild properties were threatened, but only one, Salomon's suburban château de Suresnes, was pillaged and burned. Uncle Salomon, Metternich's banker, was on business in Vienna. There a family courier communicated the news from Paris to old Metternich. *"Eh bien, mon cher, est fini,"* he conceded before fleeing in disguise with a handy Rothschild letter of credit in his pocket.

Metternich's castle at Johannisberg, Charlotte wrote unsympathetically in the diary she kept in German, perhaps for privacy from servants, "has been appropriated because he has not paid his taxes for the past nine years." Despite her naturally conservative leanings, she hoped for much good to come. Germany might become "prosperous, united and free," and might be able to repel "Cossack invasions" and inhibit "the warmongering of the French." The means which the French masses were employing might be "mistaken," she acknowledged, but if "a foundation of prosperity and happiness" resulted, she would be grateful for that outcome.

The American historian and diplomat George Bancroft was to dine with his wife at the Rothschilds on Sunday, February 27, when at noon, Elizabeth Bancroft wrote, "I got a note from the beautiful baroness saying that her sister-in-law [Nat's Charlotte] and her mother [Baroness Betty] with three children, had just arrived from Paris at her house in the greatest distress, without a change of clothes, and in deep anxiety about the Baron [James], who had stayed behind." Dinner was put off. (It had to wait until June, after which Mrs. Bancroft reciprocated, and Charlotte dined in company with Lord Rosse, the astronomer; Agnes Strickland, the historian; A. W. Kinglake, the celebrated travel writer; and William Polk, brother of the American president and the chargé d'affaires at Naples. Polk was a familiar figure to Charlotte's family, and was more interesting than her dinner guests knew. In his home town of Columbia, Tennessee, he had killed a local lawyer who had called him a drunk, in a pistol duel in the streets, and thanks to frontier justice Polk was sentenced to six weeks in prison. His brother in the White House had sent him to Naples with instructions to live on half his salary, bank with Charlotte's father, and pay his debts.

The coolest head known to James sat atop his nephew Lionel, whom Uncle James urgently telegraphed that chaotic Sunday, February 27, to rush to Paris. Lionel (now dignified by a short, clipped beard) calmly remained in Paris several weeks, telling Disraeli on returning that the Communists had gained no power, and that the problem was to find work for the unemployed, to get them off the streets. Fearing calamity ahead in Austria, Salomon sent to Frankfurt for his shrewd son Anselm. In the German states, many rulers offered liberal constitutions to save their thrones, hoping to reverse the concessions later. It was a strategy to be successfully employed by the autocratic Frederick William IV in Prussia, who kept control of his army. In the largest state not under Austrian domination in Italy, the Kingdom of the Two Sicilies, Ferdinand II acquiesced to a parliament in Naples, but Charlotte's father, Carl, misread nationalist agitation as "the stupid projects of a few deranged minds."

Concerned that the protests in England led by Chartist reformers would also turn violent, the Rothschilds saw Disraeli's *Sybil* as prophecy—the two "nations" of Rich and Poor about to clash. After the routing of the Orleanists in Paris, demonstrations in English industrial cities grew more strident. Prospects for Rothschild solvency across the family houses looked grim, and Charlotte made domestic economies that were more symbolic—in tune with the times—than substantial. "We had three nursemaids," she wrote in her diary late in March, "and sent away two of them, keeping one to do the dirtier and heavier chores." (The annual savings would have been about £100.) "We shall dress the children ourselves. Our hands shall certainly lose some of their whiteness and beauty in the process, but they will still be of use to us, I hope." Charlotte even cut back, for the moment, on the children's music lessons with their fashionable ten-shillings-an-hour teacher, then a huge sum, prompting a wit (since servants often talked) to remark that the impoverished Rothschild girls had been seen playing together on the same piano.

Little in Charlotte's lifestyle altered. Merchants sent in orders placed by servants; clothes were fitted for the family by dressmakers and tailors who brought in patterns and cloth; Charlotte went out (but more rarely) to concerts and exhibitions, and more regularly to sites of her benefactions. With the Great Synagogue in Aldgate too far for walking, and no driving or riding done on the Sabbath, prayers were said as a family at home on Saturday, when Lionel did not go to New Court, and there were always household prayers on Sunday mornings—a German practice—at eleven-thirty. Even writing was considered "work"—and improving lessons for the children on Saturdays were limited to reading, often aloud. Weekends were often spent at Gunnersbury, where there was much that the children could properly do. The High Holy Days in the autumn were often marked at Gunnersbury, including the Yom Kippur fast. Passover, like Easter, was celebrated in late March or early April, and the festive Seder was usually held at 148 Piccadilly, with other family members joining Lionel and Charlotte. A guest rabbi[2] would read the service from the traditional Haggadah, and everyone would join in the familiar songs.

April 1848 promised to be more extraordinary. On April 10, following a demonstration on Kennington Common, south of the Thames, the Chartists planned to carry to Parliament, while marching in the hundreds of thousands, a petition of grievances about disenfranchisement and its price. The evening before, Charlotte had

---

2. After 1848 it would be the future Dr. Kalisch, who at twenty-one, and a republican radical, fled from Germany during the disturbances. He resumed studies in England, supported by income from Lionel and Charlotte, whose children he instructed in Hebrew and German.

Louise to dinner, along with the recovered Hannah Mayer, no longer ostracized (except in a token fashion) by her mother. The talk was of revolution, and the hope that a massive police presence would curb the worst excesses. Thousands of special constables were deployed, so many that they outnumbered the actual opposition. "Every gentlemen in England was sworn," exaggerated Charles Greville in his diary. Among the more raffish gentlemen walking security rounds was exiled Charles-Louis-Napoleon Bonaparte, biding his time for another try at Paris.

Louise hoped that the massive preparations would "alarm the mob," and indeed the English radicals, few of them incendiaries anyway, shied from violence. Rain had dampened enthusiasm for a march—and the police had closed the bridges across the Thames to anyone on foot. Chartist leaders delivered their cumbersome, rolled-up petition to Parliament in a four-wheeler cab. "The stirring wind of revolution that destroys old injustices," Charlotte wrote in relief, "[did] not blow in England."

Soon after, she had the smug Austrian ambassador, Count Moritz Dietrichstein, to dinner. Seeing the buffeting that royal houses on the Continent were experiencing, he suggested that the Rothschild financial network was no less immune to crises than were crowns. The Count, she wrote in her diary for April 12, also

paid me some compliments in poor taste, saying, "Looking at you it is obvious that you no longer enjoy such a high position in the world. Now you are grateful if someone calls you beautiful whereas in the past you would have laughed your head off at such irony."

I replied, "And why is it that I no longer enjoy such a high position? It is because I no longer have a money-sack for my throne or my footstool? Or is it perhaps because I no longer am a money-sack?"

"The money-sack is still there, but the revolution has half emptied it."

"The world will not trouble itself about that, your Excellency, provided we do not delay our payments and make no claims upon it."

Charlotte ignored the unconcealed anti-Semitism beneath the arrogance, having long applied her father's injunction to learn usefully about the family business. The power of the Rothschild houses, she wrote after the Ambassador's carriage had departed, "does not lie in our wealth alone, and God the Almighty will not withdraw his protecting from us. Amen!"

In Paris, Lionel, Nat, and James had concluded expediently that the way to ward off French nationalization of railways and banks was, as James was widely quoted as saying, "to offer [their] cooperation to such a good and honest Revolution." Lionel and James walked unhampered to the office of the new Prefect to offer two thousand francs to distribute to the needy, and asked no questions about where it would actually go. Once the ransacking of royal and government buildings had taken some of the steam out of the uprising, the Provisional Government concluded that governments ran on popular confidence, and that nothing established this better than money. Soon James walked undisturbed and alone to the Ministry of Finance "to see," he told the novelist Ernest Feydeau, deployed at a commandeered National Guard post on the rue de la Paix, "whether they may not need my experience and my counsel." His inelegant French amused Feydeau, but no one could mistake it—and the Rothschilds at each house knew that the health of their enterprises required adhering to the government in power, whatever that was.

The nephews and uncles also realized, as did Charlotte, that although paper losses could be regained, their aura of authority, if lost, would be difficult to restore. Two months before, she noted ruefully, their paper wealth "exceeded the reserve of the Bank of England." While that seemed gone, the potency of stability and of information access, and their multinational unity, would remain once the revolutions had depleted their momentum. By the end of May, despite the red ink in their books, Charlotte saw "a bright, European and Roth-schildian future."

Alarm remained the mood through the summer months. The family firms on the Continent took heavy losses, yet they had the capital to weather them. Railways had to run; streets had to be policed; workmen had to be paid. The Rothschilds were there to help regimes cope. Stability slowly returned. The Rothschild mystique survived.

With the fading of fear, press interest in England again focused upon the House of Lords and the oaths bill, so fervently opposed by Tory grandees and Anglican bishops. For its first reading, Lionel and his brothers, and Hannah and her sister Judith Montefiore sat in the Strangers' Gallery from late in the afternoon until long after midnight to listen to the arguments about diluting a "Christian" parliament. Charlotte and Louisa had been warned away.

Louisa was waiting with Charlotte at 148 when Lionel, Anthony, and Mayer returned at 3:30 A.M. Lionel, Charlotte wrote in her diary, wore an unconvincing smile—for "self-control," she thought. Anthony and Mayer were "crimson" and cautioned the women not to read the speeches likely to appear in the next day's papers, as they were "scandalous." When the bill failed by thirty-five votes, they added, "a loud, enthusiastic roar of approval resounded . . . throughout the House." Charlotte fell asleep at 5:00 A.M. in the first light of morning "and woke again at 6; I had dreamt that a huge vampire was greedily sucking my blood."

"Surely," she wrote when she was up to adding to her diary, "we do not deserve so much hatred. I spent all day Friday weeping and sobbing out of over-excitement."

She and Louise were in the visitors' benches for the second reading of the Jewish Disabilities Bill on May 25, 1848. Colonel Charles Sibthorp, the ultra-Tory M.P. for Lincoln, had already set the tone for the debate with his foreboding that if "Sheenies" could speak in either house, "Farewell to our greatness!" *The Times's* support of the Rothschild cause, *The Satirist* charged—"the influence of Israel in

Printing House Square"—had been purchased by Lionel. It had already claimed that he had paid for his majority in the City through such intermediaries as a "Mr. Elgar," who allegedly confessed that he had purchased fifty-six voters at ten shillings each. Yet the large Rothschild majority in the City did not need such petty tinkering.

With increasing anguish, Charlotte and Louisa sat in the gallery with Lionel while further variations on the familiar themes thundered below. The tirades continued until the London sky began to lighten in early dawn. Wretched and weary, the Rothschilds left just after three. Again, Louisa wrote, the arguments against the bill "were intolerant, and bigoted and calumnious. The Bishop of Oxford, [Samuel Wilberforce,] in particular, spoke like a fiery, zealous, unscrupulous, *party man*, not in the least like a clerical one. I was quite sorry that [William] Wilberforce's son should have made such a display."[3] "Soapy Sam," as he was known, had warned, "If you destroy the groundwork of Christianity . . . in order to gratify for a time a handful of ambitious men you will destroy Christian England."

The bill again failed in the Lords, again by a majority of thirty-five, and was doomed to rejection on a third and final reading. *The Weekly Dispatch* deplored, "The City of London has been insulted—the popular will has been made of no account." Undiscouraged, Lionel prepared to contest the vacated seat again, and his City constituency was willing to renominate him. "I am not at all surprised," Lionel was quoted as saying wryly, "for history and experience show that the lock of the English constitution is very hard to open. It is a Shy-lock, and [make] no mistake!"

Although Charlotte sided with him about running again, she was emotionally worn, and this showed in her attitude toward both Lionel and her determined mother-in-law—who was also pressing Lionel to stay the course. Louisa, too, felt that Lionel was more and

3. William Wilberforce, a wealthy, devout Evangelical layman, had become an M.P. and philanthropist, and until his death in 1833 was a leading force in campaigns to end the slave trade.

more deferential toward his spirited mother as she aged, and that Hannah in turn became more the matriarch. "We came here [to Gunnersbury] last night," Louisa once wrote. "I felt my usual *chill* creep over me when we advanced through the stately carriage drive to the stately mansion and were received in rather a stately manner by Aunt.[4] By degrees, however, I became accustomed to the changed atmosphere. They were in good spirits, Charlotte as ever, very amiable, and the evening passed pleasantly enough." Yet it was a forced geniality, as was clear when Charlotte sent a snappish note to her husband about visiting Mayer's new country seat. "You ask, dear husband, if I am going to Mentmore. As your mother wishes to go there for a few days, I have no choice but to go with her. Ever since I became your wife I have had to do what others want, never what I would like to do. Pray that I shall be compensated in heaven." It was a rare outburst.

As her nerves frayed, she began to worry unduly about the children's minor ailments, and she asked Lionel to permit Mr. Marriott, a fashionable phrenologist, to examine the conformation of their skulls. Lionel knew when to give in, and Charlotte happily had their bumps "tested." Marriott was even permitted to palpate Lionel's head, after which he produced an analysis that revealed that he read the newspapers and had an ear for gossip.

Marriott also examined "Mrs. L." in what was either a triumph of phrenological science or of hearsay information. Like an astrologer playing to his audience, he combined flattery and platitude with acceptable quibbles. She had, he determined, "an artistic and fertile imagination and enjoys greatly the sublimities and beauties of nature, the reflections of poetry and the romance of history."

> She has a great thirst for information. She may be fond of money and her acquisitiveness [may] be misdirected. Friendly disposed to

4. Although Hannah was also their mother-in-law, Charlotte and Louisa always referred to her as "Aunt," as they had first known her.

those who are in distress. Very fond of method and order and [is] tidy. . . . Some taste for music and would play with feeling. She has good talents for learning. . . . Although she thinks upon what she sees and hears yet she is more influenced by imagination than by judgement.

Charlotte filed the diagnoses signed "L. Marriott" among her papers but did not employ him again.

In May 1849, a new "emancipation" bill was introduced in the Commons. Despite his party's open hostility, Disraeli reaffirmed his support. The gesture prompted Charles Dickens, once a parliamentary reporter and long a critic of Disraeli's slippery ambition, to declare himself delighted that the Tory stalwart "has done such justice to his conscience-less self in regard of the Jews." Again the bill passed in the Lower House by wide majorities, almost all Liberal votes, but in the Lords the stern new Archbishop of Canterbury, John Bird Sumner, recalled the faithful to their duty. God, Sumner charged, did not regard with the same favor those who accepted Jesus and those who had not. "Was there [with Charlotte] from five until twelve-thirty," wrote Louisa. "The debate, though interesting to us, was rather dull and cold; however there were some very good speeches. The Duke of Argyll spoke in his fine, deep voice very impressive words; the Bishop of Oxford poured forth an eloquent torrent of not very sound argument; the Archbishop of Dublin reasoned well, though without any *entraînement*;[5] but Lord Brougham's was the great speech of the night, alternately witty and grave, he amused and delighted the House, but alas! Did not persuade—for we lost by a majority of 25."

Lionel was overworked at New Court, and with politics added, he may have been the busiest man in London, but he was battling for a principle. Trying a new tactic, he resigned his seat so that he could set up a by-election, and the friendly *Times* published his charge to

5. Enthusiasm.

the City's electorate: "The contest is now between the House of Lords and yourselves. . . . You alone can decide whether you will continue this honourable struggle, or give up your own declared wishes and the cause of freedom together."

A week before the balloting on July 4, Baroness Hannah, as usual looking as aristocratic as old money, gave a dinner party at 107 Piccadilly, and had both Lionel and Charlotte, and Lord John Manners, an affable Young Englander, among her many guests. Knowing that Manners was seeking a seat, Mayer, who was also at the table with Anthony and Louisa, said teasingly, "Well, I suppose you'll stand against Lionel." Several days later, on June 30, Manners discovered at the Tory club, the Carlton, that he was indeed to be the "country party's" opponent to Lionel. "I think it only due to the private friendship that has existed between us," he wrote from the Carlton, "to lose not a moment in apprising you of that intention and of the duty which it imposes on me of not shrinking at this crisis from coming forward as the assertor of the rights of the House of Lords.[6] Would that it were otherwise! For I can honestly say that there is no one with whom I should more regret being brought into collision." He hoped that their contest would be conducted with "friendly feelings" that would outlast the election.

On nomination day, July 2, what was apparently a hired mob employed by Tory managers, the embarrassed Manners wrote, "made Rothschild inaudible by applauding me, [and] by groaning. . . ." Almost certainly without Manners's sanction, anti-Semitic publications also surfaced in the streets. In his candidacy address, following Lionel, Manners confessed his unreadiness to serve and promised, if defeated, never to stand for a City seat again. He would collect only 2,814 votes to Lionel's 6,017, but victory meant nothing more than another remedial oaths bill introduced in both houses the next year.

As reward for his sacrifice, Manners would be offered a safe Conservative berth at a by-election at Colchester in February 1850. He

6. He knew that he would be by inheritance 7th Duke of Rutland.

would have no oaths problem taking his seat, but Lionel was still barred by the "form of words."

Before the Rothschilds, in a respite from politics, left for Paris and Frankfurt, Lionel thanked the voters of the City for having

> emphatically pronounced their determination to uphold the sacred principle of perfect religious liberty; and, as I proudly acknowledge, they have not less emphatically declared their confidence in myself.
>
> To be selected as the representative of the enlightened opinions and the vast and varied interests of the City of London, is, I feel, the highest honour to which a constitutional ambition could aspire; and deep would be my gratitude, under any circumstances, to those who have confided to me so important a trust. But at this moment, and in the peculiar position in which I am placed, I feel your generous kindness with increased force.

He saw the City as having drawn to itself "the proud distinction of being the means of removing from our statute book the last remnants of those intolerant laws which have gradually yielded to the force of public opinion," and he remained their "faithful servant." In the limbo of the parliamentary recess, he returned to urgent personal business and the need to reclaim his health—a disturbing new reality he had been concealing. The growing family, Charlotte's increasing involvement in Jewish philanthropies like the school in Bell Lane, and the responsibilities of New Court and its affiliates gave Charlotte and Lionel sufficient cares until the next oaths debates, but Charlotte realized her husband's half-hidden new anxiety while on the Continent. On business in September, Lionel was at Lille, a major junction on the Northern Line in which the houses had a controlling interest, when he collapsed with what was first feared to be cholera. Charlotte, with the children in Paris, was sent for by telegraph and rushed to him on the next train. The attack turned out to be only a stomach upset, but after years of anxieties, Lionel was feeling more than his age, which was just over forty, and his considerable importance put what seemed a small matter into the French and English press. He was plagued by severe arthritis, but knew he could not slow down, nor could he afford to evidence any signs of disability. Public life was now too important to him, and he was also the fulcrum of the interlinked Rothschild houses.

As conditions in France and Germany and Austria had returned almost to the old authoritarianism, Charlotte and Lionel had taken their children on long family visits, Charlotte writing letters to Louisa on the state of the "Caucasian" population—her wry code for Jewish coreligionists, including the "utilitarian members of our worthy family." Her family, to her continuing pride, strove and worked, and dwelt in homes that were "un-English certainly," but tasteful, attractive, and comfortable. Charlotte had become, in little more than a dozen years, utterly English herself. She was appalled by the squalor of the Frankfurt she had known as a child, repelled by the gambling spa of Homburg, and now shocked by what she learned about "Uncle A."

Seventy-six and childless, Amschel had lost his wife, Eva, the year before. He was very lonely, very rich, and accustomed to the Rothschild practice of marrying within the family. He wanted, Charlotte discovered, to wed his own grandniece, Julie, who was pretty and almost nineteen. Rothschilds wrote their own rules. Although the free-spirited Julie was willing to become a rich young widow, as long as she had piles of money (a hundred thousand francs for each kiss, she proposed) and utter freedom to do as she wanted, including eating nonkosher "forbidden food," the alliance "would be a misfortune," Charlotte wrote angrily, "an indelible stain on our escutcheon and on her fair fame, an eternal disgrace, but with that one exception I do not see why our Uncle should be thwarted in his desires. What he most requires is a lively companion to accompany him out walking and driving, and do the honours of his house and table. Why should he not contract an alliance on platonic, poetical principles? He would have hundreds and thousands of young ladies to choose from." Happily, Julie married Charlotte's young brother Adolph a year later. Unhappily, Amschel spent six final, disconsolate years alone.

Charlotte had found the Frankfurt Jewish community in confusion after the 1848 risings. "I have been twice," she wrote, "to the dirty crumbling synagogue of this place which is a disgrace to the Frankfurt congregation. Each time it was full to suffocation, and Lionel noticed a sprinkling of Hebrew soldiers wearing the Austrian or Prussian uniforms." All were in the ranks. It was no more possible for a Jew in either country to be an officer than for Lionel, at home, to be an M.P.

They went on to Homburg where Baron James took another cure—like everything he did, to the ultimate. "He has the courage to drink eight glasses of sulphurous water every morning, after which he takes interminable walks and winds up the day's work by dictating innumerable letters. . . . Uncle James is heartily tired of being what is called an idle man in search of health." He would not, however, succumb to the Homburg vice of the gambling casino, preferring to place his sums on railway shares and government bonds. Despite her revulsion, Charlotte was drawn to "the green tables . . . surrounded by horrible faces; every countenance . . . convulsed with the workings of the lowest, most frightful passions." She imagined the bettors as "demons condemned for past crimes to unholy pursuits—the lurid glare of the eyes, the twitching of the muscles, the large brown and bony hands, with long black nails more like claws, clutching the bright florins and golden stars with which the green cloth was bespangled, the looks of horror and of rage when the madly acquired wealth flowed back to the croupier's bank!" Curiosity getting the better of her "disgust," she watched with fascination as a "desperate gambler" dropped £30,000.

At Wildbad, Lionel consulted with new physicians about his "infirmities," the worsening rheumatoid arthritis now slowly crippling his knees. "We walk along like tortoises," Charlotte confided to

Louisa, "which up the mountains is not a disagreeable pace, although on even ground it becomes fatiguing and irksome."

They remained into October, Lionel being warned by a doctor at Grafenberg promoting then-fashionable hydrotherapy that if he didn't "submit to the horrors and hardships of the water-cure in Silesia, he would ere long lose the use of his hands and feet, and become hopelessly crippled, and never . . . be able to leave his armchair any more." Charlotte viewed the zealous *Arzt* as an "arch-charlatan" and urged Lionel to consult "the best physicians in England and Germany."

Lionel was now a public man beyond banking and beyond politics, as the Irish relief and the slave emancipation crises validated. Early in 1850, just after his return from the Continent, a new challenge arose. Prince Albert had been promoting the idea of a great exhibition of the arts and industry of all nations in London—the first world's fair. Technology—steam, railway, telegraph—was changing the world. The Society of Arts, for which the Prince was an activist president, duly set up a planning committee for an international exposition to open May 1, 1851. Widely derided in the press as overly ambitious and grandiose, its prognosis was best symbolized by a *Punch* cartoon showing Albert, hat in hand, as "The Industrious Boy" seeking donations. A humorous verse described him as bemoaning the "blank subscription-lists."

At his urgent recommendation, the Queen appointed a Royal Commission on January 3, 1850—bankers, engineers, architects, merchants, artists, and politicians whom Albert had consulted throughout December. When it met on January 11, among the treasurers, for public reassurance, were Arthur Kett Barclay and Lionel de Rothschild. A fund-raising scheme was proposed at the January 18 session, and a premature contract was canceled. At an open meeting, a resolution moved by Lord John Russell in his private capacity rather than as prime minister, and seconded by Lionel—identified by Delane in *The Times* as an M.P. from the City of London—declared in part that "the large funds requisite for this purpose ought to be provided by the voluntary contributions of individuals, rather than from the public revenue." Planned with Lionel in advance, it passed unanimously, and a prepared announcement of early subscriptions was released, beginning with £1,000 from the Queen and £500 from Albert. Jointly, Lionel and Anthony subscribed £1,000, and the bankers Joshua Bates and Thomas Baring each offered £500, as did several other financiers. The Chancellor of the Exchequer, Sir Charles Wood, and Lord John Russell each subscribed £100 while the Governor of the Bank of England, H. J. Prescott, promised a paltry £50. Charles Chubb and Sons, the prosperous manufacturer of safes in which each City mogul safeguarded his money, managed only £25. Prince Albert's hat would remain extended for many months, but the connections of the bankers on his board assured that the Great Exhibition would be fully financed.

While fund-raising continued, so did Lionel's efforts to be seated in the Commons. Radical M.P. J. A. Roebuck, in a feisty speech on March 4, 1850, encouraged Lionel to appear and claim his place. Others suggested the precedent of the Quaker militant Joseph Pease, for whom an exception to affirm had been made, as his sect forbade oaths, but some Members contended that Quakers as Christians of a sort maintained the character of the legislature. Learning of a hostile speech delivered in Edmonton, near the Newington suburb in east London where Lionel's parents had once lived, Charlotte apparently had her fill of exasperation. Her draft of an undated letter to "My Lord" survives. "I have no words sufficiently vivid to express my astonishment at your speech of the 1st of April," she began:

> . . . You stated that "you had never met a Jew who declared that, if he had the opportunity of inflicting a serious injury upon the Christian faith or of preventing its spread, he would [not] fail to do so"—I am always unwilling, indeed I am quite unable to doubt the veracity of an English gentleman, and I . . . believe that, in the somewhat bewildering excitement of electioneering movements,

you were unfortunately betrayed into expressions at variance with well-ascertained and universally acknowledged facts.

The Jews never try to make proselytes. Faithful to their own creed, they do not, either directly or indirectly, endeavour to undermine the religious opinions of others. Why should they make the attempt? They are taught to believe that Almighty God, the fountain of all mercies and of all blessings, judges all human beings according to their works, and the pious and the righteous on earth, whatever be their race or faith may all hope to enter the Kingdom of heaven. That those who profess the Christian religion should endeavour to make converts, I fully understand, and while I am firmly convinced that they will not be successful in winning my co-religionists from the faith of Israel, I candidly confess that I honour their motives and appreciate the exertions of zealous missionaries. They labour indefatigably to diffuse the tenets of their own religion, because they believe that there is no salvation out of the pale of their church. The Jews, however, who respect all religions and all varieties of religious belief, and are truly convinced that a conscientious obedience to the dictates of same, is not merely compatible with, but pre-eminently productive of the noblest virtues, can have no motive for wishing to make proselytes.

Charlotte signed her letter "A Jewess."

Lionel conferred with Pease and others about what course to take. He remained in an electoral vacuum. On July 25, a year after his victory, a meeting of City supporters considered whether he should resign so they could be represented in Commons by a successor who could be seated, or whether he should return to the House and insist upon his rights. The feeling was strong that the City deserved its legally elected representative.

The next afternoon Lionel came to the floor of the Commons and asked to take his lawful place. In the gallery above, Charlotte and Louisa watched tensely. At the bar, Lionel walked slowly to the table of the Clerk of the House, who asked him whether he wished to subscribe to the Protestant or the Catholic oath. "I desire," he said, "to be sworn on the Old Testament."

Excitedly, the ultra-Tory Sir Robert Inglis, rose, shouting "I distinctly object!"

C. S. Shaw-Lefèvre, the Speaker, directed Lionel to withdraw so that the House could consider his admission. "I believe," Inglis began, "that I heard distinctly the words pronounced, 'I desire to be sworn on the Old Testament.' I am not mistaken as to the purport of the words? Sir, from the time that this has been a Christian nation and that this House has been a Christian legislature, no man—if I may use the word without offence—has ever presumed to take his seat here unless prepared to take it under the solemn sanction of an oath in the name of our Common Redeemer. I for one will never give my sanction to his admission." Loud cheers erupted. Lionel and the ladies left, to return three days later after new arguments on the floor.

When Lionel returned to the bar, Shaw-Lefèvre asked him formally, "Why do you demand to be sworn upon the Old Testament?"

"Because," said Lionel, "that is the form of swearing that I declare to be most binding upon my conscience."

Again the Speaker directed Lionel to withdraw, and Charlotte and Louisa left with him. After further debate, by a vote of 113 to 59, the House determined that Rothschild would be allowed to take the oath in accordance with Jewish religious custom, if the wording of such oath was appropriate to the House.

When he appeared the next day, July 30, 1850, the Clerk administered, as Charlotte and Louisa watched, the oaths of Allegiance and Supremacy. His hat on his head according to Jewish custom, Lionel swore in the prescribed form. When the oath of Abjuration was read, he repeated all the words until the Clerk came to "upon the true faith of a Christian."

"I omit these words," said Lionel, "as not binding upon my conscience. So help me God!" And he kissed the Hebrew Bible he held.

"Baron Lionel Nathan de Rothschild," the Speaker directed, "you may withdraw." Appeals of "No, no: take your seat" intermingled with cries of "Withdraw!" rang out, and again Lionel left the Commons with Charlotte and Louisa.

"I beg leave to move," shouted Sir Frederick Thesiger, a prominent Tory lawyer, "that Baron de Rothschild, one of the Members returned for the City of London, having refused to take the oath prescribed by the law before a Member can sit and vote in this House, Mr. Speaker be instructed to issue his warrant to the Clerk of the Crown to make out a writ for a new election for the City of London in place of the said Baron Lionel Nathan de Rothschild." The motion failed.

When the House took the issue up again on August 5, 1850, Disraeli reaffirmed his support for revising the oath, but took only his friend Lord George Bentinck, among the Tories, with him. Prospects remained hopeless.

CHAPTER SIX

OATHS AND ELECTIONS

1850–1858

Baroness Hannah had attended only a single session of Parliament to listen to the oaths debate. She had been active behind the scenes for twenty years and may have conceded that change would not occur in her lifetime. Many of her hours were now spent surveying her beloved orangery and gardens, and cultivating Gunnersbury pineapples. There, while playing with Charlotte's daughters, she suddenly collapsed.

Hannah died on September 5, 1850, at sixty-seven. She had barely outlived her venerable mother-in-law, Gutle, who had died in Frankfurt on May 7, 1849, nearly ninety-six. "I had new, very pretty dresses made for my little girls," Charlotte wrote, "that poor Aunt might be pleased with their appearance at breakfast." But "the new dresses they wore were black." She took the children, all but little Leo, to Hannah's deathbed to kiss their grandmother's cold hands.

Gunnersbury Park finally belonged (through Lionel) to Charlotte, long its chatelaine, although the otherwise businesslike late baroness left no will. Perhaps this was slyly intentional. Most of her property was tied up by N. M.'s own dispositions, but she had accumulated, on her own, since, a six-figure fortune. By Hannah's not designating any of it, Hannah Mayer Fitzroy would share equally among the four sons and three daughters—a parting blessing. Disraeli called it "an unexpected *cadeau.*"

The inevitable resolution to reconsider Abjuration in a new session of the Commons kept the matter alive. On May 1, 1851, a bill introduced by the Prime Minister, Lord John Russell, passed a second reading, 202 votes to 177. The rather small assembly was a disappointing augury for final passage. Russell had chosen a poor date for the division. With royal panoply, the Great Exhibition had opened that afternoon.

The Exhibition commission had stubbornly labored on through a series of frustrations as there could be no public perception of failure. Exhibitions from around the world in the tens of thousands had been offered without a structure to house them. Then, just after Prince Albert asked for a guarantee fund of £200,000—Lionel would furnish £50,000 of it—for what he and the commission expected would be an expensive, yet temporary, masonry shell, came Joseph Paxton's striking concept of a prefabricated building of iron and glass. In effect it was a huge greenhouse based upon his work at Chatsworth for the Duke of Devonshire. Albert had visited Chatsworth and was enchanted by Paxton's extrapolation of his Great Conservatory for Hyde Park.

The commission happily supported the design. *Punch*, which had often poked fun at "Albert's folly," reversed course on seeing Paxton's sketches, christening the structure a "Crystal Palace." The name caught on, quickening the excitement of crowds that gazed in awe at the assembly of the vast enterprise, 1,848 feet long—more than a third of a mile—and 408 feet wide. A technological marvel, it was one of the great architectural achievements of the century. During its thrilling 140 opening days, as light penetrated its roof of 18,932 panes of glass, six million people passed though. For working people more opportunity might have been made, but Sabbatarian restrictions kept the Crystal Palace closed on Sundays.

On May 22, a Thursday, Charlotte and Louisa and their children went to the Great Exhibition and—like most visitors—were dazzled. To help pry funds from businessmen to get the project started, Lionel at the second meeting of the organizers early in 1850 had downplayed ideals and promised that the exhibition—the first world's fair—"would have the effect of ensuring a great many orders" for British manufacturers. In part, by promoting the financing that moved the fair from idea to reality, Lionel and Anthony had made Albert's dream possible.

Perhaps as an antidote to anxieties about oaths and elections, which the Crystal Palace allayed only briefly, Charlotte wrote two lectures to give to the girls at the Jews' Free School in Spitalfields. Public education barely existed in England. The school, with nearly nine hundred students, a third of them female, had been a special benefaction of Nathan Mayer and Hannah. In the tradition of systematic self-help efforts within the Jewish community, their sons had assumed much of its support. Anthony had become president of its board of governors in 1847, and Louisa and Charlotte visited "the little learners in Bell Lane" almost weekly. The students, "indescribably dingy and dirty," were from poor families in the East End. "It is quite disheartening to be perpetually trying to improve those caucasian arabs," Charlotte would say as late as 1865, "and without ever being able to descry any real progress in them." (She had no more faith in expensive tutors, writing of her son Nathaniel, a future financial eminence, at ten, "I do not think he will ever be a clever man, but I hope he may become a cultivated, well-informed one, a useful member of society.")

Preparing a small book for Free School use, *Addresses to Young Children*, she wanted to try out her ideas. Some of her strictures meant less for the very poor than for her own peers, who needed to give of themselves, not merely from themselves—"not only gold, but time,

which is life." On June 10 and June 14, 1851, one of Charlotte's listeners was someone unaccustomed to the hard, narrow Bell Lane
benches—tall, stooped, bespectacled W. M. Thackeray.

Louisa had met the novelist of *Vanity Fair* on a Rhine steamer en
route home from Frankfurt. On July 15, 1848, she noted in her diary,
"We talked of literature, drawings, Jews, of whom he has a bad opinion, politics, etc., and we parted very good friends—at least I fancy
so. He seems a good and an honest man, notwithstanding a large
fund of satire. I like him better than his works." Among his works
was his celebrated *The Book of Snobs*, published that year after appearing as a series in *Punch*. One of the popular magazine series omitted
from the book referred to "the Baron de Houndsditch's *déjeuner* at
Twickenham" as an opportunity for the "best society" to learn the
latest political gossip. As Houndsditch was an East End area associated with Jews, it was easy to link the baronial title and the suburban
setting with Baron de Rothschild and Gunnersbury. In the book itself are the City Snob and the Banking Snob—and the Rothschilds
appear transparently as the Scharlachschild financial houses (*schar-
lach*, or "scarlet," in German plays on *rot*, or "red"). Thackeray's
spokesman, Mr. Snob, observes, "For instance, everyone knows the
princely hospitalities of the Scharlachschild family at Paris, Naples,
Frankfort, &c. They entertain all the world, even the poor, at their
fêtes." With less ambiguity he adds in his "Country Snobs" chapter,
"To hear Miss Wirt herself, you would fancy that her Papa was a
Rothschild."

In London, through Louisa, Thackeray met Charlotte. Although
an allusion to "a Jewish Lady . . . with a child at her knee" in *Penden-
nis* (1848–1850) was almost certainly a bow to Lady de Rothschild,
the uneasy Louisa was often jealous of Charlotte's social successes,
including her instant friendship with Thackeray. A diary entry by
Louisa refers to Charlotte as "amiable and unaffected. She is an accomplished hostess and understands thoroughly making her house
agreeable, which I do not at all." Even earlier she had written that at a
wedding both had attended, "Charlotte Lionel was *much admired* by

all the guests and she certainly looked strikingly handsome. I went home early, tired, nervous and out of sorts."

Thackeray never entirely dropped aspersions upon, and ambiguities about, Jews from his armory of ethnic wit, yet in his "Mr. Brown's Letters to his Nephew" series in *Punch* in 1849 he praised a City banker who votes for Lionel de Rothschild not only in defiance of the outdated Test Acts but to discomfit his bigoted mother-in-law. Soon another challenge to the statutes emerged. In June 1851, David Salomons of the London & Westminster Bank, elected Sheriff of the City of London in 1835, then a breakthrough, contested a by-election in Greenwich and, with no Tory opponent, easily won a seat in the Commons. On July 18, 1851, he proceeded to take it, physically. Ignoring the oaths requirement which had excluded Lionel, he claimed that he was defending the rights and privileges of the constituents who elected him. On July 30, with a gentlemanly tap on the shoulder by a House official, he was expelled and his seat declared vacant.

In July 1852, Lionel tried again, in his election address reminding Londoners that "the voice of the people has been disregarded." Although City electors realized that they would be disenfranchising themselves by electing him, he was again returned.

In the Lords, Baron Lyndhurst, now feeble and tremulous but tenaciously active, introduced the Alteration of Oaths bill, hoping to slip in a liberalizing amendment, but Bishop Wilberforce led another successful negative campaign for the status quo. In the Commons, futile debate on seating Lionel persisted into the next year. The emotional toll on the family was high, but somehow he managed New Court and concealed, at least publicly, the increasing arthritic crippling of his legs. Had it been alleged that he was disabled physically as well as legally from performing his functions in Parliament, his cause would have been lost.

The family did not know what to make of Disraeli's role, and nonrole, in the matter. Whatever he did, or did not do, would anger either his Tory colleagues or the Rothschilds, whom he had adopted as informal family, whatever they thought of his showy style. Without them, his "Young England" trilogy might not have existed, or at least would have taken a very different form, and as he claimed to the elderly Sarah Brydges Willyams, of Sephardic ancestry but widow of a wealthy Anglican, *Tancred* was "a vindication, & I hope a complete one, of the race from wh[ich] we alike spring." Yet in the oaths debates he had sometimes been cautiously silent even when voting apart from his party, and he had defended the legal right of the Lords to deny Lionel a seat in the other house. Charlotte accepted Disraeli's tangled motives more easily than did Louisa, while Lionel kept silent, understanding the political hazards to his ambitious friend.

Although Disraeli dined often with them, even at Brighton, to which they imported their cuisine and their cooks from London, he lacked understanding of what made certain fish and flesh inappropriate for observing Jews—except for the obvious examples.[1] Just before he and Mary Anne left London for the remainder of the summer late in July 1851, a gift of venison from the Duke of Portland arrived at Grosvenor Gate. "Not knowing what to do with it, with our establishment breaking up" he explained to his sister, Sarah, "I thought I had made a happy hit & sent it to Madame Rothschild (as we have dined there so often, & they never with us)[2] it never striking me for an instant, that it was unclean meat, wh[ich] I fear it is." Charlotte thanked the Disraelis for the venison, which possibly was used, as Lionel and his brothers were not strictly observant. Dizzy had confused his fears. The moral discipline of kashrut permitted the eating of animals with a cloven hoof—as was the buck—but the deer had been shot, rather than ritually slaughtered.

It was difficult, given the external pressures, for Charlotte to de-

1. His father, Isaac, in protest against what he considered anachronistic dietary laws, had even raised pigs at Bradenham, his country home.

2. Disraeli exaggerated Rothschild dietary strictures. Charlotte was reluctant to dine where nonkosher food was served, but did. And she had been a dinner guest at the Disraelis'.

vote herself utterly to her family, but as a loving mother she decided, at long last, that she liked even Natty, who was now, in the diary accounts she kept for each child, her "beloved son." He was "tall and strong" as he reached his bar mitzvah (she called it "confirmation") age of thirteen, and read "con amore." She also had Natty study German with extra diligence, as he was already tagged to take over at New Court. (Alfred and Leopold were still boys, and were being tutored, like Natty, for Cambridge, which Mayer had been the first in the family to attend.) Anthony had no sons, and Mayer, who had only recently married his cousin Juliana Cohen, would have only a single child, another Hannah Mayer.

Charlotte's daughters were nearly young ladies, and Leonora, she recorded proudly in mid-1852, when Laury was nearly fifteen, was already "thought to be very beautiful." Although Charlotte employed the best tutors money could buy to convince her daughter that "a highly educated lady" should read geography, literature, and history, "the only books she reads for pleasure," Charlotte conceded, ". . . are novels, or romances." Leonora's talents were more physical. In a charade at Gunnersbury she reminded Charlotte "forcibly and delightfully" of the French actress Élisa Rachel[3] in *Adrienne Lecouvreur.* When Laury danced, as at Mentmore, she was "rapturously" pursued by admirers and had to flee. At Frankfurt she was "surrounded with flatterers and admirers . . . who made no impression on her heart." When she played the piano, "It is difficult if not impossible to hear anything more perfect." By 1854, Charlotte added, "No one has seen her without admiring her oriental beauty"—an image echoing Disraeli.

"Who will the Caucasian suitor be?" Charlotte wondered unnecessarily as Leonora approached sixteen. Assumed was another

3. Élisa Félix (1820–1858), called "Mlle. Rachel," of Alsatian-Jewish background, was the great classical actress of her time. She died, at the peak of her reputation, of tuberculosis. Charlotte refers to what may have been her most triumphant role, in a play by Augustin-Eugène Scribe.

arranged marriage within the cousinhood, which eliminated any suspicion that a suitor was more interested in making a fortune than a
marriage. No one yet worried about the genetic price of consan-
guinity.

Betty and James had already reserved their eldest son, Mayer
Alphonse, for Laury. Charlotte knew and concurred: "I have seen no
one, heard of no one superior, or even equal to Alphonse. He is not
handsome; what man need be an Adonis?" She "fanned the flame,"
although neither Alphonse (who was nine years older than Laury,
and long a partner at Maison Rothschild) nor Leonora was in a rush
to marry. The designated bride felt that Alphonse preferred hunting
and horsemanship to matrimony, and when the family took the salubrious waters at Carlsbad, Laury—neglected by Alphonse—was delighted when (in Charlotte's account) she "lost her heart" to a visiting
young Englishman, who as "her faithful knight" took her along romantic mountain paths and streams. The episode would hasten her
cousin's proposal.

Evelina, two years younger than her sister, had lost her childhood
prettiness. She was also "lamentably ignorant," her mother deplored,
without "talent for languages." Mrs. Daleken, her increasingly impatient teacher, considered her a failure. Yet, Charlotte conceded, she
was "kind and warm" and undemanding. But for her propensity for
pimples, from which (in Charlotte's account) she was "never free,"
life satisfied Evy. When she was eleven, after a summer in Brighton
became a catastrophe for her complexion, Charlotte had asked the
children's doctor to recommend a skin specialist, who "gave her such
an enormous quantity of medicines that Evy declared she could not
go on taking . . . applications to be attended to every day. Pills, powders and draughts, black doses, ointments, and lotions, among them
cod liver oil, which disagreed . . . so much that I became impatient,
thanked Mr. Gascoigne for his kindness and sent for Mr. Erasmus
Wilson."

Eventually, Wilson had the problem "down to a few pimples."
Evelina filled out in the right places and a few wrong ones, and Char-

lotte decided that although Evy "was perhaps less generally admired than her sister," her attractiveness was of a sort "more appreciated in England" than on the Continent. Perhaps her likely dowry magnified her appeal, but that may not have been the case when she received a premature proposal of marriage, even anticipating the expected one to Leonora.

Evelina was only twelve when she was seen in the Crystal Palace by a young, admittedly self-educated civil engineer, Frederick Glass, in the vicinity of the notorious sculpture *Greek Slave*, by the American Hiram Powers.[4] It drew large crowds. A work of Victorian-era soft-core pornography, when nudes were acceptable if they were classical and fig-leaved, or discreetly modest, the young woman in marble drapes her left hand over the censorable portion of her anatomy. Although Evelina looked nothing like the statue, Glass, Charlotte wrote, "fell desperately in love with her and ventured to claim her hand." (By then Evy was an immature thirteen, but her epistolary swain may have known nothing of her age.) "The letter is a curiosity in its way. I own it interested her and almost touched my heart. Lionel believed it to be a hoax." Poor Glass got nowhere, but Charlotte could not help "feeling flattered because my daughters are thought beautiful & fascinating."

As long as Charlotte retained some control over their lives, her children were destined for betrothal within the family. "I assure you the family is everything," her uncle James agreed; "it is the only source of happiness which with God's help we possess; it is our attachment, it is our unity." After James, with Lionel's emergency assistance, had survived 1848, the Rothschilds had gathered in Frankfurt to reassess the partnership, where Charlotte admired her "worldly and canny" uncle, still "so mentally and physically active and indefatigable. She marveled at his having so completely eclipsed his Judengasse upbringing. Self-taught in languages and business skills and even in the arts, he appeared confident that he could cope with any-

4. Now at the Corcoran Gallery, Washington, D.C.

one and anything. He seemed unique. She wanted her own children to have the educational advantages which James had been denied. She also wanted them to enjoy the finer things in life, so long as they kept the faith and the family. The next generation would lack nothing but the fire in the belly that energized its elders.

Despite her adolescent disadvantages, Evy remained fun-loving. The European uprisings of 1848 had meant nothing to her and the other children. They confronted poverty only on visiting the Jews' Free School in Spitalfields with their mother, aunt, and cousins. The dark cloud of the oaths issue was also invisible at twelve, and prejudice had not entered their consciousness. Curiosity, on the other hand, certainly had. When Evy's cousin Annie, Louisa's younger daughter, suggested visiting a convent at Hammersmith, as Christianity intrigued Annie and her elder sister Constance, they invited Leopold, only ten to Annie's eleven, if he dressed as a girl. "Leo entered [as] a pretty young lady with a graceful tournure and with modestly downcast eyes. I thought," Annie recalled, "that it was wrong to impose upon the good nuns, but . . . Leo entered the carriage amidst the laughter of the servants and the coachman." At the convent gate they were met by the Mother Superior, "who took no notice of the transformed boy."

After visiting the chapel, with Leo clutching his skirt "rather bashfully" (according to Constance) round his knees, they peered into "a roomful of penitents who wore blue gowns and white caps. These poor girls are rescued from their sinful lives and are brought back to paths of happiness and peace. The faith that the nuns evinced is marvellous; they look on death merely as a happy release from the sorrows of the world and do not grieve when one of their sisters dies. Such faith must be delightful to have: no uncertainties, no doubts." Leopold's gender remained undiscovered, even when Father Heneage, priest and confessor at the convent, received them in his parlor. "And is this yet another niece?" he asked, but the dark-eyed Leo remained shyly silent. Charlotte "scolded and cried" when she found out about the naughty escapade, but blamed Leo for "following" rather than the scheming Annie and her friend Tishy Probyn.[5]

To minimize interruptions in the children's tutorials, Charlotte kept them at Gunnersbury as much as possible, but the distractions of a Rothschild can be seen in a sampling of Charlotte's calendar for the first half of 1853 alone, when "relations of all ages" visited and the family made four trips to Brighton, one to St. Leonards-on-Sea, "two expeditions into Bucks, several drives to Richmond, Petersham, Windsor, Greenwich, Hampton Court, Chiswick, Lygon, several visits to Charity Schools, to the British and Foreign Schools at Brentford." Still, both boys and girls underwent examinations almost every evening they were at home "in the respective histories of France, England & Rome . . . and Sacred history & Mythology . . . [and] Modern Geography." And every six months Charlotte commissioned a fashionable new phrenologist to palpate the subtle conformations of the five children's heads.

Charlotte also had in writers and musicians and politicians, who ate and drank splendidly and were a continuing education to the children, if they listened. One scholar who was there even more often than *The Times*'s J. T. Delane was "the little doctor" Rabbi Kalisch, almost the Rothschild equivalent of a Roman Catholic household priest. He taught the children, officiated at prayers, explained Judaic theology to guests, and, like Disraeli, read and advised on Charlotte's sermons for children. After one of Thackeray's extended stays at Gunnersbury with his two daughters[6] Charlotte wrote to Louisa,

Did I tell you that Thackeray, whose tender inquiries after you and yours I am afraid I never transmitted, carried off our excellent little doctor's commentary into his room and fell delightfully asleep over it. He had passed several restless nights without closing an eye, but

5. Tishy—Letitia—was from a Court-connected, staunchly Anglican family.
6. Their mother, Isabella, was mentally ill and institutionalized.

"Exodus" acted as a powerful narcotic by broad daylight, and Evy, who entered the study of the great writer one sunny morning with a message to his daughters, found the latter [one, Anne] perpetrating a portrait of their slumbering, dreaming sire, who must have had enchanting visions, for he talked [in his sleep] of Venus and Cupid and not at all of Moses and Aaron.

For the Rothschild children, unplanned travels also happened. Leonora's entry "into society"—once impossible for unconverted Jewish girls—was delayed by the death of Charlotte's mother in Frankfurt, then by the death, at nineteen, of the youngest of her four brothers, Amschel Alexander. In 1855, Charlotte's father and her uncles Amschel and Salomon all died within nine months, rearranging the heads of the European houses (but for James's Maison Rothschild) among Carl's and Salomon's sons. Succession arrangements had been planned in Frankfurt in 1852, when Charlotte's brothers Mayer Carl and Wilhelm Carl were authorized, with Anselm, to sign for the Frankfurt house, and Alphonse and his younger brother Gustave for the Paris house. Carl had been hopelessly morose after the deaths of his wife and son; his own death released Naples for his son Adolph. Although the houses had recovered from the trauma of 1848, the deaths required revised partnership agreements.

Leonora came out socially with other well-connected girls of sixteen at a Mardi Gras ball. Her escort was her father; Charlotte remained at home in mourning. Yet she thrilled at reports that the ballroom, in which there were such connoisseurs as Count Alexandre Walewski, the French ambassador, "rang with admiration" for the beauty of the "Jewish belle." Leonora waited anxiously for her engagement as her eighteenth birthday approached, cultivated patience by learning needlework, read Pope and Schiller (because her mother insisted), "and in the City she reads my sermons to the children in Bell Lane and her voice is so clear that every word is heard through the building."

Although Lionel's political career remained in limbo, he exerted persuasive influence behind the scenes, and even lobbied reluctantly (at Charlotte's urging) to promote the career of his brother-in-law Henry Fitzroy, who gained posts at the Admiralty and then the Home Office. Aiming too high, Lionel even tried in 1857, through John Delane's connections, to have Fitzroy named Speaker of the Commons. Little seemed to work out for Fitzroy despite Hannah Mayer's Rothschild riches. In 1852 their only son, Arthur, was thrown from his pony, injuring his spine. His sister Blanche's life, warped by the family tragedy, became one of traveling with her mother in hopeless search for cures for Arthur. He would be a pain-wracked invalid until his death in 1858 in Paris at sixteen, when Lionel and Anthony assisted Fitzroy in bringing the body back for burial.

Oaths bills again lost priority when, in early 1854, a war with Russia in the Crimea began, dominating parliamentary business for two years. Lord Macaulay, to whom Russell had appealed, saw no likelihood of success, despite his sympathies, for a resolution or a bill, and wrote back in exasperation, "I really cannot consent to perform a rhetorical exercise over the subject of religious liberty for the amusement of the ladies [in the gallery]." Russell gave Lionel the letter. There was a chance, Russell had thought, that the distraction of the war might make it possible to slip oaths legislation through the Commons. Since a veto in the Lords was inevitable, even Disraeli voted against the doomed bill as a piece of procedural chicanery—and to demonstrate his Tory loyalty while doing Lionel no harm.

However mishandled and bungled by the bureaucracy in Whitehall and the incompetent generals who led troops with equipment and ideas obsolete after Waterloo, the conflict in the Crimea to block further Tsarist expansion into the Balkans had to be financed and fought. Once Britain committed itself to aid Turkey and France, although its immediate interests were as remote as the Black Sea battlefields, Lionel remarked (March 31, 1854) to Cabinet officials with whom he was close that "a country with £800,000,000 of debt should

have considered much and seriously before it involved itself in another war." The struggle was unexpected to the Rothschilds, as the
ostensible provocation was the rivalry between Russia and Western
religious factions over holy sites in Jerusalem under control of the
crumbling Ottoman Empire.

Since stability remained the Rothschild watchword, the partners
were worried, but they need not have been. As did other belliger-
ents, Britain had to resort to the bond market, and the multinational
Rothschild houses, to pay for its military expenditures. Even Ottoman Turkey had to go to New Court and the rue Laffitte. Since
Barings, a Rothschild rival, had long bankrolled Russia, where anti-
Semitic outrages were common, the Rothschilds seldom involved
themselves in the Tsar's finances. Barings made the large commissions. W. E. Gladstone, the new Chancellor of the Exchequer, went
instead to Lionel, who over two years arranged loans totaling £26
million. All were at terms within the government's guidelines, which
established New Court as loyal rather than greedy. Similarly, Maison Rothschild arranged large loans to the new regime in Paris, that
of a former deputy constable in London during the anxieties of
1848, now Emperor Napoleon III. Austria and Prussia, although
anti-Semitic in practice, found it necessary to float bonds through
the Rothschilds. Charlotte's brother Mayer Carl received from
Prussia—neutral but busy rebuilding its army—the order of the Red
Eagle, Third Class (minus the symbolic cross). An honor nevertheless, it implicitly recognized him as court banker.

When the war ended in 1855 with Russia the ostensible loser—
although it lost none of its ambitions for aggrandizement—the
Rothschilds, even the Naples house, had made money. In Paris, rec-
ognition of rue Laffitte came when Alphonse became a regent of the
Banque de France.

To help pay for the war, Britain had to negotiate a further loan,
which New Court arranged. The outcome prompted Lionel's neighbor at 97 Piccadilly, Viscount Palmerston, who had become prime
minister when Lord Aberdeen's wartime government faltered, to

congratulate the Queen in February 1856 and in effect to validate the public standing of the Rothschild bank:

> It is satisfactory to have as a proof that the revenues of the country are not exhausted, that it being known that Messrs. Rothschild were about to offer [a bid] for the loan of five millions, a sum no less than twenty-eight millions was offered to them by parties wishing to have shares in the loan, and upwards of three millions was actually paid into their hands yesterday as deposits by those wishing to be contractors.

With the end of the Crimean War came two major events for the family. The first was Leonora's second coming out, a requirement among the right sort. On April 10, 1856, at a royal drawing room soiree at Buckingham Palace, 122 young ladies were presented to Queen Victoria, to be introduced and to make their bows. Charlotte escorted Laury. "Nobody very striking," the Queen noted in her journal, "excepting Mlle. de Rothschild, Baron Lionel's daughter, who is extremely handsome."

Alphonse proposed to Leonora that autumn—"in almost ungentlemanlike manner," her mother thought, as immediately after he went off to Turkey on business, leaving the bride's family to plan the wedding. Still, Charlotte was "pleased and satisfied" at her daughter's "prospects of happiness." Baron Alphonse, she told herself, was "really an excellent young man." He was twenty-nine to Laury's nineteen, about the same difference in years as her parents, but with more high-level banking experience than Lionel had acquired at the same age, and with considerably more experience of the "world," as women were politely referred to. "I hope that with God's blessing," Charlotte wrote, "my Laury may be happy. Marriages are made in heaven and I trust the good Angels of the Lord may watch over my child. Amen."

As the family looked toward a grand wedding, Lionel and Charlotte anticipated, too, a General Election which might put more

Palmerstonian Liberals into the Commons and create further pressure on the obstinate Lords, some of whom, despite political differences, would be wedding guests. The ceremony, at Gunnersbury on May 4, 1857, was described by John Delane as a "very splendid affair indeed." Thackeray, another invitee, wrote to Louisa afterward, "What a fine wedding you had in your family! What a parasol! What a pretty bride! We met them all at Aix-la-Chapelle last autumn, and I think we all liked each other. I know I did." The outdoor "parasol" was the *chuppah*, the wedding canopy, supported baronially at each corner by Nathaniel and Alfred, brothers of the bride; Ferdinand James, son of Anselm and Lionel's sister Charlotte; and Edmond James, eleven, the bridegroom's youngest brother.

Workmen had labored through the winter and early spring to ready Gunnersbury for the largest throng it would ever receive, temporarily extending the dining room thirty-five feet into the magnificent park. The Oriental garden, especially admired, was unbreached. On his first visit to Gunnersbury the ambassador from the Mikado had said politely, "We have nothing like it in Japan." All the draperies in the addition were white and rose, while the mansion itself was decorated in white and gold. Since the technology to reproduce photographs in the press did not yet exist, the London illustrated papers sent artists to cover the spectacle.

A reporter gushed that the bride had the complexion of a tea rose. The groom, it was reported, was the only man in Europe worthy to raise the bride's veil—the future head of Maison Rothschild. The band of the First Life Guards serenaded arriving guests, who were the cream of the *corps diplomatique* (including the Hanoverian ambassador); princes, generals, and admirals; a past prime minister (Russell) and a future one (Disraeli); Cabinet ministers; Church of England clerics; what the press called "a large portion of the aristocracy"; and every close Rothschild relative who could travel to Gunnersbury.

Four rabbis, including the Chief Rabbi of England, the Reverend Dr. Adler, seemed necessary to consecrate the marriage, as well as sixteen bridesmaids, including a Miss Copley (Lord Lyndhurst's daughter), a Miss Probyn (Letitia's family served the royal household), the Misses Boyle (sisters of the Earl of Cork), a Miss O'Hara ("a celebrated beauty"), and a Miss Maxse (granddaughter of the Earl of Berkeley), as well as Rothschild cousins.

Rabbi Adler offered an introductory address in English, extolling the mother and father of the bride, after which the ritual in Hebrew paralleled that which had united Leonora's parents. At the close, guests erupted into cheers at the bridegroom's shattering of the wine cup "into a thousand pieces," according to *The Times*. Baron Alphonse then lifted Laury's veil and "saluted her," followed by her parents "and the fair sisterhood in attendance upon her."

As the Life Guards played, guests clustered about the bride to admire her much remarked-upon diamond necklace, "the design, which is perfectly novel, . . . furnished by the mother of the bride, the Baroness Lionel de Rothschild, the execution . . . entrusted to Messrs. Hunt and Roskell, of Bond Street." While they waited to be summoned to the wedding breakfast, actually a sumptuous feast, celebrants poured into the gallery where bridal gifts—according to a gushing press account "rivalling the wealth of the Indies"—were displayed.

After grace chanted by Rabbi A. L. Green, the French ambassador, the duc de Persigny, offered a toast to the bride and groom, fully printed in French in the English press (an unusual exception to custom), even to identifying Leonora as the new "Madame la Baronne Alphonse de Rothschild." Alphonse responded, followed by "the Right Hon. B. Disraeli," who spoke in his most florid manner. "Under this roof," he declared, "are the heads of the name and family of Rothschild—a name famous in every capital of Europe and every division of the globe—a family not more regarded for its riches than esteemed for its honour, virtues, integrity and public spirit." Lord John Russell then toasted Charlotte and Lionel for their public and private conduct, and Lionel replied that much as he felt the loss of a beloved child, he had confidence in her husband and in her future happiness.

After a plethora of toasts, guests filled the ballroom. There the newlyweds danced until ten, departing then for the Willesden station of the London and North-Western Railway, where a special train was to convey them, for their wedding night, to Baron Mayer's mansion at Mentmore, in the Chilterns.

Under the nom de plume "A Sufferer," Thackeray wrote jocularly in *Punch* for May 9, 1857, about the Rothschild nuptials, "that gorgeous Judaic family ceremonial at Gunnersbury, in which God Hymen and God Mammon were equally honoured." Thackeray's usual bite was muted. He blamed the newspapers for excesses—that if one accepted press reports, "the altar must have been of solid gold, . . . the bridal couch stuffed with bank-notes. . . ." There was no altar, and no bridal couch, nor any of the other Thackerayan inventions. "I felt for once," he went on, "that such display was not out of place. There was something grand in the Oriental magnificence—the insolent splendour—the parade of 'money-power.' Dukes and Lords, and Prime Ministers and Secretaries of State were summoned to bow down before the Golden image that Rothschild the king had set up; and they came and bowed dutifully."

Whether dukes and lords would bow at all when it came once more to the oaths matter remained on the family's agenda. Laury had hardly been married a week when she wrote, from France, "I am afraid, my dear Papa, that the election will give you a great deal of trouble and anxiety; how charming it would be if you were at the top of the tree." In the City, Lionel would be three hundred votes short of the top, but ninety ahead of Lord John Russell, who was third.

The new oaths bill introduced by the Palmerston government differed from earlier formulas devised by Russell and Lyndhurst in that it provided for consideration of Jewish seating separately from other anomalies in the law. In debate Palmerston himself ridiculed the contention that a few Jews in Parliament could bring down Christianity. In a culminating speech he reminded Members that a man's religion

The wedding portraits of Charlotte von Rothschild and Lionel de Rothschild, 1836. Oils on canvas, painted by Moritz David Oppenheim in Frankfurt, Charolotte's has a symbolic Bay of Naples setting. Lionel's suggests the English countryside. *Israel Museum, Jerusalem*

The Rothschild's humble beginnings—the Judengasse in 1845, during Gutle Rothschild's years of residence. The ghetto seems artistically cleansed and somewhat depopulated in this watercolor by Carl Theodor Reiffenstein. *Historisches Museum, Frankfurt am Main*

The Rothschild baronial coat of arms, recognizing the ennoblement from the Emperor of Austria. In one generation the Rothschilds were able to move from the ghetto to wealth and even nobility. *The Rothschild Archive*

(*Facing page*) "N. M. Rothschild, Esq."—an unsigned caricature by W. M. Thackeray in the *National Standard*, May 18, 1833, accompanying his satirical verses. N. M. Rothschild skillfully ran New Court in London and was the able head of the Rothschild partnership. His wealth and standing often resulted in newspaper caricatures such as this one.

Lithograph by Hermann Raunheim from a portrait by Moritz David Oppenheim of Gutle and Mayer Amschel Rothschild's five children: Amschel (*top*); Nathan, or N. M. (*upper left*); Salomon (*upper right*); James (*lower left*); and Carl (*lower right*). *Historisches Museum, Frankfurt am Main*

(*Below, right*) The 1837 extension of New Court by John Davis commissioned by N. M. before his death as seen through the arch rebuilt in the 1860s. A tower and cupola of a Wren church are seen behind it. *N. M. Rothschild & Sons*

N. M. Rothschild and his family in a group portrait by William Armfield Hobaday, 1821. Standing to Hannah's left are Charlotte (to marry Anselm von Rothschild in 1826), Lionel, Anthony, and Nathaniel. Mayer is the child in arms. Sitting are Hannah Mayer and Louise. *The Rothschild Archive*

A portrait of the young single Lionel (*right*) and his brother Anthony (*left*). Painted by Moritz David Oppenheim in 1828. *The Rothschild Archive*

(*Facing page*) Neue Mainzer Strasse in Frankfurt in 1868, where Charlotte lived at the time of her marriage in 1836. *Historisches Museum, Frankfurt am Main*

(*Left*) Charlotte's mother, Adelheid von Rothschild, a portrait painted in 1834, two years before Charlotte's wedding, when Adelheid was thirty-four. *Private collection*

(*Right*) Charlotte at eleven, in 1830, with her brother, Wilhelm Carl, then two. The background is the Bay of Naples. *Private collection, artist unknown.*

N. M.'s illness cast a shadow over Charlotte and Lionel's wedding. Shown here is the last sheet of their wedding certificate. The younger Mayer stood in for his bedridden father and signed the *ketubah* (wedding certificate) with Hannah Mayer. Rossini enthusiastically and boldly added his signature although he was not a member of the family. *The Rothschild Archive*

(*Below*) After Lionel and Charlotte were married, Gunnersbury Park became their country home. This is a view from the south of the mansion in 1840. Gunnersbury would later become more than just a country home. It would be the setting for many glamorous parties and dazzle all who visited. *From a watercolor by an unknown artist. Gunnersbury Park Museum, London*

The commemorative lithograph "The Shadow of a Great Man," by Edouart Mons, was sold in London immediately after N. M.'s death in 1836, shortly after Charlotte and Lionel's wedding. *The Rothschild Archive*

(*Below*) The silk cloth, symbolically golden in color, printed in N. M.'s memory and sold at the time of his funeral in August 1836. He appears in silhouette next to "his pillar" at the Royal Exchange. The citation, in French, Spanish, German, and English along the borders reads, "Equally distinguished for his commercial skill & enterprise & for his charitable and benevolent disposition."

Lionel at thirty-eight in an engraving in *The Illustrated London News*, July 31, 1847, on his abortive election as M.P. for the City of London. Lionel would fight for years to be seated in Parliament without having to take a Christian oath.

(*Below*) Although Gutle Rothschild never reached her ninety-ninth birthday, an anonymous German satirist depicted local obeisance to the matriarchal grandmother of Charlotte and Lionel in "Der 99ste Geburtstag des Grossmutter." From the *Fliegende Blätter*, Frankfurt, 1848.

Charlotte with her children in 1843, before the addition of Leopold, the youngest. From left to right are Leonora, Evelina, Nathaniel, and baby Alfred. *Oils on canvas, by Christina Robertson, The Rothschild Archive*

(*Right*) Communication between the Rothschild houses was fast and efficient. The Rothschilds were privy to the latest news, often receiving word before heads of state. A cartoon by J. J. Grandville, published in France in 1841, shows how the Rothschild bank branches communicated financial data before electronic telegraphy came into use. Optical systems such as semaphores are shown as well as the famous Rothschild carrier pigeon. *Hamburger Kunsthalle*

(*Above*) The entrance of the bride, Leonora de Rothschild, at her wedding in March 1857 at Gunnersbury Park. From *The Illustrated Times*, March 14, 1857.

Lionel de Rothschild being introduced in the House of Commons on his being seated by Lord John Russell (*left*) and J. Abel Smith (*right*) on July 26, 1858. His long battle was over; he had been sworn in on the Hebrew Bible. *N. M. Rothschild & Sons*

(*Facing page*) The marriage of Leonora de Rothschild to Baron Alphonse de Rothschild at Gunnersbury Park, 1857. The groom holds the wine goblet high, as he is about to ceremonially shatter it. From *The Illustrated Times*, March 14, 1857.

(*Below*) "Baron Rothschild's New Mansion, Piccadilly," in *The Illustrated London News*, 1862. The building appears unoccupied. Interior work was still ongoing.

Photograph after the completion of 148 Piccadilly. The Duke of Wellington's Apsley House is the grand building with the columns; to its right is the Rothschild mansion. *The Rothschild Archive*

(*Left*) The entrance to Piccadilly House, with stairwell, in a photograph from a Sotheby catalogue when the contents of 148 Piccadilly were being sold prior to the dismantling of the mansion for the widening of Park Lane in the late 1930s. *Sotheby catalogue, sale of April 19, 1937*

Lionel's last great achievement: "The Lion's Share," a cartoon in *Punch* late in 1875 showing Disraeli handing £4 million borrowed from Lionel to the Khedive of Egypt. Without Lionel, Britain would not have been able to finance purchase of the Suez Canal shares.

(*Right*) Pleased with himself after arranging the purchase of Suez Canal shares, Disraeli, holding a key reading "Suez Canal" with a ribbon identifying it as "The Key of India," contemplates a Sphinx which has an uncanny resemblance to himself. *Punch*, December 11, 1875.

Baron Mayer de Rothschild in his fifties. Portrait engraving from *The Illustrated London News*, February 21, 1874.

(*Below*) Lionel de Rothschild as "The Modern Croesus" in the series "People of the Period" in the July 5, 1870, issue of *Period*.

Sir Anthony de Rothschild in
his sixties. Portrait engraving
from *The Illustrated London News*,
January 22, 1876.

(*Below*) Lionel de Rothschild in
1879, the last year of his life,
painted for the bank by
"WFH"—initials which match
no known Victorian painter.
N. M. Rothschild & Sons

Nathaniel de Rothschild as head of the London house, succeeding Lionel. *Constance, Lady Battersea's Reminiscences (London: Macmillan, 1922)*

The marriage of Leopold de Rothschild to Marie Perugia beneath the wedding *chuppah* at the Portland Street Synagogue, London. From *The Graphic*, January 19, 1881.

was of parliamentary significance only if it swayed his political conduct, but that Liberal logic, by mid-June, failed to sway Tory proponents of exclusion.

An amendment to retain "the true faith of a Christian" was, nevertheless, rejected by a majority of 140 in the Commons, with four members of the Tory front bench present in the emancipation lobby for the tally—Disraeli the most senior of the renegades, and the Earl of Derby's son and heir, Lord Stanley, the most junior. Three Cabinet ministers voted at their hazard with them; four did not. As Derby was Tory leader in the Lords and prime minister, his son's position opposed his own.

On a third reading of the bill itself, the Commons reaffirmed Palmerston's bill by a resounding majority of 123, sending it once more to the Upper House. There, Lord Lyndhurst, frail at eighty-five and a veteran Lord Chancellor of every Tory Cabinet since Canning's in 1827, recalled the unfulfilled fears about Roman Catholic erosion of Anglicanism. Breaking ranks, some bishops supported him. "Justice and reason, and tried citizenship, and intelligence, and peaceful behaviour, and the assent of the whole country besides back the Jewish claims," Thackeray wrote, "but my lords block the door up, and—unless he chooses to come here, Baron Rothschild has no place where he can exert his eloquence." Lyndhurst observed that historically the Lords were a check against rash and hasty change, but he "never thought . . . that this House ought to be a perpetual barrier against sound and progressive legislation." A young reactionary, Lord Robert Cecil, who as the 3rd Marquis of Salisbury would be Victoria's last prime minister, argued otherwise. A sincere Jew, in Cecil's view "a peculiar animal," was bound to consider Christianity as false and blasphemous and work to subvert it. On July 10 the peers rejected emancipation by only 32 votes. The gap was shrinking.

When the Commons resumed deliberations on July 21, 1857, Russell proposed that the body proceed by unilateral resolution. To dramatize the issue, Lionel offered to resign and fight a new by-election. At a public meeting at the Guildhall on July 29, 1857,

nominations were called for the vacant seat, and no rival material-ized. The Sheriff of the City of London then asked for a show of hands, and every one was raised for Baron Rothschild. Yet the issue dragged on into the spring and summer of 1858.

For Lionel and Charlotte, the religious, social, and political biases that elsewhere restricted them did not exist in their own environs. They frequently hosted outspoken (but influential) antagonists, inviting them only if there was a likelihood they would come. King Ernest Augustus openly despised the Rothschilds, but his ambas-sador to the Court of St. James's, Count Kielmansegge, was at the head table at Leonora's wedding. It was important to be on reason-able terms with Napoleon III, but that did not stop Lionel and Charlotte from remaining friendly with the family of his exiled pre-decessor. Disraeli wrote to Lady Londonderry of a dinner in January 1858 at which the guests were the late Louis-Philippe's children and their spouses, a covey of dukes and duchesses, counts and count-esses, with "the guests to meet them choice, among them, by-the-by, Cardinal Wiseman, and the banquet not to be surpassed in splendor or *recherche* even at Windsor. . . . It was rather curious to dine with a Cardinal at Gunnersbury."

Since the Commons remained insistent on legislating its own membership qualification, it made that point boldly, voting that Baron Rothschild, a Member, although unsworn, be appointed to a Commons committee to draw up formal "reasons" for its disagree-ment with the Lords on oaths. In France in May to relieve her anxi-eties about the oaths matter, Charlotte visited Baron James's palatial country seat, Ferrières; the "great apartments" reminded Charlotte of "the large gambling rooms at Homburg" although there were "beautiful pictures," "extraordinary Chinese vases," and "wonderful Italian clocks." Returning to Paris, she found a message from Lionel about his extraordinary appointment. "The committee should en-able you to sit and vote in Parliament," Charlotte answered. "It is breaking my heart not to see you take your seat. I do not think you would be so cruel as not to telegraph to me to come back." She

signed it, "Most affectionately your old wife." And she hurried back to London.

Two days after being charged, the committee came forward with its report, observing that the obsolete oath had been framed to exclude Catholics, now seated, rather than Jews; that freedom of conscience had to be allowed; that no disloyalty to the government was ever imputed to Jews; and that Jews had long been declared fit for other public offices. When the report went to the House of Lords, the agreeable Earl of Lucan, a Crimean War general, proposed independently a formula making it lawful for either House of Parliament to modify the oath for its own members. As a strategic sop to Tory diehards, he included lines contending that the Commons had been provocative by "something very like an insult" when it named an unseated member to its "Reasons" committee.

The unexpected initiative was discussed on June 7, 1858, along with a Lyndhurst alternative proposing a comprehensive modification of the oaths. With one or the other certain to pass, the Earl of Shaftesbury wrote bitterly on July 1, faced with the first reading of Lucan's compromise, "This evening Jew Bill in Lords. Had signified my intention, to many, of offering no further resistance. It is in vain, and altogether useless, nor is it wanting in a tinge of peril, to deny, pertinaciously and hopelessly (for the country is, and ever has been, quite indifferent) the yearly demands of the Commons." After further weeks of delay, the Lords passed a second reading of Lucan's face-saving bill by a majority of forty-six. The Archbishop of Canterbury and ten bishops voted against the measure although seven bishops deserted to vote in favor. When the Lords discussed the bill in finality on July 5, the Earl of Derby reluctantly backed Lucan's compromise while adding a spiteful amendment:

Without imputing any Disloyalty or Disaffection to Her Majesty's Subjects of the Jewish Persuasion, the Lords consider that the Denial and Rejection of that Saviour in whose Name each House of Parliament daily offers up its collective Prayers for the Divine

Blessing on its Counsels, constitutes a moral Unfitness to take Part in the Legislation of a professedly Christian community.

Lord Granville, leader of the Liberals in the Lords, protested that the language offended the Commons and insulted the Jews, branding them as unworthy to be seated. Yet the meanness worked. Derby's malicious amendment passed on July 12 by eight votes; the next day Lucan's bill as amended passed by twenty-one votes. The Commons reluctantly accepted the bill while declaring that the Lords had not acted "fairly and handsomely." On Friday, July 23, the act became law in both houses, and after eleven years Lionel prepared to be sworn on Monday, July 26. From Paris, Laury wrote to Charlotte joyously, "Today is the grand day and I ardently hope that you & dear Papa may be satisfied with the proceedings in the House of Commons. . . . Pray tell Papa that he must not make his maiden speech till we arrive."

Disraeli's inability to carry more than a few unenthusiastic Conservatives with him although he was his party's leader in the Commons remained an embarrassment for him and a source of covert ill feeling among the Rothschilds. When "Mrs. Dizzy" dined at the Mayer de Rothschilds, Lionel had written on July 18 to Charlotte, then in the country, that Mary Anne insisted upon "how much Dizzy had done for us and how angry he was because we wouldn't believe it." Refusing to review all the details, Charlotte accepted with relief what had become inevitable. "For eleven years we've had the M.P. question screaming in every corner of the house." It was over. Lionel would be followed by David Salomons, and Mayer himself, in 1859, and Francis Goldsmid in 1860. Only Dizzy's urging moved the hidebound Earl of Derby, whatever his ungraciousness in letting change happen.

Charlotte's relations with Disraeli's distant sister and dependent brothers were almost nonexistent, although Sarah would see various Rothschilds on rare visits to her brother at Grosvenor Gate or in the country, at Hughenden in Beaconsfield. In the year of Lionel's seating, Charlotte had published, privately, her *Addresses to Young Children: Originally Delivered in the Girls' Free School, Bell Lane,* sermons that would have been described in their time as "of an improving nature." The eldest of the D'Israeli siblings (born two years before Benjamin) and the most unwilling—and last—to be converted by their father when they were children, Sarah penned a poignant response. "I have read your little volume with sympathy & admiration," she wrote; "the tone of tenderness which pervades the Addresses & their devout and elevated feelings must touch the hearts of all of every creed. I had the gratification to read one aloud last Evening (on the holiness of the Sabbath) & its piety and eloquence deeply touched my auditors"—who, she went on to explain, put aside their farming implements in the twilight to listen. The picture of the Baroness de Rothschild's Shabbat prayer being read by a D'Israeli,[7] however Christianized, to Herefordshire farmers, encapsulates the alienation of the lonely Victorian spinster, who at fifty-seven would be dead the next year and almost unmourned.

Leonora had already given birth to her first child, Bettina Caroline, in February 1858. Charlotte had arranged for nursing bottles to store "nocturnal meals" for the infant so the new mother could sleep through the nights. The grandmother-to-be and Evelina had gone to Paris to await the birth, staying at the posh Hotel Bristol for privacy, and for Charlotte to be able to write letters there after evening dinner at the rue Laffitte. At the table she talked politics with James and learned the latest gossip from everyone else. She worried that Napoleon III was seeking provocations for war with Prussia, or even England, as a diversion for the French from joblessness and a poor economy. "War is most assuredly out of the question," James insisted. "No one thinks of it, and if mentioned by chance, the very idea is considered absurd." She passed on the informed opinion to Lionel, who undoubtedly passed it on to Whitehall.

Gossip focused upon Empress Eugénie's flirtations, since her hus-

---

7. Sarah did not elide the apostrophe in her name as did Benjamin.

band's infidelities were public, and about his secret police "in disguise" everywhere, even at fashionable balls, to listen for treasonable talk. The Emperor feared assassination, for an Italian revolutionary, Felice Orsini, had attempted to shoot the imperial couple that January. The implications of the affair, reported by Disraeli to Derby, very likely came via Lionel or Charlotte. The "alarm in the City," Disraeli wrote, was affecting the value of securities and the entire Mediterranean trade, as it seemed a provocation for French intervention in Italy, where much of the north was still an Austrian domain. Confidence would need to be restored in Paris, where—Disraeli seemed to be quoting New Court—"we were on the eve of immense prosperity." (The Emperor was priming the economic pump with a building boom, reshaping Paris under the imaginative but controversial supervision of Georges Haussmann.) Word of the shooting had reached the worried Austrian ambassador as he was dining with Alphonse in his new home in the rue Saint-Florentin. The Rothschilds seemed everywhere news was made or information surfaced.

From the Bristol, Charlotte wrote to her sons, claiming to herself that her discipline and privacy were necessary. "I must exert myself to work after dinner," she explained to Leopold, thirteen, who would be deluged with letters for decades, "for a life of idleness, of so-called *dolce far niente*, is foreign to my habits, repugnant to my feelings and entirely distasteful to me." Her mail went by bank courier, as did that of the newly married Princess Victoria, bride of the future king of Prussia, Prince Frederick William. Since she and her husband were considered too liberal-minded for Berlin, she worried with reason about her letters being read, which they were, by the king's agents, even before she sealed them. She had told her aide-de-camp, she wrote to her mother, Queen Victoria, "to give the post letters to my banker here who sends them to Rothschild in London."

The last act of the parliamentary drama, now close to farce, began on the afternoon of July 26, 1858, when the Clerk of the Commons formally announced that a Member waited to take his seat. Lionel had been through it all before. The Speaker directed him to advance, which Lionel did—ignoring his arthritic pain—in company with his two sponsors, John Russell and Abel Smith. As he reached the table, an M.P. shouted on cue, "I rise to a point of order!"

"The question of a Member taking his seat is a matter of privilege," said the Speaker, "and should not be interrupted." As the Clerk automatically began administering the old oath, Lionel protested—it was a choreographed charade—and the Clerk announced loudly to the unsurprised Speaker, "The Honorable Member says that he entertains conscientious objections to taking the oath in the form presented."

"Then the Honorable Member will please to withdraw."

Slowly, Lionel withdrew below the bar, whereupon Lord John Russell moved a resolution to permit the Clerk to omit the words objected to from the oath and to allow the Member to take it in a manner binding upon him. The House duly divided, and a majority of thirty-two for the resolution was declared. Cheering arose from the benches and descended from the Strangers' Gallery where Charlotte had sat through so many earlier and unhappier ordeals. Lionel then stepped forward grimly and was sworn on the Hebrew Bible that he had carried to Commons for eleven frustrating years. It was vindication. He could see on the benches his brother-in-law Henry Fitzroy, who was born a Christian; his friend Ralph Bernal Osborne, whose father had become an Anglican, making his son's career possible;[8] and his closest friend, Benjamin Disraeli, whose father, while not converting himself, had had his son baptized at twelve. For the first time an elected Member who had tenaciously kept his faith was there as a Jew.

As Leader of the House (the Conservatives were still briefly in power), Disraeli, who had negotiated Lucan's compromise through

8. The younger Bernal took the surname of his Irish wife, Catherine, when they married in 1844.

to passage, rose to shake hands silently with Lionel as he made his way to the Opposition benches. Both men were too moved for words.

Future legislation would make oaths less cumbersome and permanently continue the new principle. This was now as inevitable as the future candidacies of other Jews. Eventually, even an atheist, the fiery orator Charles Bradlaugh, would not be denied a seat. In honor of taking his own seat, Lionel endowed an open scholarship at the City of London School, which he could not have attended as a boy. By 1866 the Rothschild Scholar was a Jewish pupil, Israel Davis, then captain of the school.

With one house now decided, Lionel and Charlotte could turn to modernizing another kind of house. The M.P. Fitzroy Kelly lived at 147 Piccadilly, adjacent to the Rothschilds. He was willing to sell the property, and Lionel commissioned the firm of Nelson & Innes to design a residence that would combine 147 with 148, and include up-to-date amenities. There was only one problem. The new M.P. and managing director of the Rothschild bank had to live somewhere else while the extensive rebuilding was accomplished. In more than twenty years of marriage he and Charlotte had collected art and furniture almost royally. While Lionel could escape to New Court to work from his wheelchair, or attend debates in the Commons, Charlotte would have to reestablish their corps of servants and supervise the transfer of everything movable or detachable to wherever they would relocate.

CHAPTER SEVEN

KINGSTON HOUSE

1858–1863

Before purchasing the Fitzroy Kelly property on Piccadilly adjoining his own, Lionel had tried to acquire Kingston House. Its stateliness belied its history. Ten acres of greensward on the south side of Knightsbridge fronted Hyde Park and backed upon Ennismore Gardens. Although he offered £300,000—an enormous sum in contemporary terms—the absentee owner the Earl of Listowel refused to sell, agreeing only to a temporary lease. Built about 1770, when the rural district was called Brompton New Town, the sprawling mansion, with conservatory, almost unseen behind a high brick wall, had once been the home of Elizabeth Chudleigh, Duchess of Kingston, who lived scandalously until she was tried for bigamy in 1777. After claiming the privilege of her peerage to escape punishment, she fled to Paris and then St. Petersburg, where Catherine the Great protected her. The Duchess never returned to England, leaving Kingston House unoccupied until her death in 1788.[1]

As Lionel and Charlotte took up residence in Kingston House, Nelson & Innes of Whitehall were commissioned to design a new Piccadilly House, with a façade of Portland stone, to be built by George Myers and Sons on the combined Rothschild-Kelly site. Charlotte wanted new kitchens as removed as possible from living and social areas, constructed beneath the terraces in the back garden. Female servants' quarters were to be topmost, garrets only by definition. Male servants would share the basement with the elaborate wine cellar. The marble entrance hall with grand staircases eight feet wide would lead to a floor with ceilings twenty feet high, containing four reception rooms, saloon, dining room, and library. Above was the spacious private living area. Since cost was less a consideration than quality, the meticulous (yet sometimes sloppy) construction work would keep the family at Kingston House far longer than anticipated.

An irony of family life is that parents often enlarge their residences, or relocate to grander ones, just as their children begin to empty the nest. The Rothschilds' elder daughter had now married and was living grandly in Paris. The first of their three sons was about to take up university life, to be followed by the others, and none was likely to live at home afterwards. Alfred, Leopold, and Evelina remained, and her marriage and departure were inevitable. For Charlotte the loss of her boys would be a greater wrench than she supposed. She was unhappy that they were quickly maturing beyond her oversight. A year earlier, exasperated, she had written to Lionel from Paris, "Our sons have outgrown my jurisdiction. For their own sake, I am anxious. They will not take any lessons. . . . The won-

---

1. Curiously, Charlotte's friend W. M. Thackeray had just published, in parts (1857–1859), *The Virginians*, a sequel to *Henry Esmond* (1852), in which the notorious Elizabeth Chudleigh is novelized as the young, coquettish Beatrix Esmond and then (as she would be later) the elderly and dissipated Baroness Bernstein.

ders of Paris bore them. . . . They will do nothing but run about in the streets, which is not an improving way of passing one's time."

Although Leopold was closer to his mother than were his elder brothers, he looked up to them, and Natty and Alfred as teenagers were uninterested in cultural improvement when there were livelier attractions in Paris.[2] Leopold was then thirteen. On October 23, 1858, he had celebrated the traditional bar mitzvah, after which Lionel and Charlotte had held a reception at New Court, convenient walking distance from the Great Synagogue in Aldgate. Strictly observant attendees would not ride on the Sabbath.

Both "well and jolly," according to John Delane, Charlotte and Lionel were in Paris in November 1858 as the razing of the old Piccadilly structure began, Lionel on business with his agent Charles Villiers, a younger brother of Lord Clarendon. In command at New Court were Lionel's brothers, often only nominally. Sir Anthony, Delane told Bernal Osborne, was "in full bloom as High Sheriff of Bucks." Mayer, whom Anthony had succeeded as High Sheriff when his brother became an M.P., had a large party at Mentmore to meet Disraeli, then Chancellor of the Exchequer. In Paris, Lionel and James discussed what they felt was the irresponsibility of Napoleon III, but saw nothing they could do but accommodate to his ambitions for the profit of the firm. Gala events and spectacles manipulated public opinion and masked the Second Empire's emptiness. Without Lionel and Charlotte in London to rein him in at home, Delane thundered in *The Times* against Napoleon and his designs against Austria on behalf of Italy (and himself), leading to a withering if polite letter from Palmerston recommending that he "slacken *The Times'* fire. . . . The continuance of attacks will not dethrone him, and there would be no advantage to England in doing so, even if it were possible."

An early visitor to Kingston House on the return of Lionel and Charlotte was Lord Macaulay, who was awed by what his hosts con-

2. As adults, both Natty and Alfred would be connoisseurs of the arts.

sidered an inconvenient rental. "What a paradise he lives in," Macaulay wrote to a colleague. "I had no notion of the beauty and extent of the gardens. . . . A palace ought to be built there." Lionel agreed, noting that he had tried to buy the property but had been turned down. Dinner there, Macaulay thought, was a "curiosity" because no pork was served, yet there were compensations in the cuisine and wine. "I do not believe that Solomon in all his glory ever dined on Ortolans farcis à la Talleyrand. I may observe in passing that the little birds were accompanied by some Johannisberg which was beyond all praise."

For Lionel, Kingston House had an additional drawback beyond its unavailability for purchase. In the new Piccadilly House the most anticipated new facility would be a mechanism for which its American inventor coined a word which failed English usage. Elisha Graves Otis had demonstrated an "elevator" at the Crystal Palace in 1851. It went into commercial service in New York in 1857. Lifted by steam power, it had a safety clamp that gripped the guide rails on which the device moved and could climb five stories in less than a minute. Lionel's legs often failed to propel him unaided. On good days he walked. On bad ones, both at New Court and at home, he used his wheeled chair, which he could manipulate himself and in which, also, he could be carried up and down stairs. It went with him in his carriage and on his travels.

In no way was Lionel the most afflicted brother. Although Mayer and Anthony seemed to flourish, if girth was the measure, Nat, who by marriage to James's Charlotte had cast his lot with Maison Rothschild, had been an invalid in Paris since the early 1850s. While hunting he had been shot accidentally, a common tragedy that seldom made the newspapers as the assailant was often a friend or a relative, or a guest unused to the field. Nerve damage led to partial paralysis, which grew worse, and to Nat's increasing blindness, which would become total. Through the 1860s he remained actively interested in banking affairs and was regularly consulted for advice, yet he became more of a vicarious Englishman each passing year, eagerly having the sporting papers from London read to him. Despite their fraternal warmth, Lionel's visits often seemed gloomy affairs with invalid chairs placed arm to arm. Anyone looking in would have had cause to wonder what use their excess of millions was to them.

Their Parisian uncle—also Nat's father-in-law—seemed ageless and driven, stubbornly ignoring his infirmities but for his sampling the sulfurous waters at spas and summoning expensive physicians whose advice to slow down he dismissed. Failing sight did not restrain James's buying art, and his new country estate was a showplace meant to outshine Mayer's Mentmore. Even Lionel was tempted to Ferrières, where he left his chair and walked in the deer park with James, shooting two hares, two pheasants, and a partridge. The next day he was exhausted, and his arm black and blue. "He had not touched a fowling piece for the last ten years," Charlotte explained to Leopold. Yet later, when Lionel was "quietly seated in the Baron's pony phaeton, he accidentally killed a gigantic wild boar, whom a party of 20 eager sportsmen had been chasing all day." He even went on with Evelina to Nat's famous vineyard at Château Mouton, adjacent to the village of Pauillac in the Médoc, before returning to Paris for the High Holy Days.

Despite Nat's immobility he kept up with his vintages, and Baron James's eagerness to have his own chic vineyard to outdo his son-in-law remained extreme. He had tried to buy the Château Lafite vinery, with its *Premier des Premiers Grands Crus*, as early as 1830, the year that 19 rue d'Artois became 19 rue Laffitte. He would bid for it nearly every year for thirty-eight years, all the while loyal to it by the barrel through his pocketbook. Only in the last months of his life was he successful, caring little about the 4,140,000 francs he overpaid. Despite gout and glaucoma, James raised his goblet in pride. The wine was as good as ever, and it was his.

Lionel now traveled less, and Charlotte more. Once, from Paris, she wrote frankly to Lionel of some family connections she met, "I hate parasites who curry favour by speaking against one's relatives." As the parliamentary session wound down, she hoped that her husband was not hazarding his fragile health while enjoying his hard-won seat. "I trust," she wrote, "that you are perfectly well and that you do not fatigue yourself too much with political visits. Your health is of far more importance than the right & pleasure of sitting & voting in the House of Commons." The principle had been won. She was content with that.

Charlotte did not want to be severed for long from the umbilical cord that was her adopted London. At Ferrières with Laury she visited the vast acres being landscaped under the direction of Sir Joseph Paxton, of Crystal Palace fame, who described the future farms and gardens, and the "innumerable glades and glens and emerald turf." It would be splendid, she thought, but artificial, lacking the "picturesque and romantic charms" of the villages about Aston Clinton or Halton—which Lionel had bought for a future Buckinghamshire seat for one of his sons. Still, Ferrières would be a "noble property" when its expensively manicured greensward matured.

"I have told you the news," she closed, "and have nothing to add for you but my love, for you do not care to have descriptions of moonlit nights with sheet lightning through the trees of the forest and illuminations on the lake."

Returning to the temporary home in Knightsbridge she disliked, Charlotte received, as if still at 148 Piccadilly, inquirers, friends, and supplicants almost without pause. On one quiet summer day alone in 1859 when London, early into the parliamentary recess, seemed "deserted by the gay and brilliant world," she discussed construction details for Piccadilly House with the head carpenter, met with "the whole domestic staff," and had four supplicants without appointments, one a rabbi. They asked for funds for a new religious school for the "rising generation," for a new Sabbath school, for "a burying-ground in Wales," for the distribution of Christian Bibles in England, and to send sermons "to the Colonies." Two years later, discovering from a visitor that young Jewish immigrants were being apprenticed into sweatshops, she gave the Board of Jewish Guardians funds for ten sewing machines, another invention that had been exhibited at the Crystal Palace. Hired out for token sums to small entrepreneurs who bought them with their earnings, the sewing machines set a self-help pattern for more purchases. Soon there were hundreds in use.

Like Charlotte, Lionel believed that good work as well as good works was essential. At the Fortieth Anniversary Dinner of the Jews' Free School, he declared that the "public and private virtues as well as the happiness" of the graduates should not have to depend "upon the few who [are] especially favoured by fortune, extraordinary talents or conspicuous influences," but rather "upon the many who advance themselves upon the path of progress" and in a "faithful and enlightened" manner "discharge . . . all obligations . . . which may be placed by Providence." Lionel, separately, received so many supplicants for charities that in order to conduct business at New Court he now had to employ someone to review applications and make recommendations.

While he was away in France with Evelina and Leonora, Charlotte enjoyed a private holiday at Sandown on the Isle of Wight. Then, for Rosh Hashanah and Yom Kippur, she took a ferry to Portland, to stay where there was a synagogue. Her overriding preoccupation on returning to London was not, for the moment, Piccadilly House, but Cambridge. Natty had matriculated at Trinity College at the Michaelmas term in 1859, soon to be followed at Cambridge by Alfred. Since Prince Albert had become chancellor, the hidebound university had been liberalizing more quickly than archaic Oxford, still sunk in medieval torpor. Although there was no longer a religious test for the B.A., other covert bars remained. Mayer had bent the rules for Chapel but left before getting his degree in the later 1830s because at least minimal attendance was required. In 1859, Natty objected to his parents that taking the sacrament "as a member of the Church of England" was still mandated. This seemed equivalent to the discarded oath in the House of Commons, and he questioned "why a national institution like this which is the stepping stone to legal and political preferments as well as ecclesiastical ones should be ruled by priests as if it were a Jesuit's seminary or a Talmud school."

Another religious hurdle, disguised as an academic one, was the "Little Go," the second-year examination based in part upon William Paley's *Evidences of Christianity* (1794), long demolished as logic. Paley had claimed that what he saw of design in nature evidenced Christian truth. Although advances in science had made his contentions absurd, the requirement was not dropped until 1871. (The "Little Go" also included one of the Gospels in Greek, and Euclid.) As a student attestation of Anglican faith, *Evidences* had as much meaning as nominal attendance at Chapel, but seeing the examination as a cheap price to pay for a coveted degree, Charlotte appeared more willing than her sons to be complicit in the hypocrisy. This was not the same to her as the public swearing of an unacceptable oath before the bar of the Commons, as their father had refused to do. When Leopold, the last of her sons at Cambridge, also bridled at the religious barriers, Charlotte responded pragmatically that she was "annoyed" with him and that it was "an insult to the Reverend examiners," even "reprehensible, and indeed unpardonable." She saw no objection in his becoming "acquainted with the subject," and professed to be "grieved" and "sorry" at Leo's resistance. A small hypocrisy seemed to her strategically acceptable. Her boys had erred in objecting to a trivial technicality. Natty, however, disagreed, recalling his "rage" one evening at the Cambridge Union when a student attacked the "too great power of the House of Commons [in] the passing of the Jew Bill. I had hoped that the day was gone by for all [prejudice] of this kind and if I had spoken [in return] at once, I might have aroused religious passions, not so easy to quell as arouse."

One undergraduate who expanded Natty's social world at Trinity was Albert Edward, Prince of Wales. Although the Prince was isolated from undergraduate life at Madingley House, four miles from the university, the Master of Trinity, William Whewell, brought him into closer contact with students by making rooms also available in the Lodge. There, Natty discovered, "the different Regius professors come and lecture to him." The Prince by fatherly fiat was "not allowed to take any notes but has to write the lectures when he gets back to Madingley." It was a difficult way to become educated for a young man who had suffered learning disabilities from boyhood. "I fancy," Natty told his parents, "the little spirit he has is quite broken, as his remarks are commonplace and very slow. . . . He is excessively fond of the chase but Windsor does not approve of the national sport and allows him but one horse and does not even find horse flesh for his equerries. He is very fond of riddles and strong cigars and will I suppose eventually settle down into a well disciplined German Prince with all the narrow views of his father's [Coburg] family. . . . If he followed the bent of his own inclination, it strikes me he would take to gambling and certainly keep away from the law lectures he is obliged to go to now."

Natty was soon a crony of the Prince's, thanks to a mutual friend at Cambridge, the young Duke of St. Albans, descended on the wrong side of the blanket (via Nell Gwyn) from Charles II. His widowed mother and his sister were frequent guests of Charlotte's. At the University Races, Natty wrote, the Prince's presence deflected discipline by proctors, and one of the winners was St. Albans. "I acted as judge and handicapper and was very pleased with the results." Afterwards he went to a party at the Master's Lodge, where he found the Prince and his friends, and many privileged outsiders, up for the races, including the Dowager Duchess of St. Albans with her daughter, Lady Diana Beauclerk—to Charlotte the "lovely Di"—and other lords and ladies.

For the younger Rothschilds, this was a social breakthrough. Although Natty resented the unearned advantages of birth and rank he saw in practice all around him at Cambridge, he himself had become part of that exclusive group. Later in the term he described "a grand Gala" on Whitsunday, at which "the Dons appear in their scarlet robes, and the Prince of Wales and the [other undergraduate] Noblemen in blue and gold gowns. A stranger coming down here would take all the world for maniacs." At the Prince's dinners at the Lodge, where dons, dignitaries, and undergraduates mingled awkwardly, the atmosphere of cautious gentility made for dull evenings, which Natty endured to remain within the elite orbit. "The music and the company not being compatible with my tastes," he confessed to his parents, "I escaped at an early hour unnoticed."

When the aristocratic elders left early, Natty was often the Prince's partner at whist, one evening winning twelve shillings and sixpence. "We ought to have won twice as much," complained the budding banker, "but His Royal Highness threw away the game." Bertie was no better at tennis or at field sports, but improved as a horseman despite alleged penny-pinching at Windsor Castle, which allowed the heir to the throne only a single "old" nag, "Comus." On occasion the Prince was permitted to have friends at Madingley House for lunch or dinner, or to make up a cricket eleven. "I expect I shall have a fine leather hunt and a duck's egg," Natty wrote pessimistically before one match. Football, a working-class pastime, Leo would say was "by far too vulgar." Shooting was the preferred sport "for wealthy gentlemen and aristocrats," and accommodating tutors of the well-born would make exceptions for assignments that conflicted with shooting parties.

The friendship with "Wales" would be taken up by Alfred and Leopold, and the Prince remained part of their lives. After the Prince of Wales's marriage to a rather dim, if pretty, Danish princess, Alexandra, in 1863, the Queen and her courtiers often sniffed at the company the young Royals kept as the wrong sort for a king-in-waiting. The haughty Earl Spencer as Master of the Household would advise Victoria that the Prince of Wales and his Princess should not attend a ball at Piccadilly House given by the baronial parents of Bertie's Cambridge friends, as "the Prince ought only to visit those of undoubted position in society." Lionel and Charlotte de Rothschild were "very worthy people," he conceded, "but they especially hold their position from wealth and perhaps the accidental beauty of the first daughter they brought out." Leonora may have been ravishing, but she was a Jew.

The Prince and Princess of Wales ignored such prejudices, but, born to bigotry, their attendants persisted. Natty, Alfred, and Evelina would be invited to balls at the Prince's Marlborough House, and the Waleses, when presiding later at royal levees that his mother, in persistent mourning for her husband, Albert, refused to hold, invited both Natty and Alfred. Charlotte reported sardonically to Leopold that "the Prince was gracious, as usual, smiled and shook hands—but H.R.H. has accustomed them to much kindness and cordiality; what amused them, however, was the rebuke he gave to Lord Sydney, who fine gentleman and jew-hater as he is, announced Natty as Monsieur 'Roshil'—'Mr de Rothschild' was the correction he received from royal lips." Sydney, Charlotte fumed, "though fed from time immemorial upon all the delicacies in and out of season by all the Continental Rothschilds, and not disdaining our dinners either, never thought us worthy of being asked to court."

At an even lower level of bigotry was the crabbed Thomas Carlyle, still seething over Baron de Rothschild's seating in the House of Commons. On visiting Charles Dickens he was venomous about the ongoing construction of elegant Piccadilly House. Writing to his actor friend W. C. Macready on June 11, 1861, Dickens reported,

Carlyle has greatly intensified his aversion to Jews, and is greatly enraged by beholding the gradual rise of a Mansion that Rothschild is building next [to] the Duke of Wellington's. He was with us the other day, representing . . . King John as an enlightened Sovereign in respect of drawing the teeth of Jews, to make them shed their money; and was comforting himself with an imaginary picture of Rothschild haled to the Court of Queen Victoria, and having several double teeth drawn, and being addressed, "Sir, you sow not, neither do you work, nor make any useful thing upon the surface o' God's airth; you merely accumulate; and Sir we do require to have such accumulation out of ye, and, by the strong dentist hand and the permission of the Eternal Ruler o' this Universe, we will draw every tooth out of your Mosaic head unless you here and now put down seventeen millions of ill-gotten Money, which shall be held sufficient for this day and this day only, for tomorrow we will have other teeth or other millions."

Macready, who had played Shakespeare's *King John*, would have understood Carlyle's allusion to the story that John once demanded a thousand marks from a Jew, on the refusal of which he ordered one of his teeth to be drawn each day until he consented. The Jew allegedly lost seven teeth before paying the extortion money.

Another passerby curious about Piccadilly House was a visitor from New Hampshire. He had heard about "the famous palace that the Rothschilds were building" and, through "the kindness of the master builder, was shown over it." Afterwards, as the unidentified American stood on the sidewalk admiring the façade, he recalled,

I noticed a gentleman, a few feet from me, watching. . . . I thought, from his appearance, he might be the contractor. . . .

"Good morning, sir," I said, approaching him. He bowed politely, but without speaking. "I am a stranger here," I went on.

"You are from America," he said, smiling.

"Indeed I am," I replied, "and I am proud of it, I assure you. I have just been looking over this building, and I would like to ask you some information concerning it."

"I shall be happy to oblige you," he said politely. He was very kind in telling me much that was of interest. At last I said abruptly, "I suppose you have seen Rothschild, sir."

"Which one?"

"The old fellow."

"I see the old fellow every day," he replied dryly, giving me a strange glance.

"By George, I should like to have a look at him," I went on. "People say he's a gay old chap, and lives high. I wish I had him in my power. I'd not let him get away until he had shelled out a pile of his money."

The New Englander, who wrote anonymously about his encounter in the *Portsmouth Journal* four years later, could not have known of Carlyle's diatribe to Macready, yet he echoed similar odium. The gentleman, his short black beard going grey, took it lightly. "Baron Rothschild had to work for his money, and deserves to enjoy it," he said with a laugh.

"Maybe so, but I reckon he did a heap of gouging and squeezing to get it."

The old man's face flushed. "I never heard the honesty of the house called in question," he said stiffly.

"Didn't you? Well, to tell the truth, neither did I. But I wouldn't be surprised if I'm right, after all. It's in the blood of his race, you know. Ever since the days of Judas Iscariot, the Jews have had a hankering after pieces of silver."

The old man's face grew as black as a thundercloud, and he bit his lip without speaking. "People tell me," I continued, not heeding this, . . . "that the Rothschilds have made two fortunes. Now, as most people can make only one, I feel somewhat interested. to learn the manner in which this was done. Can you tell me, sir?"

The old man's face brightened instantly. . . . "Certainly, sir. People do say that the House of Rothschild made one fortune by being careful to mind their own business, and the other by letting that of other people alone. Good morning, sir." With an elegant bow, he turned, and left me . . . and [I] looked for someone from whom to ask the old gentleman's name. He had stopped at the upper end of the building, and was giving some directions to a workman.

I saw a handsome man of about thirty . . . looking up at the building. . . . "Excuse me for troubling you," I said, "but I am a stranger in the country. . . . Can you tell me the name of that old gentleman," I asked. . . .

"Certainly," he replied. "That is Baron Rothschild, the head of the house of that name."

"Whew!" I exclaimed. . . . "I have got myself into a scrape." I told him what had occurred between the baron and myself. He laughed heartily. . . . "That was awkward."

"He's a crusty old chap," I said. . . . "He's as cross as a bear."

"Oh, that's only his way. . . . He is a good, kind-hearted man, but is rather eccentric."

"I should say so. . . . Do you know Baron Rothschild?" I asked. . . .

"I have met with him several times, and I have an appointment to wait upon him at his office today."

"Then I wish you would say to him . . . that I did not know whom I was talking to today, or I would not have said so much; and that he need not have been so huffish about it."

"I will do so," replied my acquaintance. . . . "You must not mind him. He was a little nettled at it, but will be the first to laugh at the adventure when he recovers his good humor. Good morning." With a bow and pleasant smile he left me. Just then a workman passed. . . . I stopped him and asked if he could tell me the name of the gentleman who had just left me.

"That was one of the younger Rothschilds," he said.

Since Lionel would not permit intermittent disability to slow him down, he was away often on business in the early 1860s, in Germany and France as well as in England, reporting local political gossip to his "Dearest Wife," and (despite Delane) so pleased with Napoleon III's remaking the face of Paris that he wished sluggish London could have him for a few months, "just to make a few alterations." The children worried about Charlotte's loneliness during Lionel's absences, but she went off in her carriage just after the new year of 1861 to present dressed turkeys to friends, visited new mothers to coo over infants, dined at the country seats of other Rothschilds, visited France to see the again-pregnant Leonora, returned to entertain dozens of the "stronger sex" (her own), and wrote enormously long letters and apologized for short ones by observing "as the good Frankfurters say, half an egg is better than nothing."

With Lionel she spent some of the summer in the Lake District. Increasingly lax about importing their diet from London, they stayed at a hotel in Grasmere just above Lake Windermere. Even their dogs accompanied them, chasing after their carriage as they bumped almost daily along waterscapes "wild in the superlative degree." Taking her carriage to the post office in Windermere one day to pick up packets of mail, Charlotte found herself with no money for the turnpike. Her coachman paid.

On his long vacation, Natty joined them from Cambridge, in retreat from detested mathematical studies for the Tripos, yet accompanied by a maths tutor. Even Uncle James turned up, en route on business to Scotland.

"We . . . expected the great Baron"—Charlotte's invariable term for him—"by every train," she wrote (August 14, 1861) to her other children, "for there were some inaccuracies about the telegrams— he did not come[3] and the great gun was fired for the good of the public, instead of being kept sacred to announce his arrival. You can have no idea of the magical effect of the echoes. It was grand and startling. We went out on the Lake—and not wishing to call in loud tones the names of our beloved [children], Natty enumerated the heroes and heroines of "Great Expectations"—also our dogs.

Dickens's novel had just finished its long serial run in *All the Year Round*.

3. Until a later train. A "time gun" at Kendall, nearby, was fired every afternoon at one.

René, the infant son of Leonora and Alphonse, had his Brith Mi-lah (ritual circumcision) in Paris on October 21, 1861, the customary eighth day. Lionel James Mayer René was registered in the syna-gogue as "Nathan." Charlotte was distressed, but helpless, at the French fashion for cosseting new mothers who did not need to re-turn to farming or cooking that kept Leonora imprisoned in her bed-room for two weeks in near darkness, without being allowed to read, write, or do work of any kind. Lionel also crossed the foggy Channel for the usually joyous event, and remained unhappily as the infant declined, dying on November 3. By tradition René was buried the next day, a wintry one for autumn. Although his parents maintained that the child was ill from birth, Charlotte contended that infection from the token surgery was responsible. (Application of sacramental wine was the only antiseptic in pre-Lister days.) She decided that the ritual was abhorrent, and hoped it would be abolished.

Lionel stayed with James, who had become more like an elder brother than an uncle, and drove consolingly with him along Hauss-mann's broad new boulevards, still under construction. Charlotte worried about James's "very bad poulticed eye"—a family weak-ness—under the wet and grey mid-November skies, but the stubborn master of the rue Laffitte received his usual fifty clients a day, in a darkened room. Late in November Charlotte and Lionel returned home together; they were in London on December 14, 1861, when Prince Albert died and life in the city came to a halt. Black bunting was everywhere. They escaped the gloom for Gunnersbury, where they found that their gardeners, who appreciated Albert better than did most politicians, would not work on the Monday of the Prince Consort's funeral at Windsor.[4]

---

4. For Lionel, whose business dealings with the efficient Albert, whom he ad-mired, were warm, the Prince's death, at forty-two, meant the end of his and Char-lotte's presence at royal functions. As Charlotte recalled to Leo, "[D]ear Papa used to apply to him—when forgotten or omitted." Now she would decline to "trouble" the perpetually mourning and distant Queen, and become subject to the prejudices of Lord Sydney.

The children commiserated to Lionel about his "troublesome pains" and reported on their doings to both parents, Leopold ridiculing a student named Montagu Corry, an inept horseman who held up his riding party. "I believe he had never been on horseback before or at least not very often. He was fortunate enough to escape with few falls." The Rothschilds would later see much of Corry, who became Disraeli's factotum and secretary.

The talk at Cambridge, and even at Gunnersbury late into December, focused upon the American war, and whether Britain would be drawn into it. A Union gunboat had seized a British mail packet, the *Trent*, on the high seas and removed Confederate emissaries en route to London and Paris. Russell and Palmerston drafted a bellicose ultimatum which, from his deathbed, Prince Albert had made more pacific. Still, troops were being sent to Canada, including some students with whom Natty had drilled in Stowe Park. Charlotte worried about the Rifle Corps' gunnery practice upon bales of hay, and Natty assured her that it was merely like taking exercise, and safe. He was more concerned about Southern victories over faltering Union forces: If they continued to have it their way, they might go on to seize Cuba and Mexico.

The early 1860s were dominated by the American war. The blockade of the rebel states depleted stocks of imported cotton and led to mill closings and economic hardship. Belligerent talk from the Liberal government followed, and more, as Palmerston and Russell averted their eyes from the arming of ships destined for the South as commerce raiders. Gladstone, perhaps third in rank among the Liberals, Lionel's party, claimed that the South had "made a nation," and Delane also railed against the North, which could have peace by conceding secession. Natty would complain to his parents about the anti-Union irresponsibility of *The Times*, not so much Delane's doing as that of Mowbray Morris, the newspaper's manager, and John Walter, the proprietor. On visits to England, the Rothschilds' agent in New York, August Belmont (once Schönberg), now an independent, Americanized banker living in New York as a *grand seigneur* but still undertaking commissions for New Court, was entertained with his family at Kingston House, talking Unionist politics with Lionel's influential friends. Since Caroline Belmont (daughter of the American Commodore Matthew Perry) had brought her two daughters, Charlotte arranged entertainments, including tableaux vivants in which the girls appeared as serving maids, nymphs, and angels.

From a business standpoint, Belmont had fashioned a course for himself that was separating him, despite his considerable charm, from the Rothschilds. The London brothers, and James in Paris, had abandoned every opportunity to establish a house in New York, for none of James's sons was interested, nor were Lionel's brothers. Once, at fifteen, an apprentice in the Frankfurt house, Belmont had exploited the vacuum. The Rothschilds suspected, he confided to his wife, that "I have realized immense profits by contracts with the United States government and other business, which I might have given to the House. . . . This interferes very much with that confidence which is indispensable for our mutual relations." He deplored the cynical encouragement for the Confederate cause he saw among leaders in Lionel's party who coveted Southern cotton and who smugly envisioned a breakup of the Union as making competition for English manufactures more advantageous. Alarmingly candid, Palmerston told Belmont, "We don't like slavery, but we want cotton."

In writing on his return to Lionel, who was unsympathetic to Palmerston's pro-South leanings, Belmont admonished, "Let your statesmen and Southern sympathizers go to Cuba and see the fearful barbarity and misery of slavery there, and I fear they would find it more difficult to satisfy their consciences as easily as they seem to have satisfied their constituents for the course they have pursued to our people in our hour of trouble." Had England assisted the North, he cautioned the innocent Lionel, "she would have secured forever the abolition of slavery throughout the world, while now instead she is assisting in riveting the fetters on the poor Africans for another century." After listening to the variety of opinions on the war, especially from the usually well informed editor of *The Times*, Charlotte wrote to Leopold late in July 1862, "Mr. Delane paid a long visit to Papa yesterday; he talked of the sad cotton famine, and of the far more distressing American war. The unfortunate soldiers are dying by the thousands, cut down by the sword and still more decimated by the yellow fever. It is, therefore, thought that the carnage and the horrors of the war cannot be protracted beyond the end of the summer."

In pro-secessionist Cambridge, Natty assured his parents that he was still occupied by lectures and private tutors unsuccessfully trying to fill his head with algebra and trigonometry, for "to get on here one must be wedded to Mathematics and think of nothing else." With his friends also cramming, he sent to the college kitchens for carrot soup and roast turkey to supplement their sherry. As for Paley's *Evidences of Christianity*, it was "the most absurd conglomeration of words I ever broke my head over, so that there is *no* danger of my being converted as many up here have prophesied." But he finally got through the "Little Go."

Natty would get through little else at Cambridge. Rather than "just *scrape* through," he wrote to his parents, he would leave. He would miss only the "drag"—a pseudo-hunt in which hounds chased after a scented lure that substituted for the elusive fox. After the Michaelmas term of 1862 he did not return for his examinations in 1863. Alfred and Leopold would be wary of Natty's experience and chose a different college at Cambridge—King's. Yet Alfred would not last as long as did Natty. He was a success at the Dramatic Club, and Natty's friends took easily to him, but in the summer of 1862 he became ill and had to return to Kingston House, where a succession of expensive physicians visited Lionel's study, which had become Alfred's sickroom, and pronounced his "wound"—an incision following a painful "stoppage" (as described by his mother), with fever and nausea—as healing satisfactorily. During the summer months Charlotte often took her meals with him, and her visiting ladies gratified her, if not him, by bestowing kisses on the convalescent Alfy. "Poor boy!" Charlotte told Leopold, "it is his fate to be embraced by all the old women; but as the young ones come and sit by his arm-chair, he has not too much to complain [about] from the fair sex." Nothing was likely to better speed his recovery.

With Alfred still ill, Charlotte fended off Disraeli's continuing pleas for a Rothschild visit to Hughenden Manor. Mary Anne had been adding expensively to the house, which had insufficient entertainment space. Outdoors, "Mrs. Dizzy" was planting new gardens. In a long letter to Leonora and Leopold that August, Charlotte gossiped in her usual unawed fashion about "the great Disraeli, who rhapsodizes about the enchantments of his dear country home, the silver river, where rose-coloured trout disport themselves, the ever-growing, ever-improving and really beautiful trees." With Hughenden no more than twenty miles from any of the Rothschild country homes in the Vale of Aylesbury, exchange visits were frequent. Constance de Rothschild, daughter of Sir Anthony, and seventeen miles distant at Aston Clinton, recalled Disraeli in his costume as squire, "in his velveteen coat, his leather leggings, his soft felt hat, and carrying his little hatchet for relieving the bark of trees from the encroaching ivy." The "only fault of our party," Disraeli wrote to Charlotte, away in Torquay, "was that it contained no Rothschilds—but that was not our fault, for we tried not only the English, but the French & Austrian dynasties, but in vain." In a later letter he noted that he had named a room in the manor for Charlotte—"so now you have a vested interest in Hughenden."

More and more, Disraeli confided in Lionel and Charlotte, and found them both politically and emotionally necessary to him. Even earlier, in January 1859, Lord Malmesbury when Foreign Secretary in a Tory government that included Dizzy complained, "Disraeli *never reads a word of my papers* which go round [the Cabinet] and knows nothing but what the Jews at Paris and London tell him." Malmesbury's vituperation was both bigoted and exaggerated, yet Disraeli clearly valued his Rothschild sources.

For a time Lionel was Charlotte's second invalid, remaining home and reading such novels as Henry Kingsley's new *Ravenshoe*, about Catholic-Protestant religious rivalry and family secrets ferreted out by the family's shrewd Jesuit confessor. Charlotte knew that Lionel was recovering when she wrote to Leopold ("Poodle"), with Leonora at Spa to keep the Prince of Wales company, "While I am scribbling, Papa is enjoying an excellent breakfast—grilled sole, fried chicken, eggs, toast and tea, and Sir Anthony is talking to him about Buckinghamshire estates." By August 9 the Baron was able to accompany Charlotte and Natty to the synagogue in the evening for *jahrzeit*—the annual prayers on the anniversary of Nathan Mayer's death.

A few days later Lionel's Kingsley novel almost materialized in the person of the brother of their Spanish agent. Freshly killed game was being served for lunch on Wednesday, August 13, when Bruno Bauer's younger brother, "the Carmelite monk," called. "As he eats nothing but vegetables boiled in water," Charlotte explained to Leo, "I did not dare to venture to ask him into the dining room." The pale, seemingly austere Monsignor Marie-Bernard Bauer at thirty-three was a curious contrast to the Rothschilds' ebullient Madrid agent. In Vienna in 1851 the future abbé had abandoned Judaism to be baptized (thus the "Marie" prefix). A wealthy American expatriate in elite French circles who knew him later recalled, "Wearers of the *soutane* (especially if they be young and stalwart and enterprising) . . . can rush in where laymen—because of possible duels and divorce proceedings—fear to tread." In Paris, "all the actresses, all the demimondaines, went mad over him. He was passed from arms to arms, from lips to lips." Monsignor Bauer

reveled in it, and probably no one man in modern[5] society has ever had such close, tumultuous, intimacy with the consciences of beautiful women. . . . It was so delightful, so new, so unexpected to have a rich young Abbé to confess all your sins to; it was almost worth while confessing imaginary sins to obtain his delightful advice and

5. Julian Osgood Field is referring to permissive France in the 1860s.

forgiveness! And then when you . . . put all your sins—your temptations—before him, how kind, how comforting this experienced young spiritual guide was! He knew all about it; he had been tempted and fallen himself, so he knew just how and where to soothe, and console, and heal. . . . [In 1866] he was made Almoner to the Empress; and [in 1869] when Her Majesty went to open the Suez Canal just made by her cousin, [Ferdinand de] Lesseps, Bauer, as her *Aumonier*, went with her, and it was he, this profligate Jew mountebank, who blessed it! When the Empire fell, Bauer . . . discarded the *soutane*, and returned to the Synagogue.

In exile after 1870, Eugénie discovered Bauer's deception and confessed to Madame de Mouchy, "*Quel misérable!* And to think I let that scoundrel bless the Canal. It's enough to bring a curse on every ship that goes through it!" That adventure was six years away, and no hint of the holy father's *libertinage* seems to have been known to Charlotte when Bauer paid his call at Kingston House and took back with him to France her contribution intended for his holy order.

A great family event early in 1862 was the completion of the tallest chimney stack atop Piccadilly House, and the hoisting of a flag to the top—a centuries-old builders' propitiation of the household gods—the wreathing of a spire, the beflagging of a tower. The house was far from ready for occupancy, but by November the trade journal *The Builder* could publish an article, "Baron Rothschild's New Mansion in Piccadilly," picturing not only the façade but a floor plan showing the impressive pentagonal staircase winding up to what would be a balconied gallery of sculpture and Chinese vases.

Neither Lionel nor Charlotte was comfortable in vast, fussy Kingston House, and they retreated to the sea air at Torquay, to which deputies from New Court came daily with messages—including the sporting news—and returned with instructions. Lionel managed to keep an enormous amount of financial data in his retentive memory and seemed to carry New Court's files under his hat.

The Torquay area had no sublimity about it, Charlotte wrote to

Laury, who was holidaying in the Alps. Rather, it was "a most uninteresting spot, unhallowed by art, science, history or the beauties of nature." Paradoxically, she enjoyed it for its blandness although the citified Delane lauded the countryside as "really beautiful." Friends like Disraeli, Thackeray, Matthew Arnold, and the Duke of Cambridge, the Queen's cousin, visited happily. Some stayed only for the day; others were put up for as long as a fortnight. "There is a large society here," Delane wrote happily to his secretary, "so that we have parties every night." Happily, too, for him, there seemed no dearth of newsmakers. At the request of Mayer's wife, Juliana, kosher food was sent in from nearby Dover and prepared by "a Christian cook used to Jewish meals," which prompted the hotel manager to seek an audience with Charlotte. He "wanted to make sure his chef, [wine] cellar, waiters, chambermaids, porters, etc. were giving satisfaction. Many protestations of devotion to our family."

Often agents and clients visited Lionel at Webb's Hotel, including Nathaniel Davidson, who represented Rothschild interests in the American West from San Francisco, and the ubiquitous Bruno Bauer, who discussed Spanish and Russian affairs. On occasion Charlotte and Lionel did the visiting, lunching at Angela Burdett-Coutts's villa with her many literary friends.

Lionel was still unable to put on his boots, but Charlotte's lowering the intensity of his lifestyle worked at least a temporary cure through October and November. At New Court, behind his cluttered desk, he seemed masterly, but elsewhere he had become, when he lost the use of his legs (which was increasingly often), one of Charlotte's children, although her solicitude had to be administered privately. One of the most powerful men in England, Baron Lionel had to retain his public mystique.

By early December he felt improved enough to be able to ride again, and sent for his horse from Gunnersbury, which remained at Torquay until the family (the recuperating Alfred included) left on January 28, 1863. It was Lionel's longest absence from St. Swithin's Lane since his wedding in 1836.

But for its Saturday closing for the Jewish Sabbath, New Court was typical of the Victorian counting houses of its time. After renovations in 1860 the partners (usually Lionel, alone) sat in "the Room"—a gaslit joint office space about forty feet long with oak paneling rising to eight feet, after which white plaster reached to the ceiling. (A partners' entrance closed to clerks admitted favored— "*hochwohlgeboren*"—clients.) At each end was a black marble chimney piece under which a fireplace housed a blaze summer and winter. Turkish carpets and armchairs in reddish brown leather completed the aura of mid-century banking respectability. Two huge mahogany writing tables with brass edges and leather tops in which were panels of bell pushes occupied the center of the room. At the far end of the farthest table from the entrance was Lionel's chair.

Adjacent to the Partners' Room was the Correspondence Department, which employed a small army of "linguists" for translation, and the coordinator of couriers. Although telegraph now accommodated most messages, the most confidential communications went by couriers, some of them recruited, still, from Folkestone-area descendants of mariners of "infinite resource" who had manned the cutters which Nathan Mayer had used to convey agents across the Channel. As a contemporary courier explained, "One day a man might have only to walk round to Bishopsgate, the next to leave on five minutes' notice for Budapest."

A "rather rusty sword," one courier remembered wryly, "a relic of the Peninsular War, which used to hang in a glass case in the front hall, was [allegedly] kept for the purpose of operating on such [clerks] . . . as were found not to have been circumcised." Wages for clerks ranged from about £80 to £120 a year; their hours began at about 9:30 and ended at 6:30 or 7:00. Among the perquisites at private banks was a staff dinner at about 5:00, when doors were closed to the public and several junior clerks worked on the balance for the day. A senior clerk took the chair and went through a litany of familiar toasts over excellent wine, "and if the Balance was agreed before dinner was over one of the porters from downstairs was sent up to make the announcement." The hope was that the announcement would be "Gentlemen, the Balance is right." If not, clerks returned to their desks until it was right. Lionel never remained for the ritual. Charlotte usually had a formal dinner waiting, and often a dozen or more guests from the highest levels of business and government.

The Paris house operated in a manner which Charlotte and Lionel found inordinately excessive. An event long in planning for Ferrières was an imperial visit scheduled for December 16, 1862, intended as a formal reconciliation with the Rothschild bank, often at odds with the "bread-and-circuses" spendthrift Emperor. Napoleon III had heard much about Baron James's château. Its galleries eclipsed most museums in France, and the state dining room, according to Leonora, who remained as militantly English as her blind uncle Nat,[6] evoked "the great chapel of the Knights of the Garter at Windsor." The bubbly Evelina, on a visit, "pleased Uncle James by telling him that [she] could find only *one* fault—the place was too royal to be without sentinels."

Baronne Betty asked Rossini for a ceremonial piece for the occasion, and he composed the pompous *Choeur de chasseurs démocrates*, marked *allegro brilliante*, for tenors, baritones, and basses, accompanied by two drums and tam-tam. On the festive morning the imperial flag was raised on all four towers as Napoleon III and Eugénie arrived from the railway station at Ozouer-la-Ferrières in five carriages emblazoned in the Rothschild racing colors of blue and yellow, the Emperor attired in what his attendants assured him was traditional hunting garb for Brittany.

Of N. M.'s sons, only Anthony was in the greeting party, with Natty and Evelina representing Lionel and Charlotte. Luncheon, Leonora wrote to her parents, was to last exactly one hour and exceeded the schedule by only twelve minutes, although the servants were so flustered by the presence of the Emperor "that they called all

---

6. Juliana, Baroness Mayer, wrote to Charlotte from Paris in May 1862, "Nat is very pleasant to talk to, and *very, very* sad to look at."

the visitors by the wrong names. Fortunately the cook did not lose his wits." The elderly diplomat next to Laury at the table "talked all the time about you, dear Papa, & was happy you had exchanged New Court for Torquay." Because of assassination worries, "There were police agents in every corner but I fancy that precaution was unnecessary." (Natty wrote that "paid agents" at the station had cried "Vive l'Empereur" to suggest popular enthusiasm.)

Following dessert, Napoleon planted the traditional cedar, and then took part in a great shoot in the manicured forest of Ferrières in which nothing resembling hunting was involved. According to Natty's letter home, "There was an enormous show of game; but as most of the sho[o]t[er]s had drunk 10 or twelve different kinds of wine, they shot very badly. Altogether some 800 pheasants were murdered; they ought to have killed 1500." Leonora added, "The Emperor had 8 guns, and was asking for a 9th. . . . The poor birds are so tame that they come and meet the carriages as they move through the park."

On the return of the shooting party, the hired chorus of the Paris Opéra sang under Rossini's direction, swelling to a mighty *fortissimo* on the closing phrase, *"Amis! Le cerf est pris!"* Beginning with the Emperor, dignitaries signed their names in the Ferrières golden guest book. Taking his cue from the marriage of Charlotte and Lionel, Rossini signed boldly just below Napoleon III. After the Emperor said his good-byes to the family, the frail Baron, who at seventy had lost little of his Frankfurt accent, responded (according to Prosper Mérimée), in his fractured French, "Sire, my chiltren and I vill nefer forget dis day; de memory of it vill remain tear to us."

By mid-January 1863 Lionel, who—like Charlotte—had evinced no interest in the imperial occasion across the Channel, was weary of his protracted absence from New Court, and impatient, also, to occupy Piccadilly House, so long in reconstruction. He planned a dinner in London in March for the workmen at the site, to offer thanks and speed them along. Thanks to her book account at Hatchards in Piccadilly, Charlotte managed through the winter, finally giving in to

Lionel's entreaties to return on January 27. Desperately, while waiting, Lionel read one of the books she ordered, Wilkie Collins's sus-
penseful *No Name,* replete with sentimental complications in the life
of a girl who, after her parents die, finds that her birth was illegiti-
mate. It could not take his mind off his increasing crippling. The seaside cure was fading, with winter, and he did not want to spend the
rest of his days in an invalid chair reading cheap puzzle-plot novels.

CHAPTER EIGHT

PICCADILLY HOUSE

1863–1866

Just before the celebratory dinner for the workmen at Piccadilly House in March 1863, which turned out to be premature, Charlotte wrote to Leo that "[Papa's] knees, alas, do not improve, and he seems to move about with difficulty this morning. The complete absence of [supportive] bandages and kneecaps may account in some degree for his debility." From Leonora came a letter to Papa: "I was much grieved . . . that you have again been a prisoner to the house." But he refused to remain a prisoner, even to Kingston House, as the year quickly proved to be the most fateful for the family partnership since the chaos of 1848.

Charlotte referred to "debility," but the unspoken reality was *decline*. Only fifty-four, and at the peak of his intellectual and political powers, Lionel faced the certainty of continued physical erosion. No medical panaceas, however expensive, arrested, let alone reversed, painful rheumatoid arthritis. He had spent all of the 1850s fighting for a principle that would seat him in Parliament, yet to reach his place on the Liberal benches would become more difficult day by day. Commons and its committees met in the late afternoon and evening, into the night, after his work at New Court, where he was a major force in the financial world. Although he refused to give up an iota of either responsibility, Charlotte would remind him affectionately that the political cause was won and that he had also proved he could take much of his financial concerns home—or on holiday—in his hat. She had taken on almost all supervision of the work on Piccadilly House. When the workmen convened for Lionel's appreciation dinner, all he had to do was preside.

About the only matter going well, while Charlotte and Lionel waited impatiently to move from Kingston House, was—for Lionel, a passionate reader of the sporting papers—the outcome of the Tom King–John Heenan prizefight. Otherwise, he warned Leo that May, "you will . . . find us as grumpy as we were last week." Heenan's historic mill with Tom Sayers, the self-styled English champion, in April 1861 at Farnborough, had gone forty-two rounds before being stopped by the police, with the exhausted American seen as marginally superior. Seduced by a guarantee from promoters of a thousand pounds, win or lose, Heenan returned to the ring in May 1862, at Wadhurst in Kent, to take on Tom King, a burly sailor from Stepney. To Heenan, King had seemed clumsy in winning over Jem Mace. But like Mace, the groggy Heenan fell to a crippling punch in the nineteenth round, and withdrew when he could not continue. "The great topic of conversation has been the great fight," Leo was advised, "the account [of] which you will see tomorrow in the papers."

As with his financial intelligence, Lionel, from armchair or wheelchair, his dog Jacky at his side, learned most things from well-placed informants before the news was in print. "They say," he added, "the American got famously punished; it will be some time before he forgets Tom King's right hand."

In 1859 the gossipy Goncourt brothers had noted that at the marriage of Baron James's son Gustave to Cécile Anspach, seventy-four

Rothschilds—excluding small children—sat at the banquet. Disraeli would be endlessly quoted for his remark at a family wedding that "there cannot be too many Rothschilds." Yet Charlotte's brothers, heirs to the Naples house, had no sons; and the Naples bank itself seemed without a future. The unification of Italy, beginning in 1860 when Giuseppe Garibaldi's Redshirts seized Sicily from its Bourbon regime, rendered Naples irrelevant. On his own, seeing only a down-hill trend and no heirs, Adolph von Rothschild announced that he would withdraw from the partnership and shut down. To the others, having long preached binding ties and cooperative business, the shock was profound. Baron James wanted his errant nephew anathe-matized, but Adolph held all the cards. He had capital; he held loans in tandem with the other houses; he could defect to a rival firm or operate, anywhere, independently. The first Rothschild to cash in his shares, he was retreating from the inevitable. Italy no longer paid off. From his point of view, the withdrawal made sense; for the family it was a blow to the prestige of the houses, another sign of decline.

After months of negotiations by courier and telegraph, a family conference convened in Paris. For Lionel it was, as he wrote to Natty and Leo—Natty was now taking a hand in New Court affairs—an "awful passage" in rough seas across the Channel on September 7. Lionel's poor condition must have been even worse than intimates in London realized, for at Calais he was met by Joseph Moses Levy, proprietor of the *Daily Telegraph*,[1] who, according to Charlotte, "compliment[ed] him on his improved looks." A week later she blamed herself for not having had "sufficient courage to brave all . . . reproaches and prevented him from leaving England."

Adolph's demands were making family compromises difficult. Charlotte's cantankerous brother insisted upon three months to ex-amine the accounts of the London, Paris, Frankfurt, and Vienna houses before he would consider any financial settlement. "Dear

---

1. His son and successor, Edward, took the name Levy-Lawson, soon dropping the "Levy." He became the first Lord Burnham.

Papa," Charlotte wrote from Paris's posh Bristol, "must be a Hercules to endure successfully," for the deliberations went on "from the earliest hour to the latest" in his disabled brother Nat's Paris residence. Although as sharp as ever, Nat was increasingly blind and immobile. Lionel "really is better," Charlotte insisted to her sons; "he not only sleeps well, but he actually shrinks from being carried, and walks upstairs—with assistance—to Uncle Nat's room every day, and on his return to the hotel, to this entresol. I have even seen him struggle . . . without any help at all but that is by no means a pleasant sight." Her words revealed faint optimism.

Despite his crippling handicaps, Nat was more active in the family enterprises than were his brothers Anthony and Mayer in London. Both were assiduous overseers of their farms and livestock, and rode, hunted, and raced. When necessary they undertook dealings for New Court across the Channel, as Lionel's legs, or they replaced him on call at St. Swithin's Lane. Both brothers were effective negotiators, but both also had public duties, and none of Lionel's drive.[2]

All three brothers in London contributed to the building of the new Jews' Free Hospital in Lower Norwood, but it was the Rothschild women who visited the site and oversaw the work. Although Lionel had designated someone from the Great Synagogue to be his almoner at New Court, few days went by when Charlotte wasn't called upon at home by petitioners ranging from blatant schnorrers to Rabbi A. L. Green of the Central Synagogue, often her own almoner, who asked for funds for a new Torah for the ark. He told her frankly "that formerly there were religious persons who had great generosity—and superstitious people, who though not very wealthy or liberal, gave to the Temple out of feelings of awe or dread; but now that superstition has been annihilated by civilization, and that religious Jews have ceased to be generous[,] . . . the generous Israelites allow their bounty to flow into secular channels. I dare say he

---

2. In a close vote (as in July 1864), Charlotte noted, a government could now be "saved by the Jews." Mayer was now one of several Jewish M.P.'s.

is right. I would infinitely rather give twenty pounds to a school than expend it for a *sepher* [Torah]." She found, too, from her experience at the Free School that most people, even the rabbi himself, felt awkward at personal involvement with the rabble, and as soon as they could "rushed away as if a plague had been in the building." That was not her impression at the Roman Catholic House of Charity, and she felt impatiently that "among us there is no heartiness."

As business piled up on Lionel, who thrived on arranging state loans, and like James at the rue Laffitte was consulted by dozens of clients with imposing titles, Charlotte, in Paris, was exasperated by her bucolic brothers-in-law, who lacked Lionel's enthusiasm for New Court. They did whatever Lionel asked of them, but the passion for grand entertainment evidenced by Juliana and Mayer at Mentmore was something she reserved for great occasions, and she put aside the reality that Lionel, although less often than earlier, still raced thoroughbreds as "Mr. Acton." "Though I have, not a prejudice against, but a well-founded dislike to racing," she confessed to Leo, "I am glad that Uncle Mayer has been successful; whatever one does, one should do well." She was pleased, nevertheless, when Baron Salomon, Lionel's elderly uncle now retired from the Austrian house, arrived in his Victoria to take her husband to the races in the Bois de Boulogne. It was a break for him from the "endless" partnership conferences. And Salomon, "with his usual good luck," she reported, ". . . won thirty thousand francs." Lionel's bets were on bonds.

With the women excluded from the men's financial deliberations in Paris, Charlotte visited Versailles, St. Cloud, and Ferrières, went shopping but purchased nothing, visited friends, and attended Betty's "grand dinner in the rue Laffitte," where the principal course was "quails and partridges and pheasants put to death in the orthodox way, and stuffed with truffles."[3]

The mortality tables had juggled the generations around the con-

---

3. Kosher preparation not only required slitting the throat with a clean cut, but also hanging the fowl upside down to drain off the blood.

ference table. Only James, of the sons of Mayer Amschel, the founder of the dynasty, remained active. Some of the third generation already seemed old and querulous and cranky, not only Lionel's Neapolitan cousin and brother-in-law, but also Anselm Salomon, widower of N. M.'s daughter (and Lionel's sister) Charlotte since 1859. Only sixty, he seemed to be ageing rapidly. Anselm would head the Vienna house for a further eleven years, but to Lionel's Charlotte he seemed "not exactly morose and taciturn, but shy and embarrassed" and he "spills much snuff over chairs and carpets." Fortunately, younger Rothschilds were present, and also the partners' shrewd attorney, Monsieur Guibert, who drafted and read a new contract to the conferees just before the Rosh Hashanah holiday.

Finally, Lionel wrote of the agreement, "it was more satisfactory than expected." On September 22, 1863, Adolph relinquished his partnership for a sum in excess of the worth of the Naples house. He was authorized by the other partners to withdraw £1,593,777, although the capital at Naples was actually £1,328,025. The contract was formalized on September 26, a Saturday, following the close of the Sabbath. "We have finished and signed [off] Adolph's affairs," Lionel reported to New Court after an interruption for the Yom Kippur fast, "and are very glad this is all over." "Dolly" would sell his residence in Naples, buy another at Pregny on Lake Constance just above Geneva, and occupy himself for thirty-eight further years in collecting art. Lionel and Charlotte would not discuss him.

To Leo and Natty, Charlotte wrote from the Bristol, this time frankly, "Your dear father is, alas, not as well as when we came across the water, and the warm, dry, bright climate of Paris has utterly failed in counter-acting the effects of the conferences. If money could purchase health, it would indeed be a treasure. . . . What cannot be cured must be endured."

On the evening before the signing, Baron James, Charlotte wrote to London, "gave the most extraordinary dinner imaginable to fourteen Rothschilds and Mme. Castiglione," a repast "which included every delicacy in and out of season." The Countess de Castiglione,

one of the great beauties of the Second Empire, was known for the opulence of her bosom and the delicacy of her feet, and the dazzling garb with which she flaunted both. Charlotte described the countess's décolletage of pearl and coral ornaments, her black draperies fastened by a cherry velvet sash, and the "devices" by which her amplitude was flaunted. "Evy and Emmy [of Frankfurt] knelt down at the beauty's feet; took off her velvet over-shoes embroidered with gold, then her little slippers, lastly her black silk stockings to admire a fairy-like white marble foot. When her loveliness was praised, the Countess smiled and laughed, and became good-naturedly animated; otherwise she was silent and dull, and nothing seemed to interest her. Her vanity is quite as absurd as her beauty is transcendent; she worships herself incessantly." In her narcissism she epitomized the hollow excess of the Second Empire. To Charlotte its men were no better. Their "busy tongues and pens" spread "hatred, envy and jealousy"—she deplored to Leo—"about this favoured land." She was eager to return to England.

In September the Michaelmas term at Cambridge was just beginning, and Leopold settled in at King's College, exhorted by his father to "work like a man" and "get a good place." Recognizing his slow deterioration, he wanted his sons equipped to take over at St. Swithin's Lane. But Leo would work hard at riding and cricket and partying while writing letters to his mother full of unpersuasive optimism. Charlotte hesitated, berating him, criticizing only his sloppy script. Referring to a twelve-page letter just received from Disraeli, she admonished Leo, in her own spiky handwriting, "I only wish you could see it, and notice, and remember that a great man, while lavishing the pearls of thought and the gems of style, does not disregard the graces of penmanship." But she had much more to do than to hector Leo from afar. From Knightsbridge Charlotte went off to Thames Street, near the docks, with Mr. Joyeau, her Piccadilly House majordomo, "to look at some stoves," doing as usual the "constant superintendence" of which Lionel was physically incapable. She hosted dozens of the social, political, and intellectual elite, as well as dozens of Rothschild relatives by blood and marriage, and she employed her wiles to find a discreet solution to the financial dilemmas posed by Lady Lyndhurst's recent widowhood. (Baron Lyndhurst had died at ninety-one, "persecuted" at the end, according to Disraeli, by his wife's Low Church zeal.) Georgiana's pride excluded even Charlotte's covert charity, and a practical solution seemed to be an income raised by sale of her husband's property, and a grace-and-favor residence bestowed by the Queen. Lionel hardly wanted the difficult Lady Lyndhurst about, but reluctantly used his good offices, more for Charlotte than for Georgiana.

Charlotte's drawing rooms also welcomed authors W. M. Thackeray and Matthew Arnold;[4] politicians William Calcraft, Bernal Osborne, Lord Henry Lennox, and Louis-Adolphe Thiers; New Court retainers Daniel Weisweiller, Bruno Bauer, and "the eternal" Charles Villiers; New World agents August Belmont and Benjamin Davidson; newspaper editors Peter Borthwick of the *Morning Post* and John Delane of *The Times* and its proprietor John Walter; dandies Count Maffie ("the greatest fop under the sun") and Lord Calthorpe ("his silk stockings, his lavender gloves—his snowy hands when the covering was removed—and his turquoise rings"); aristocrats Lady Molesworth, Lady Cadogan, the Duchess of St. Albans, and "old Countess Stackelberg who knew me shortly after I was born"; relatives Hannah Fitzroy, Baron Mayer, and Anna Waley.[5] "Clever people," Charlotte concluded, weighing the most interesting of the lot, "are always more agreeable and more indulgent than mere men of fashion and the world, not merely because, as a rule, they are more amiable and more amusable, but also because they have so many more resources." She

---

4. "What women these Jewesses are," Arnold wrote to his mother in October 1863, after a visit to Aston Clinton, where he met several Rothschild ladies, one of them almost certainly Charlotte. They were possessed, he thought, of "a force which seems to triple that of the women of our western and northern races."

5. Anna Waley was the wife of Simon Waley, a member of the Stock Exchange, a gifted amateur composer, and an activist in Jewish parliamentary emancipation.

also relished the personalities who were entertainments in themselves—like a titled lady considered a bore by Lionel but who to Charlotte was "blooming and beautiful and giggliferous."

Physicians, too, were regular visitors, usually to check helplessly upon Lionel but sometimes for gossip. Old Sir Henry Holland, the Queen's physician, returned from observing the carnage in America, talked of "the whole country laid waste, and appearing covered with the dead bodies, or with the bones, of thousands of horses and mules." The imperious Dr. Ferguson of Baker Street, once assistant accoucheur to Victoria but now thought of as the literary man's physician, found Lionel "far better in health" than before, but added, "he will be a rheumatic man all his life." Not up to attending the annual Lord Mayor's dinner at the Guildhall on November 9, Lionel sent Natty, despite his son's protestations that he was unready. Twenty-three the day before, Natty was proving more proficient at New Court than at Trinity College but still lacked self-confidence. As the Baron's representative he had "a first-rate place" from which to observe the elderly Prime Minister, Lord Palmerston, deliver what Charlotte called a "bumptious" speech, which from Natty's account was "rapturously received."

Always special and beyond category were "Mr. Hermann the famous conjurer," hired to entertain at a party, and "the Dizzys," who on November 29, 1863, came to dinner attired, surprisingly to Charlotte, in black—"for the good old lady who left him £20/m—just enough they say to pay his debts." Disraeli, who could turn an odd friendship into a fortune, was an even better conjurer than Hermann, who could only turn cards into doves. Early in November, the Disraelis had learned of the sudden and alarming illness of Sarah Brydges Willyams, now ninety-four, and had rushed off to Torquay, "but too late," Charlotte wrote to Leo, "to receive her blessing." "The old lady expired," Charlotte exaggerated, adding a decade, "at the age of one hundred and two, and none of us could wish to live longer . . . I put down my pen," she added—it was then November 13—"to take it up again and write Mrs. Dis a letter which sincerity prevents me from making one of condolence, and which from motives of feeling and delicacy cannot be one of congratulations. I wish the Emperor of the French would give me some of his epistolary talent."

Mrs. Brydges Willyams (née Mendez da Costa) had initiated her largely epistolary friendship with Disraeli in 1851. Lonely, childless, and long widowed, she had made the chronically impecunious Disraeli her heir and had arranged to be interred in his plot at Hughenden. "The female Croesus," Charlotte had written earlier to Leo, "has piercing black eyes, wears a jet black wig, with an enormous top knot, no crinolines, is quite a miser, . . . keeps neither horses nor carriages, nor men servants—only an enormous watch-dog to protect her and her gold." Her only exercise, Charlotte as a habitué of Torquay had learned, was to walk, on two sturdy leashes, two large and very ugly bulldogs, possibly the origin of her Cerberean legend. Two weeks after Mrs. Brydges Willyams's demise, Charlotte gossiped to Leo that Sir Hugh Cairns, out hunting with the Rothschild hounds, had told Sir Anthony "that the legacy of Mrs. Willyams might jeopardize Mr. Disraeli's pension, . . . as the legislature had never contemplated pensioning rich men." But, she added, "For once in my life I have talked to some purpose. . . . I have this fortnight been repeating what is the truth, namely that the inheritance will do nothing beyond paying the great and illustrious adventurer's debts. This is now generally believed." Charlotte had seldom lobbied her husband's powerful friends, but as she had quietly assisted Lady Lyndhurst, who would achieve her grace-and-favor residence at Hampton Court and not have to sell her diamonds, Charlotte rescued Disraeli's pension.

Lionel, too, wrote to Leo about Dizzy's good fortune, and with more fiscal accuracy. From his wheelchair the Baron seemed to know everything. His letter on November 30, 1864, noted that the Dizzys had dined with them the evening before, and he described the inheritance as his friend had not. "They are in the black," the Baron confirmed. After bequests, Disraeli had been left £40,000 rather than Charlotte's imaginative sum, about which he fudged to others as he

could not to Lionel: "She left many legacies, chiefly to her god-
children. . . . I am obliged to undertake the management of her affairs." Disraeli, however, had charmed his way toward solvency.

With Natty and Alfy beyond university studies, neither with any
glory, it seemed up to Leo to conjure his way through King's College,
and as early as February 2, 1864, Charlotte wrote to him, "Papa sends
you his love but he is quite determined not to write one word until
you should have passed your May examination to his entire satisfaction. . . . You ought really to make an effort, and not to sleep and loi-
ter seven-eighths of your time away. After a week's lessons Papa
would like to have a letter from your new tutor." Lionel's health had
left him in low spirits, and his disappointment in the academic lapses
of his sons, who were intellectually capable of better performance,
was profound. Their access to wealth had given each entrée to the
aristocratic racing and hunting set, young men who needed little
more than to live into inherited titles. New Court needed capable
sons. Success, Charlotte would explain to Leo with what seemed loving futility, "is far more important than popularity—which is won, I
am ashamed to confess, by bidding streams of champagne to flow and
truffled pies to circulate."

Despite expensive doctoring and months of rehabilitation, Lionel
in 1864 remained unable to climb the stairs of the House of Commons. That would not keep him away. As Parliament reopened, the
subterfuges that allowed him to be on the Liberal benches resumed,
and he was carried, little noticed, up a back staircase, from which he
walked a few steps to the benches from behind the Speaker's chair. "A
good precedent for him," Charlotte told Leo, "as he will, please God,
be able to attend in his place whenever there is an important debate."
She would attend from the gallery and discuss the issues with Lionel.

Charlotte was seldom afflicted by boredom. Her responsibilities
were too many, and her family seemingly always in motion—on occasion too much so. On February 7, an express from Paris to Calais on
which Evy and Natty were traveling was struck by an oncoming train,
loaded with coal, which plunged through a signal. "Our dear trav-

ellers were separated from the engine," a letter to Leo reported, "only by the tender—and the violence of the shock sent them up into the air to fall from their shattered carriage on the locomotive, where the heat was terrific, and the danger, after having escaped destruction, that their clothes might take fire." The railway line was largely owned by the French and English Rothschilds. "Natty disappeared almost completely—and poor Evy could see nothing but the soles of his feet. . . . When she found herself on the [ground] she had not any garment on except her shift and her drawers—the remainder of her wearing apparel had been torn off to extricate her."

Pinned under the "crushed carriage" was Bruno Bauer, who with two other Rothschild agents was en route to London. Aided by the bruised Natty, they somehow extricated Bauer, who elected to return, on a stretcher, to Paris to be nursed by his mother and sisters, and perhaps prayed over by his brother, the Monsignor. Only the carriage guard was killed. The others, including the badly bruised Evy, continued to London to tell their tale. For Charlotte it meant days of visitors to congratulate Natty and Evy on their escape; and Evelina's writing table "groaned" under the weight of solicitous letters. Responses delayed a few days noted also her next close call—when her brougham, waiting at the Kingston House gate, was struck by the tilbury of a commercial traveler and upset in the road.

When Charlotte herself escaped, it was to oversee children's examinations at Bell Lane, to take Lady Lyndhurst to consult Lionel at New Court, to oversee interior work at Piccadilly House, or to do what she recorded as "various domestic and charitable missions," which sometimes lasted from nine to six. On occasion her appointments secretary, Augusta, failed to remember that Charlotte was not "at home" (although she was), and her private afternoon solaced by a book vanished. Only a violent snowstorm slowed down the visitor count for luncheons and dinners, yet she was miffed when some well-fed but indiscreet guests on February 23 "rushed off afterwards for Lady Palmerston's assembly." Emily Palmerston, nearby, was not known for her cuisine, but her husband was prime minister.

The only guest of authentic Rothschild importance was Baron Ferdinand, Salomon's grandson, and the child of Anselm of Frankfurt and Lionel's late sister Charlotte. Anselm had returned to Vienna after the unsettling of family houses in 1848 to take over his father's bank. Born in December 1839, "Ferdy" was four months younger than Evy, and was beginning his suit for his cousin, initiating what he knew would be formal relocation from Austria. (He already spent much of the time in London.) In conversation with the Prince of Wales, he would describe Evy's glamorous sister, Leonora, as one of the four most beautiful women in Europe[6] but conceded he would have to settle for her sister. Charlotte was at first puzzled when Ferdinand wrote that he was coming to spend his last season in London—she called it "a curious expression"—but he may have meant his last fling as a bachelor. Unhelpfully, on his arrival Evelina became "giddy and faint" and went to bed for a week, but Ferdinand went out instead with Natty and Alfy and met the Prince of Wales at a levee.[7] The low-key courtship would prosper—so low-key that on one day in early April 1864, Natty went to a play with Ferdy while Evy attended the opera (Charlotte kept a box) with Nelly Baring and Alfred. Despite such beginnings, the arranged Rothschild match would evolve into deep mutual love.

April, Charlotte had hoped, would finally see their relocation to Piccadilly House. Sawing and plastering and hammering were still ongoing, and after an inspection on the seventh she wrote to Leo, "I am out all day and am more weary than I can possibly say—but it cannot last for ever this perpetual vibration, and provided the house is comfortable and dear Papa satisfied, I shall be contented." The next day she escaped Piccadilly with dust and plaster to remove "not

6. The others were Lillie Langtry, Empress Elizabeth of Austria, and the American Alice (Mrs. Mahlon) Sands.

7. When the Prince was to revisit Cambridge, Charlotte wrote to Alfred (May 30, 1864), "Do not allow the Prince of Wales to interfere with your studies." Early in July, Alfred, who was in the Prince's unit of the Lancers, rode with him in fashionable Rotten Row.

only from my old wrinkled cheeks, but from my equally old skirt." And each time she returned to Kingston House, there were people for lunch or dinner. Some visitors remained for both.

As she oversaw the frustrating progress on Piccadilly House, entertained guests from duchesses and marchionesses to Delane and Disraeli, employing her Sèvres dinner service for ninety-five, work on the house kept falling behind. On April 12 the workmen all abandoned work to cheer the visiting Italian revolutionary Giuseppe Garibaldi, a popular hero. The next day she oversaw Edward Corbould of the noted painting family as he did canvases of her dogs Brill and Jacky for the new house. Visitors eager to see the last of Kingston House "overwhelmed" her—not only Continental nobility but what seemed like much of the annual *Court Guide*. Happily, for a week her inspections ceased as the family went to Gunnersbury for Passover. Lionel preferred that to a hotel. After Passover, the wooing of Evy warmed, and she returned with Ferdy from a ball at three in the morning.

Although the lease on Kingston House expired on April 30, 1864, the house at 148 Piccadilly remained unliveable. Lady Eleanor Macnamara, the sixth and youngest daughter of the Earl of Listowel, owner of Kingston House, had arranged to be married there to Edward Heneage. Lionel and Charlotte had to withdraw to Gunnersbury, where to her surprise Lionel mounted and rode, gingerly, his old and much slowed horse Dicky, whose coat—a reflection of his master's decline and greying—had turned almost entirely white. When Lionel's legs stiffened, he returned to his wheeled armchair. That evening, time on his hands, he played whist—for the first time in fourteen months—with Ferdy and the visiting New Court agent Benjamin Davidson. It was further evidence of his giving in, reluctantly, to physical reality.

When Charlotte and Lionel finally spent their first day in Piccadilly House, just before Sabbath eve on May 6, they found few spaces but the bedrooms and grand dining room usable. "The occupation," she explained to Leo, still away at Cambridge, "is full of humiliating circumstances. Every nook reveals a mistake not to be remedied now, but which might have been avoided, had I been more watchful, more careful and attentive, had I possessed more forethought." She hoped to be able to dine, later, "habitually in the library and to keep the somewhat sparkling [formal] room for festive occasions only."

Charlotte, however, was accommodating her lifestyle to what was as much a museum as a mansion. On her walls were Murillo's *The Good Shepherd* and *Madonna and Child*, and canvases by Rubens, Pieter de Hoogh, Wouwermans, Nicolaes Maes, Jacob van Ruysdael, Pieter Breughel, Albert Cuyp, Jean-Baptiste Greuze, Thomas Rowlandson, Phillip Dawe, and Edwin Henry Landseer. She also hung engravings by Dürer and Rembrandt, and although her Rembrandts included an *Abraham and Isaac* and a *Triumph of Mordecai*, the eleven by both masters were largely pious New Testament scenes. That disturbed neither Charlotte nor Lionel. The pictures were high art, not liturgy.

That weekend she reported that "thank God, dear Papa is delighted with [the house] and quite pleased and happy. He walks wretchedly, alas! But in other respects [he] appears flourishing." At first, disappointingly, the lift would not work, and Lionel had to be carried upstairs, but soon it was operating as efficiently as the Otis firm had guaranteed. Everyone wanted to try it. Visitors flooded in, most curious to see the interior but staying only briefly when they realized its unfinished state. "Mrs. Dizzy," Charlotte wrote, "was a bore at tea-time." (She called Mary Anne "decidedly the worse half.") Mrs. Baillie Cochrane came with her daughter (who had "a catlike glamour") to announce that she was to preside over a refreshment stall at a benefit fair for fatherless children and wanted "Gunnersbury cream" to sell. A five-pound note, Charlotte thought, "will be more acceptable than the produce of our dairy."

Charlotte had additional guests for the Queen's annual review in Hyde Park in late May, offering only strawberries and grapes, as cooking was not done on the Sabbath. Slipping past her, two Russian countesses—Evy's friends—ascended to the roof of Piccadilly House in Lionel's lift for a better view, evading another Sabbath ban by smoking cigars there. Sometimes uninvited, friends turned up, even during her regular Sunday prayers at eleven-thirty, and Charlotte joked ruefully that if their visitors left church too early they would be "surrounded by Rabbis."

The deluge of visitors, from "discontented" Lady Lyndhurst to cabinetmakers, gas fitters, tradesmen, salespersons, solicitors for charities, and gardeners from Gunnersbury to help out at Piccadilly House, left Charlotte wearied of "showing even homoeopathic civility" to everyone. She confessed (June 10), "I am old, and begin to love books better than human beings—I am ashamed of this unnatural taste, but cannot alter it." ("Old and musty and fusty and dowdy" was her self-assessment a month later, and indeed the slender beauty who had been the talk of London nearly thirty years earlier had become more ample and now evaded the camera.) It was three days before her forty-fifth birthday.

For Lionel and Charlotte, early summer would also be complicated by external events. The war between Prussia and Denmark over title to the buffer duchies of Schleswig and Holstein, the continuing war in America (Mayer had invested in Federal bonds for the firm), and the battle over a sweeping electoral reform bill kept Lionel close to the Commons yet busy at New Court. Political differences, even among the Liberals, threatened to topple Palmerston, and Gladstone, a power in the party, did not help by expressing "mortification" at the sinking of the Confederate raider *Alabama*, built illegally in England, or by calling supporters of the Union "negrophilists," or by extolling Garibaldi, considered by many to be a dangerous radical. The Queen was an ardent Germanophile, while the Prince of Wales, married to a Dane, lobbied Members in the Germanophobe cause. Charlotte scorned the Schleswig-Holstein dispute as a triviality—"a mere freak on the part of Kings and Emperors and royal Dukes!"

After their dinner on July 8, Charlotte accompanied Lionel to the debates in the Commons—"a purely selfish move, for I could not, under any circumstances, have been of the slightest use to him." She stood in the crowded gallery to listen (Lionel never rose to speak), too late to hear the recognized funny man of the Commons, their friend Bernal Osborne ("a consummate actor"), but enjoying Disraeli's contrary wit ("Fortunately the finest speech is utterly unable to win even one vote"). The Liberals squeaked through a confidence motion by eighteen votes. At Gunnersbury the Rothschilds held an end-of-season fête where the political talk was spirited, although in the unusual rainless heat "the lawn was brown" and the flowers "hung their heads."

With Parliament soon afterward in recess, she could leave "dear, dusty London" and its "African weather" for Paris to see Laury, who was again pregnant. When Charlotte called on Baron James at the rue Laffitte, she found him as energetic as ever, even at luncheon, where he consumed "first beefsteak with potatoes and then an enormous helping of lobster." His schedule remained "excessively exhausting"—even his cures at Wildbad, Homburg, and Nice were strenuous. Gratefully, by mid-August she was back with Lionel at Gunnersbury, which was now so quiet that she was grateful for the yapping of their Japanese dogs.

On September 14 she and Evelina were in Paris again, for the birth of Charlotte Beatrix. Sardonically, the infant's grandmother observed that Leonora was "very grateful to her husband for not showing the slightest disappointment" at another daughter. The child's first name honored her; only the second would be used. Privately, she would have "preferred any appellation" to Beatrix, "because it begins with a B." (She despised the difficult and selfish Blanche Fitzroy, Hannah Mayer's daughter, who had just wed the fortyish, previously married Sir Coutts Lindsay, an arrogant arts entrepreneur who would squander her Rothschild money and was faithless.)

From Paris she revisited the Great Baron at Ferrières, returning in a carriage with "two dirty fat Frenchmen with tiny red ribbons attached to black greasy coats, a not over-clean lady's maid, holding a large, but uninteresting, dumb parrot on her forefinger—and an un-tidy lady, who played with her sparkling trinkets, and put on her garters ere she alighted." Charlotte tried without success to focus on her less interesting copy of *The Times*.

With Piccadilly House largely empty, renewed interior work in-tensified, not altogether efficiently. A workman dropped his mallet from a great height onto the "crystal terrace," causing expensive damage, and when Alfy's servant neglected to turn off the bath, water flooded the drawing room beneath, then broke through the ceiling of Lionel's sitting room, soaking the Cordova leather of the chairs and the Boulle cabinet, leaking further down into the servants' floor, and inundating the bedroom of Lionel's valet, Gotliffe. The entrance balustrade was also broken, and Sir Edmund Antrobus's foreman es-timated that final plastering, painting, gilding, and unanticipated re-pairs would take three further months As much as possible, Charlotte and Lionel intended to remain away—in Brighton or Gunnersbury.

At a hotel window in Brighton with a view of the sea, Lionel sat impatiently in a dressing gown and again received messengers and agents from New Court, his capacious memory substituting for fold-ers and files. From Charlotte's vantage the "white powders" pre-scribed by Dr. Hilbert seemed more efficacious "than our friend Dr. Fuller's draughts." Lionel was gradually "less out of spirits" but not free from arthritic pain. They remained into late December 1864. Then, until Parliament sat again in February 1865, Charlotte, from Gunnersbury, planned the July wedding of Evy and Ferdy, set for Piccadilly House at the height of the social season. Remarkably, she recorded no visitors on January 2. But the next day she noted (it was not unusual at her table) "a medley of the most incongruous elements of all religions," from a Roman Catholic priest and a rigid Church of England minister to an ultra-Orthodox Jewish woman in a wig.

The *"Liebhaber"* (lover), as Mayer called Ferdinand, was now a per-manent guest at various family residences and intended to remain in London on his father's wealth, whether or not he would have any-thing to do. He was automatically a British subject if he chose to be, as his mother, Lionel's late sister Charlotte, had been an English-woman. His elder brother, another Nathaniel, now twenty-nine, was dismissed by their father as having no business sense. Anselm placed his hopes on his shrewd youngest son, Salomon Albert—"Salbert"—only twenty-one, who had studied at Brünn (now Brno) and was then at Bonn.

Despite late-winter snow, Evy's engagement led the lovers to a flurry of visits to galleries and shops. With Lionel unable to do so, Delane loyally escorted them, with Charlotte, to see Baron Marochetti's studio, where the sculptor had fashioned the recumbent marble effigy of Prince Albert (and at Victoria's command, also one of her, so that they would be the same age in death), and to the studio of Sir Edwin Landseer, where his lions—"magnificent monsters"—for Trafalgar Square could be seen by gaslight for the last time before being cast in bronze. Madame Doucet arrived from Paris with patterns for Evy's bridal gown and traveling garb, and August Belmont debarked from New York, quickly becoming offended when he read, over Ferdy's shoulder, a note from Alfy calling the ambitious financier a braggart. (Mayer intervened to suggest that Alfred meant that Belmont boasted of his political influence. He had become a major figure in the Democratic Party.) Lionel chastised Leopold ("Noodle" instead of the usual "Poodle") by telegram for buying new horses and taking them hunting in what Charlotte called a "strange county": Leicestershire was not Rothschild country. Charlotte explained pacifically that neither of his parents liked newness: "I begin to like and appreciate people after I have known them long and well, new servants are to me particularly disagreeable, new dresses intolerable, new shoes still worse." Worse, still, Leo was doing poorly at Cambridge, excelling only in the chase.

More happily, Charlotte returned to Gunnersbury to look over what plate, glass, and china she wanted carted to Piccadilly House for the wedding, and Ferdy went to France to purchase jewelry for Evy and Sèvres porcelain for their future home. Lionel found financial affairs "dull" as the markets awaited the impact of the now-inevitable

Union victory over the South. The only "fright," he told Leo, was the possibility that after peace the Americans, angry at less-than-covert British assistance to the South earlier in the war, "would quarrel with us." Without some reparation, he predicted, "they will not be satisfied."[8] But the immediate news from America would be the assassination of President Lincoln and the attempts on his Cabinet, which shocked and grieved Charlotte although she thought of America as a primitive backwater. She wrote of her "feeling of alarm . . . at the thought of the frightful passions, which these murders will inflame throughout the once-United States. The Vice-President [Andrew Johnson] is a drunkard, who drowns his intellect in fire-water, as the Indians would say. He was most violent and blood-thirsty; but a sense of sudden and unmerited responsibility may have sobered him."

At her dinner table, J. T. Delane, Charles Villiers, and Bernal Osborne talked with Lionel of little but the gloomy postwar future for America; and when Osborne, whom she usually found likeable, tried to change the subject to something lighter (the Princetown races), Charlotte felt offended by the "cross and rude" intrusion.

Two months of balls and dinners and receptions in honor of the forthcoming nuptials began in May, some hosted outside the family. "More than two Rothschild banquets each week," Charlotte sighed, "would be impossible as the same people would be constantly asked." Wedding gifts began to arrive—from the Duchess of St. Albans, the Countess of Ely, Lord Cadogan, Mrs. Petre. Charlotte's house steward, Mr. Joyeau, began pressing for wedding rehearsals and an estimate of attendees. "Everybody wishes to come to the wedding; many delightful persons will have to be left at home," she conceded, "while we shall be called upon to invite innumerable ladies and gentlemen who will be additions to the list, and not acquisitions in any other way."

As prelude to the nuptials, Evelina, accompanied by Charlotte in

---

8. The *Alabama* claims, unsettled until 1872, would bear Lionel out.

grey and black, appeared on May 18, 1865, at a reception at Buckingham Palace for Evy's formal launch into society. Disappointingly, neither the Queen nor the Princess of Wales did the honors. Presiding instead was Princess Frederika, daughter-in-law of blind George V of Hanover, Victoria's cousin. More happily, two days earlier, Charlotte and Evelina had attended a Catholic charity bazaar. Little Princess Blanche of Orléans, granddaughter of the late Louis-Philippe, and a favorite of Charlotte's, had penny dolls to sell. Charlotte gave her a gold sovereign, 240 times the asking price.

Both Disraeli and Gladstone, as family friends, were among the guests on July 7 at Piccadilly House for Evy's grand wedding. The sitting of Parliament had ended the day before, with a General Election to come. An overflowing crowd mounted what a historian of the family called "a tidal wave of a white marble staircase" to "a ballroom as big as the royal yacht" with "lusciously embroidered satin curtains the size of mainsails," and then filled "whole coral reefs of salons and drawing rooms glistening with marble, gold and scarlet. Each chair offered, to quote a contemporary wit, gilt-edged security." Fourteen bridesmaids represented the Rothschild family as well as some of the most venerable names in the aristocracy.

As the cantor prepared to chant his blessings over the couple, Lionel, standing with self-discipline at the *chuppah*, remarked, "Ben, there are so many of you Christians present that our *chazan* wants to know whether he should just read the prayers, or sing them as in the synagogue?"

"Oh, please let him sing them," Disraeli joked back. "I like to hear the old-fashioned tunes." Afterward he gave a predictably felicitous post-nuptial toast—this time following the Austrian ambassador, Count Albert Apponyi. Representing the government, the First Lord of the Admiralty toasted the Rothschild family. The banquet was served on apple-green Sèvres china with a silver table service by Garrard. As guests dined stylishly, Evelina and Ferdinand slipped away to Dover, then to Uncle James's château de Boulogne retreat, going on to Linz, Vienna, and Schillersdorf, Anselm's model farm in Silesia, remaining in Austria through the High Holy Days and into December. Ferdinand planned to make it their home away from England, to retain something of his Continental identity, but the auguries proved unhopeful.

Civilization as the English knew it seemed nowhere to be found. Silesia was not the Vale of Aylesbury. A synagogue for Polish peasants was only two miles from the farm, "but the absence of cleanliness in this country," Evy deplored to her parents, made worshiping there impossible. They read prayers in their sitting room. Anselm, her father-in-law, seldom went to the farm, and the servants, she wrote, were so shiftless from lack of oversight that when a fire broke out in a building on the edge of the farm, the steward had to drive them with whips to fight it. Silesia, Evy concluded, was not for her. When they returned, they would live at Gunnersbury until Ferdy located a proper residence in London.

The strain of the wedding had overwhelmed Lionel's arthritic legs, and he feared it was politically suicidal to campaign in the upcoming General Election in a wheelchair. Would the electorate in the City vote for a visible invalid? Yet he thrived on politics. What he had fought for as a matter of principle now energized him, and although he would not rise to speak in the Commons, he was a power in committees, and beyond. Whether at New Court, or Piccadilly House, or Gunnersbury, he also saw, almost daily, politicians and political journalists with whom he discussed the issues and drew useful information. When it seemed practical, he offered information himself from his network of agents, who knew most of those who made a difference in Europe. "Politics interest your father to the exclusion of all other topics," Charlotte told Leo.

On grounds of indisposition, Lionel was substituted for on the hustings by young Leopold, who employed, with enthusiasm, the thespian skills he had acquired in student theatricals, and which would get him elected to the Garrick Club. He spoke effectively for "Palmerston, peace and economy," and suggested for Lionel, who had long been exchanging letters on politics with him, that reducing the tax burden on the lower classes would leave more money for ordinary people to spend and encourage widespread prosperity. Disraeli was a family friend, increasingly almost a member of the family, but he led the Opposition in the Commons. Party politics was something apart, and for his father Leo challenged City constituents as to whether "you would rather be ruled by Palmerston, Russell and Gladstone or Derby, Disraeli and Malmesbury?" Lionel was re-elected easily, and from Paris, Leonora sent congratulations to Leo. (But in October Lionel frowned at the academic reports from Leo's dissatisfied tutors in Cambridge.)

Already at New Court, Natty seemed the obvious alternative for his father, but he was campaigning for himself in Rothschild country, for a seat from Aylesbury. From Sir Anthony's home at Aston Clinton, Natty, twenty-five, canvassed constituents in the traditional manner, as he would not have had to do from St. Swithin's Lane. "We drove over to Missenden," he wrote to his parents, "and were met by a large party who promenaded me through the town and over the hills . . . like a tame bear; friend and foe we called on alike." But he told villagers firmly that he would not continue politicking into the evening. "I intended . . . to keep well for the nomination day. Luckily they all were of the same opinion as myself and had walking enough [for] themselves."

Since Natty's opponent would not support the abolition of Church rates,[9] while Dissenters, who made up the Liberal majority at Aylesbury, did, Natty was nominated and easily elected, and would hold the seat for twenty years. It seemed only yesterday that his father was fighting to take his own seat. Now both Lionel and Natty were in the Commons.

After the election, Charlotte and Lionel went to Yorkshire on the Great Northern Railway, to stay at the Royal Hotel in Scarborough,

9. A tax upon assessed property within a Church of England parish levied by its vestry for the maintenance of the church and its operations. In 1868 the compulsory tax was abolished.

and to carriage about the countryside, lush in summer. Referring to Francesco Albani, who had painted sunny Renaissance pastorals, Charlotte described the rustic setting to Louisa as "living pictures in the Albano style." But she registered puritanical disapproval of the hordes of unclothed bathers, very likely from burgeoning industrial cities like Manchester and Sheffield and Bradford, for whom railways now made the North Sea beaches at Scarborough accessible. "In the full glare of day and sunshine," she wrote, "there is complete absence of costume as in the garden of Eden before the fall of man, and hundreds of ladies and children look on while the bathers plunge into the foaming waters, or emerge from them. I really think the police should interfere."

As the family awaited the return of the newlyweds, Lionel and Charlotte resumed their routine at New Court and Piccadilly House, and in November, as chill autumn air collided with the smoke from coal and wood fires, a "fearful" Dickensian fog intermittently unsettled London. A couple coming to 148 Piccadilly by carriage wandered for three hours from nearby Hyde Park Corner, just west of Apsley House, which was 149, to find the Rothschilds. On one evening, Lionel sent out four men with torches to find and escort Charles Villiers. A stranger, Charlotte reported to Leo, "lost his way and, in beautiful evening dress, walked into the green room as we were on the point of going in to dinner. He was to have been our neighbour's guest."

On January 29, 1866, Evelina and Ferdinand moved into 143 Piccadilly. Ferdy's sister, Alice, devoted to him, mannish, and never to marry, but then only eighteen, would eventually move next door, to 142. Parliament was to end its recess on February 6, with Victoria, in widow's cap, actually present, and Lionel and Charlotte were back, as was Natty. They had a new Liberal leader. Viscount Palmerston had died on October 18, 1865, two days before his eighty-first birthday. Lionel's City colleague John Russell, now an Earl, succeeded at Downing Street, with W. E. Gladstone as party leader in the Commons, which put him directly opposite Disraeli for the first time.

(Both men were Lionel's friends, although the relationship with Gladstone, now more and more a religious crank, was becoming strained.) On a long visit on February 29, Disraeli discussed the perennial topic of a new reform bill, predicting that the Liberals would pay lip service to reform but were divided about extending the franchise.

More immediately vital to Lionel was stimulating a sluggish economy, and he promoted a Bank of England reduction in the discount rate. But early in May, as the Commons haggled over how many in the working class should be qualified to vote, came the collapse of a major banking house—Overend, Gurney—followed by a slump in the market and a rise in interest rates to 10 percent. Lionel and Natty even remained at New Court over a Sabbath to weather the firm over the huge fall in share and bond prices, and Baron James sent London £150,000 to assure the bank's liquidity. Prospects were further soured by reports of impending war between Prussia and Austria, the government getting much of its intelligence from Lionel's listening posts in Berlin, Frankfurt, and Vienna. Sharp as usual, Baron James had warned his nephews in London in April to unload securities for cash. "I am very much afraid of war," he wrote, "and would rather make a sacrifice in order to keep and maintain my holdings of cash because in a war there is money to be made from having money." It was a lesson he had learned from their father decades before.

With key votes in Commons narrowly lost and confidence in Russell and Gladstone faltering, the Cabinet resigned. When the Queen sent for the Earl of Derby to become prime minister early in July, Disraeli became the leader in the Commons. They had had the experience of two brief previous Conservative Cabinets. During the transition, the Seven Weeks' War began, Chancellor Bismarck emboldened by his easy Danish successes to bully Austria into relinquishing its nominal presidency of the Prussian-dominated German Confederation. Quickly, Prussia absorbed Hanover, Hesse, and other statelets that had taken Austria's side or imprudently remained neutral. While the Rothschild banks preferred stability over anything else, they had no pleasure in seeing it come via Prussia, where they had no close financial ties. At first they could do little more than watch as, on July 5, Austria, its armies shattered at Königgrätz (Sadowa), asked for peace.

With Austria in danger of collapse, the Rothschild bank in Vienna became a key to shoring up the economic ruins, but it was also in trouble. Its ironworks at Witkowitz was cut off by Prussian troops, and employees could not be paid; and Anselm's vast Schillersdorf farm in Silesia was occupied by Prussian-backed Hungarian Legion troops who trampled what they did not steal. On July 17, Frankfurt, too, was occupied and looted as the German Confederation collapsed. Charlotte's brother Mayer Carl rushed his wife, Louise (Lionel's sister), and his daughters off to France. In London, Charlotte's Frankfurt sympathies overflowed into unrealistic hopes about anti-Prussian coalitions, although the new Conservative government, with its own problems at home, saw no compelling interest in any involvement. She soon heard, erroneously, that Mayer Carl had been imprisoned. "This I hope and believe is not the case," she wrote, "but the Prussians are perfect monsters."[10] Despite the Earl of Derby's "unstatesmanlike" position, she also worried to Leo on July 10 that "we may be drawn into an armed intervention, to prevent the civilized world from being absolutely divided between France and Prussia." Louise, she told him, had suggested she "ask Mr. Delane for a powerful article in *The Times*," but Charlotte dismissed that as useless, for Bismarck would not much "care for an article in our English papers."

Helpless, Charlotte solicited funds among her friends "for the poor Austrian soldiers" and, even more helplessly, heard from her former home that Frankfurt had to pay an indemnity to be forcibly absorbed into Bismarck's burgeoning empire—"the transformation," she called it, "of the good, old prosperous town of our ancestors into an insignificant addition to Prussian greatness."

10. James's reaction was, simply, "A Rothschild? It's impossible."

In London itself, protests over the failures of electoral reform and the alleviation of poverty and unemployment had been keeping the Metropolitan Police busy in Hyde Park, within listening distance of Piccadilly House and Grosvenor Gate. For three days beginning on July 24, mobs broke through railings at Marble Arch and tramped exuberantly through the flower beds in Hyde Park—a mild parallel to Schillersdorf. Alarmed as noisy crowds spilled into Piccadilly, Evelina locked away her most cherished wedding gifts, her Sèvres vases, and remained indoors. Yet she wrote to Leonora in Paris that when "some conservative gentleman said to Natty, who was defending the foolish reformers, that he was sorry all our windows had not been smashed . . . your brother replied that we were perfectly safe, as the people know us to be their friends; they cheered the house, and Natty and Alfred in the crowd." Lady Alice Peel, daughter-in-law of the one-time Tory prime minister and a close friend, expostulated to Lionel "that the soldiers ought to have shot twenty or thirty of the rabble, which would very soon have put an end to the riot." He cautioned her gently, "You may say anything to me, Lady Alice, but I advise you not to go about London with such suggestions."

The demonstrations faded when it became obvious that the new government intended to complete the unfinished business of electoral reform, and Charlotte conceded, despite the Liberal politics of her family, that "if a Tory government can but be induced to bring in liberal measures, there is no earthly reason why it should not prove as useful as the Whig administration." At 143, Evelina again set out her Sèvres vases. The collection was, in any case, no longer her greatest concern. She was expecting a baby.

CHAPTER NINE

LOSSES

1866–1870

"Coming up to London and reading that terrible message in the paper," Anthony's daughter Constance wrote in her diary on December 5. There had been an obituary on page six of *The Times*. "It was enough to arrive all trembling with fear and anguish. The house, all dark and shut up, confirmed our unhappy fear. And then, the sight of the mourners—oh, it went to my heart. Saw the bedroom, that gay, bright room with the motionless form on the bed, with the poor, tiny baby on the sofa. Oh, what a sight."

In the first stages of labor on Tuesday, December 4, 1866, Evelina was seized with convulsions. Arthur Farre, also obstetrician to the Princess of Wales, summoned two additional physicians, who could only assist in delivering a stillborn son. Minutes later Evelina was dead. The family was stunned. Ferdinand had been in Vienna with Evy since September supporting his father. After Austria's defeat at Sadowa, ending the nominal supremacy of the crumbling empire over Prussia, only the Rothschilds could extricate the collapsing Austrian economy from chaos. Evy had returned home to await her baby. In the loneliest of journeys, Ferdinand rushed to London by special train.

There had been little warning.[1] The day before, Lionel had written from New Court to Leo, "Mamma will not write today as she was with Eve who is a little uncomfortable." A week earlier, Leo had written to his parents, "I am very glad that Eve continues so well and I am in hopes of hearing ere long the best news. Cyril Flower"—his classmate who would marry Constance eleven years later—"was in London for a few hours and caught sight of your dear sister which . . . confirmed your report of her looking so well." Still in Paris because the visiting Prince of Wales had to be entertained, Leonora rushed to England. She would arrive too late.

It was little consolation to Lionel that John Delane wrote, among the hundreds of condolences that deluged Piccadilly House, only a few steps from darkened 143, that Evelina had died "in the noblest office of her sex." Lionel and Charlotte would be responding to the deep sorrow of their friends for two months. Charlotte found Delane's lines "strange and far-fetched": it was a bachelor's effort, in the editorial language he knew, to comprehend a phenomenon beyond him.

The closing months of 1866 had seemed to be filled with the happiest of auguries. As Evelina awaited her lying-in, she and Leonora had been sharing sisterly confidences about their brother's wooing of Emma Louisa von Rothschild of Frankfurt, twenty-two and Mayer Carl's daughter (thus Charlotte's niece). It was another courtship

---

1. *The Lancet*, the organ of the medical profession, described the seizure, only a few minutes in duration and followed by spontaneous delivery and coma, as sudden and without forewarning. Nevertheless, toxemic preeclampsia, the likely cause of death, is almost always preceded by warning symptoms. Portents include sudden weight gain, persistent headaches, sharp rise in blood pressure, abdominal pain, and increase of albumin in the urine. Since Evelina's discomfort occurred only the day before onset of labor, it was not considered extraordinary by the fashionable Dr. Farre.

within what Natty's mother called their "fairy circle." There was so much family togetherness that nubile Rothschild women were often close to eligible Rothschild men at resorts and spas and country places, and when they were not, Rothschild mothers and married sisters plotted pairings.

Charlotte had been hoping that Natty would become interested in his cousins Constance and Annie, daughters of Louisa and Anthony. Nat's son, James Edouard, a Parisian cousin, had hoped to secure Emma for himself. He would eventually marry Emma's younger sister, Laura Thérèse. Mayer Carl and Lionel's sister Louise had five unmarried daughters, the youngest only four years old. Because of the war, the family had stayed at Gunnersbury in late summer 1866 after fleeing Frankfurt for Paris. Both serious-minded, Natty and Emmy found themselves well matched, and—in authentic love—they eschewed their usually austere ways. Evelina had written to Laury, visiting in Frankfurt late in September 1866, that the informal engagement was no secret, that she "will be able to judge of Emma's happiness," and that Natty was already "fidgetting for letters from Emma" and feeling "spoony."

The family idyll would be brief. On the morning of December 7, a Friday, a queue of family carriages followed by sixteen private carriages, including that of the Russian ambassador, left 143 Piccadilly and proceeded via Park Lane, Oxford Street, Portland Road, Marylebone Road, City Road, and Hackney Road, past Victoria Park to West Ham Cemetery. "The bodies," reported *The Times*, "were borne to the grave with every token of grief and affection. Seldom, indeed, has a young lady been more widely and deservedly mourned." On the two coffins, one pathetically small, were bouquets of camellias and violets. Rabbi Asher Ascher of the Great Synagogue read the committal service.

Although Charlotte was desolated, Lionel's grief was so great and lasting that it would take the form of silent refusal ever to alter his will to eliminate Evelina as a beneficiary. The evidences that he was a doting father are otherwise difficult to find. In a letter-writing age, he might have written of his affection had she ever been away long enough for correspondence, but Victorian girls seldom went to a boarding school, and she was tutored at home. Legally she would always be alive to him.

The first thanks from Charlotte for a message of consolation went to the Queen, via Jane, Countess of Ely, a Lady of the Bedchamber and one of Charlotte's closest friends. Understanding Victoria's continuing anguish over the death of Albert, Charlotte treasured her sympathy. "To you, dearest Lady Ely," she wrote on the Sunday following the funeral, "I shall not attempt to speak of our grief; . . . our loss must remain irreparable, and the void left by our child can never, never be filled. You knew that blithe spirit of joy, and mirth and happiness, ever diffusing gladness and sunshine around our hearth and home; that faithful heart so full of love, so intensely happy in giving pleasure to others, a heart so large and generous that no one who ever came within the circle of our child, ever failed to find a place in it."

As they sat in mourning with Ferdy and Laury and others in Gunnersbury—Charlotte and Lionel and family could not bear doing so in Piccadilly—Lionel responded to sympathy letters from the duc de Nemours, Sir Robert Peel, Mary Anne Disraeli, and Bernal Osborne. Despite the deluge, the Baron remained a public man, and when intelligence came to him from agents that the Emperor of the French had no idea how weak his position was, he passed what information he had to Disraeli, who in everything but title, with the Earl of Derby ailing, was prime minister. In the diary of Lord Stanley, Derby's son and the foreign minister, is a line dated December 12: "Disraeli sent to see me, and said he had received from one of the Rothschild family alarming news as to the state of France. It was thought that people were getting tired of the empire."

Otherwise, the family was submerged in grief. "Every messenger, every servant, every postal delivery," Charlotte wrote to Leo, who returned to Cambridge after *shivah*, overwhelmed her with more messages—from the Irish composer (of *The Bohemian Girl*) Michael

Balfe, Mme. de Castiglione, Nelly Baring, and Mme. Walewska among an international list of correspondents. She began taking her son's advice to keep her responses to "less intimate acquaintances" short, so that the effort would not exhaust her. "All my happiness," she confided to him on December 17, "seems to lie in her grave." The first, pathetic seventy-five letters would take Charlotte a week. Ferdinand, she told him, "finds it all so melancholy to be with us, talking about darling Eve. Today was Ferdy's birthday and he intends to pay a heartbreaking visit to the grave. Poor fellow, he can only think of his loss." And indeed, although he would be one of the richest men in Europe, and was again (after mourning) eligible, he would never remarry. His castlelike Waddesdon, built a dozen years later, would be a monument to loneliness.

"Selfish as it is, in speaking of myself," he explained to Leo after his graveside visit, "yet you will forgive me for telling you how I feel that mine is a loss which years cannot repair, nor any accidental circumstances relieve." He had loved Evy since childhood, and his "wishes, cares, joys, affections" were all "wound up with her existence." Material things were now as nothing to him. "I can find no consolation in the future; it may partly come from . . . the recollection of those by-gone days when she lived, when she was with me, when we were intensely happy." He would have Edward Pugin, son of the famous Augustus Pugin, architect of churches, design a mausoleum for Evelina in which was inscribed on a wall, in Hebrew and English, lines adapted by Ferdinand from Psalm 139:

> If I ascend up into heaven
> Thou art there
> If I lie down in the grave
> Behold I find thee
> Even where thy hand leads me
> And thy right hand supports me.

Although a snowstorm battered Gunnersbury as the new year of

1867 opened, Lionel resumed daily carriage trips to New Court, wearing a heavy greatcoat, with a fur rug over his legs. Each day, at first under leaden skies, Laury's husband Alphonse—she was briefly in Folkestone—accompanied him. Sweeping snow from the roof at Gunnersbury, a workman broke a large pane of skylight glass, narrowly missing Alfred and cracking the marble floor. Still home doing nothing, although even that seemed dangerous, he claimed continuing recuperation from his summer illness, but he was doing exactly what he wanted to do—avoiding work of any kind. Even penning acknowledgments to sympathy letters seemed too arduous for Alfy. In contrast, by January 6, Charlotte, despite her burdens—life had to go on—recorded posting 234 responses, with always more to come.

In Cambridge, Leopold replaced his tutors as they abandoned him in frustration, and Charlotte sought comfort in Natty's unsuspected abilities. He had been barely adequate as a scholar and had dropped out for the bank. Now he was a bulwark at New Court, an M.P., and soon to be married to a Rothschild who would keep him working at a high standard. As Charlotte returned to her Christmas bills and household accounts two months in arrears, he was preparing to leave for Frankfurt to plan his wedding with Emma. Anthony—"goodhearted as usual"—came on January 12, the Sabbath, to discuss fundraising for the new (Central) Synagogue and for the Free School. Then he ascended his carriage, "disappearing among mountains of furs" en route to Aston Clinton. The next day, Sunday, saw the arrival of the Disraelis, which Charlotte regretted for the small talk she would have to exchange with the flighty Mary Anne. No Rothschild was ready for that, but Lionel, desperate for a change in atmosphere at home, wanted to talk politics with Dizzy, particularly about electoral reform.

Everything reminded Charlotte of Evelina. So much had delighted her daughter. If starlings fluttered along the terrace to pick bread crumbs out of the snow, feeding them—now the task of Laury's little girls while they visited—was something that Evy would have done.

At 143 Piccadilly, Ferdy was beginning to make a new life for himself while dining at least once a week at Gunnersbury, and talking politics to deflect mournful recollections of Evy. It was dreadful, Charlotte agreed, for the trades unions to discourage laborers from taking non-union jobs in adverse economic times. Any employment, she felt, was better than resorting to the soup kitchens: "To earn thirty-nine shillings a week in ship-building is surely far better than to starve."

With the family's focus now upon the wedding of Emmy and Natty in Frankfurt, recalling the marriage there of Charlotte and Lionel (the bridegroom, marrying his German cousin, was heir to the London house), most Rothschilds were eager to put aside the tragedy of Evy's death. But not Lionel, and not Charlotte. In stubborn mourning, both were absentees who cast their shadows on the nuptials.

As Natty, cultivating a dignified new beard, arrived in Frankfurt early in February, before Parliament reconvened, Lionel returned daily, under physical and emotional stress, to St. Swithin's Lane. With work his only therapy, it was a struggle for him to take any interest in New Court. A winter chill had left him with nearly no voice, and he depended now upon Ferdy, who was even more distraught. Under his wraps Lionel wore a mustard poultice. Despite her own mourning, Charlotte was expected to rove about London to purchase Emmy's furs and laces and shawls from the proper Mayfair dealers, to choose her future daughter-in-law's dressing case, and order a bridal necklace which was traditionally part of *"la corbeille des noces,"* the gifts of the bridegroom and his family. "It seems dreadful," she thought, "to be obliged to give time and care to such hard, frivolous, worldly baubles, while one's heart thrills with pain and sorrow for a loss a million times greater now than all the rubies and diamonds in the world."

Charlotte's press of consoling visitors, whom she could hardly refuse to welcome, included "the most disagreeable woman of my acquaintance, the Countess Russell." The Prime Minister's second wife, daughter of the Earl of Minto, had been married to Earl Russell for twenty-five years, during which Charlotte had seen little of her. "Lady Somers [also] came, pale and agitated," she wrote on February 18. Yet she found her friend curiously insensitive, for, though she was "full of pity and sympathy for us, she . . . might have remembered . . . she was coming to a house of affliction. No one expected funeral crape, but she wore bright green and bright scarlet and white and fashionable cinnamon coloured silk slashed with satin—colours I have not seen for many weeks past." In Charlotte's grief she wanted to see little of anyone, including Lady Alice Peel, long a friendly neighbor, for no one then could "bring any relief to a sorrow, which must be eternal."

Lady Alice "good-naturedly" lent Charlotte a book, privately printed and presented to General Peel by the Queen, *Leaves from the Journal of our Life in the Highlands.* The grieving mother was in no mood for it. "There is not a ray, indeed not the faintest glimmering," she felt, "of talent or even of pretty writing in the volume, which seems astonishing, as very great and illustrious statesmen pronounce the Queen to be remarkably clever. But the redeeming and truly interesting feature of the work is its extraordinary and almost incredible simplicity; there is not the remotest allusion to royalty or sovereign power; the most humble minded of Her Majesty's subjects might have written it; not a single word reminds the writer that the writer rules over hundreds of millions of human beings, and that the sun never sets over her dominions."

Much different was the language of the Queen's most effusive admirer, Charlotte's Dizzy, who was running the Conservative regime as the Earl of Derby remained incapacitated by gout. Disraeli's colorful, chatty letters to Victoria on the proceedings in Parliament were intended to woo his "Faery Queen" into acceptance of the Tory agenda, including his reform measures. It was less easy to placate Conservatives with Liberal legislation, but Disraeli recognized that the Tories as a minority party had no other means of surviving in power.

Putting aside his agenda for the moment and recognizing Charlotte's pain, he wrote a note on March 28, 1867, in a far different vein than the florid memoranda which Victoria now anticipated to improve her day. "Amid the struggles of my life," he told Charlotte, "the sympathy of those we love is balm; & there is no one I love more than you." He very likely meant it, and his often impromptu visits, electric with his enthusiasm, were interludes for which she was grateful. Later in the year (November 23) he closed another letter, "I would also send you my love, but I gave it to you long ago."

On April 17, 1867, Natty and Emma were married at Frankfurt. At the preliminary civil marriage, the registrar's office could accommodate few beyond the happy couple. The marriage under the *chuppah* was celebrated in Emma's parents' flower-filled mansion, and almost without the plump, black-bewhiskered father of the bride. Charles (Mayer Carl in Germany) had been in Berlin, consulted by Bismarck, who told him, Mayer Carl reported, that the Prussian army was awesomely "invincible." According to Leo, Charles had been so "tremendously feted" by the king and queen that he barely returned in time. The wedding cake imported from Vienna was also delayed, as Custom House authorities suspected that a confection so towering had to be concealing something. Even the rabbi was late, but "made an excellent speech" and—Leo reported—"said everything to the point and was not at all pompous."

At the nuptial banquet the conversation of the guests, largely in German, was punctuated by humorous family reminiscences. "I cannot say I understood all the jokes," Leo, no scholar in anything, wrote, "but everybody laughed at the intervals so I joined in."

For Lionel and Charlotte, their year of mourning was far from over. They spent the wedding week in seclusion at Gunnersbury, unwilling to see anyone in London. Leo, Alfred, and Laury remained in Frankfurt, where their parents sent expensive gifts which meant little to a pair of Rothschilds. Leo assured his mother and father that they would be gaining a daughter, and although she could "never replace the darling we mourn," Emma "by her affection & devotion [will] prove a great joy to you." Alfred wrote that Natty seemed "radiantly happy," and Leo described him as "no unworthy match" to the "beautiful" bride. At the least, Lionel recognized that his eldest son, settled in politics and banking, and now in marriage, would leave him confident about the future of New Court—and Emma made him even more hopeful by bringing Lionel Walter into the world on February 8, 1868.

The younger sons left little expectation for the kind of fulfilment to which Victorian families aspired. Leo was surviving at Cambridge, but barely. Neither of his parents was pleased with his desultory academic achievement, while Alfred, now dapper and mustached, thrived as a bachelor clubman in the Prince of Wales's Marlborough House circle. Leo seemed inclined in the same unproductive direction, excoriated by his father for arising at noon and going to bed at dawn. "I am glad . . . you are pleased with yourself," he wrote acidly to Leo on May 25, 1867, "for having guessed the winners of the two great races. Your [college] examiners were quite right in saying that you have a good hand at guessing." Charlotte confessed her sorrow that he was "idling his time away"—she had "a perfect horror" of such misuse of a life.

On the anniversary of Evelina's wedding day, June 7, Charlotte reported to Leo, she visited "the silent home where your sister sleeps." The week before, among the continuing and painful condolence visits from Anthony and Louise, and Mayer and Juliana, and from Lady Dorothy Nevill, the Lord Chief Justice, and the French ambassador, all of whom had to be entertained with food and drink and talk, came Edward Corbould, who had been commissioned to paint Evelina from a photograph. It was, Charlotte deplored, "a very ugly picture which cannot be considered a portrait of our darling Eve. He was in a distressing frame of mind, trembling and weeping." Not long before he had lost his own wife, and he had given a portrait of her to the Queen's daughter Princess Louise, one of his pupils. Corbould showed Charlotte the princess's thank-you letter, "full of tender pity and feeling," but it did not improve her opinion of the picture of Evy. The painter had not idealized her.

The passionate debates over the new Reform Bill diverted Lionel from the cycle of mourning which kept Charlotte at home. ("I ought to be able to write an ode to solitude," she confessed, "which I so infinitely prefer to society.") He spent many evening hours in the Commons, taking in the speech making and questioning, distancing himself from gloom. His servants waited patiently to help him down, and ease him in and out of his carriage, and when he returned to Piccadilly House "much at the usual hour," he would remark to Charlotte, "I am sure you have had a great many visitors; you look so cross."

In the Commons, Disraeli accepted liberalizing amendments to get the Reform Bill of 1867 through; it would double the electorate. To persuade his own party to accept the bill, he invited the distinguished statistician Sir John Lambert to put a Tory twist on what the new voters might mean to a Conservative future. In all, before the final division, Disraeli spoke or responded to questions 311 times, and when the satirical weekly *Tomahawk* scoffed at his success in maneuvering the legislation as entirely cynical, Lionel ordered that the paper not be permitted in his house.

Craving someone he cared about to share, at length, his satisfaction, Disraeli walked to Piccadilly the next Sunday afternoon and found Charlotte, who had returned from the country before Lionel. As she had been away for the weekend, there were, blessedly, no visitors waiting. On the heavy, black-bordered stationery she was still using, she wrote to Leo that "Dis" had visited, happily without the bubbly Mary Anne, "and in my opinion was so brilliantly eloquent, and so wonderfully agreeable, that I was quite sorry to be his only listener; when dear Papa came back from Gunnersbury, I made the great man repeat his anecdotes, but a twice-told tale loses much."

The next day the chief rabbi called on Lord Stanley, the Foreign Minister, with a telegram about pogroms in the Romanian city of Jassy (now Iasi), asking for British intervention. Baron Rothschild, Stanley noted in his diary, had already spoken to him about it the night before. "I promised to do what I could, and telegraphed accordingly."[2] Since the Damascus affair in 1840, Lionel was, to everyone, the central figure in British Jewry. It made no difference where he was, or what he was doing, or what his own problems were. The senior Rothschild seemed always the focal point for his people. It was no less a fact in France, although Baron James's legendary vigor was fading.

Charlotte—feeling "very poorly," according to her husband—escaped across the Channel late in July to James's château de Boulogne, and then to a seaside hotel in Dieppe, where she could be with her grandchildren. "You will have time," Lionel tried joking to her, "to read all the papers and study politics." Passage of the Reform Bill in the Tory-dominated Lords remained uncertain. Why not make the enfranchised masses a Conservative asset, Disraeli pressed the reluctant Derby, employing arguments from *Sybil*, rather than split the electorate into parties of the rich and the poor? The rich were far less numerous: They would always be an electoral minority. Conceding that the bill was a necessary risk, the Prime Minister called for a division on August 6, 1867, describing reform as "a leap in the dark." Reform passed.

Dizzy, Lionel told Charlotte, was radiant with the success, while "Mrs. Dis beams like the disk of the sun." But Disraeli confessed his exasperation with the endlessly reactionary Earl of Derby, who after recommending the usual baronetcy for the Lord Mayor of London, remarked that he was relieved that Thomas Gabriel, despite his biblical surname, was not a Jew. "Such is gratitude," Charlotte snapped, from a Prime Minister who "may be said to owe tenure of office to the genius of an Israelite." While prejudices in Derby's antique class—he was the 14th Earl—died hard, an article on the Talmud in the *Quarterly Review* offered some amelioration, Disraeli told her. It

2. At eighty-two, the tireless Sir Moses Montefiore was authorized by the Board of (Jewish) Deputies to make a trouble-shooting mission to Romania. On March 29, 1868, Disraeli sent Lionel a copy of a telegram from the British envoy in Romania reporting, "Prince Charles will not sanction laws against Jews," which he considered "a disgrace." But license and legislation were different matters, and outrages continued.

"proves that everything gentle and sublime in the religious code of the New Testament is a mere transcript from the so-called oral law of the Jews."

Parliamentary recess came on August 21. Lionel and Charlotte tried a German spa, then returned to Gunnersbury. Lionel left New Court, and also the escorting of the visiting Uncle James, to Anthony. Despite the failing sight of the uncle whom Charlotte continued to call privately "the Great Baron," he met the Prince of Wales, the Duke of Cambridge, and the visiting Viceroy of Egypt and Sultan of Persia. Ferdinand began traveling on business for Lionel, Leopold accompanying him as apprentice, dealing with the Russian-operated Bank of Finland, and acting as liaison with the Vienna house on Italian and Austrian finances. To his father, Leopold described the low status of Russian bankers under Tsarist despotism as "little better than shopkeepers." The plight of the "staring and begging Jews" he saw was "horrible." A venerable rabbi explained the ogling of the peasantry as "they had never seen a Rothschild before"—possibly the source of a story that a Rothschild, visiting a *shtetl* in Russia, was served, at a squalid inn, two eggs for breakfast. When he was presented with a bill for twenty-five rubles, a surprising sum, he objected, "This is absurd. Are eggs that rare here?" "No," explained the innkeeper, "but Rothschilds are."

As much as he could, Lionel conducted New Court business from the country, with agents and messengers from the City streaming in and out. With the gouty Derby again ailing, the Tory government was in limbo. Disraeli awaited a call from the Queen that the Prime Minister was finally relinquishing office. That Dizzy was straining to avoid saying or doing the wrong thing at the wrong time was clear from Charlotte's account of a weekend at Gunnersbury when the Disraelis were the last guests to leave. The next day, November 5, 1867, she described "the laborious exercise of speaking to the Chancellor of the Exchequer and his consort from 10 in the morning till 12 at night. The illustrious cabinet minister was most amiable but he was not at all amusing, and endeavoured to make others talk while he listened. . . . Mrs. Dis, pale, thin and wrinkled[,] was in admirable temper. . . . Her wig was irreproachable, adorned with sky blue velvet folds and gold butterflies and chains, which were not ridiculous, but very becoming." Mary Anne, seventy-five and a dozen years Disraeli's elder, was intermittently ill, and Charlotte was at her kindliest. But she herself was ailing, hobbled by a painful foot infection, and was about to leave for Jews' Hospital for treatment. Her physician's ministrations had been quirky and useless, Laury writing, "I do not understand that Dr. Ferguson should recommend you not eat meat; it seems indeed a strange prescription."

Lionel and Charlotte were at Gunnersbury as the old year of 1867 ended. A letter from Leonora sent, emotionally, "good wishes as the clock strikes midnight. . . . I pray God with all my heart that he may bless you, and give you a year brimful of happiness. I have worked a little cushion for you, my dear Papa, and a footstool on which I beg you will place your feet, my dear Mamma, when you return tired from a walk. . . . They are not so successful as they might have been, but you know that my fingers are good for nothing, and their productions are generally failures." She could have purchased the priciest cushions and footstools in France, but they would not have meant nearly so much to their recipients.

Laury furnished one of the first happy events of 1868 to her parents. On February 24 she gave birth to a son, Edouard Alphonse James, his first name a bow to her friend the Prince of Wales. But Emma and Nathaniel had preceded them with Lionel Walter, born two weeks earlier. In politics, it was no secret that the Earl of Derby was delaying his departure only to negotiate parting peerages for some of his loyalists. Finally, he confirmed to Disraeli that he would be recommending him to the Queen, and as rumors surfaced about London, Charlotte asked "Dis" to confirm who would succeed. The day after Edouard's arrival she received a laconic note: "Your devoted Dizzy—to be communicated by Lord Stanley at the House today." Certainly the only happier lady was Mary Anne. "By the time this reaches you," she wrote hurriedly to Charlotte, "Dizzy will be Prime Minister of England!"

Natty, who would later transfer his loyalties to Disraeli, was, as a doctrinaire new Liberal M.P., properly partisan, writing to his parents while on family business in Paris, "From what I can hear, . . . by fair means or foul, Dizzy will tide over this session." Lionel thought that as long as Disraeli could persuade Tories to support essentially Liberal measures, he would survive in office.

For the Rothschilds, their intimacy with the pragmatic Disraeli added to their standing with the government. They had been suppliers of political and financial information to both political sides through their links to other regimes, notably now Prussia. Mayer Carl's relations with Bismarck and his banker, once a Rothschild agent, Gerson Bleichröder, were now close.

As bankers without borders, the Rothschilds wanted no new wars, yet one loomed between France and Prussia. Luring France into believing that Prussia had no ambitions in its direction, Bismarck suggested in April 1868 through Bleichröder that on economic grounds he was downsizing its army. However misleading it was, Lionel learned of it. Nearly a year earlier he had heard from the rue Laffitte that Napoleon III, increasingly unpopular, was seeking ways to prop up a dubious prestige in his competition with ambitious Prussia. Berlin had already absorbed some of the defenseless German principalities and might pluck the rest, putting Prussia on the Rhine. The anxious Emperor eyed Luxembourg as a balance for Prussia's gains to its west, but a great powers' guarantee of Luxembourg's neutrality remained possible to ward off war in that direction. In May 1867, Britain made known its agreement via a telegram from Lionel to Bleichröder: "We wired you today that we accept your drafts which means that our government is inclined to accept the conference under the conditions as suggested. Your friend will like it."

In early September 1867, although Lionel was away from New Court, he was not out of touch, and he continued his good offices via

Disraeli, who kept the Queen informed through Lord Stanley. Baron Rothschild's "information as to what is passing on the Continent," the Foreign Minister explained, "is generally quite as early and quite as accurate as that which can be obtained through different channels." Rothschild intelligence was more than familial. Lionel had sources beyond his cousins on the Continent—such European agents as Charles Villiers, Delane of *The Times*, and informative clients.

Talk about Lionel being offered a peerage had resurfaced with Dizzy in Downing Street, and on March 9, 1868, Villiers left one Piccadilly mansion—Lady Palmerston's—for another to report to Lionel new rumors about his supposed elevation. Villiers, Lionel wrote to Charlotte, who was away, "could not understand nor could they"—the Liberal social elite—"at Lady P's that I would accept anything from the present Government. They all fancy Dis is under great obligations to us. So the best thing is to hold my tongue and let them think what they like. It is only amusing to hear all this nonsense." It would have been indelicate for Lionel's relationship with Disraeli to lead to a contentious peerage, and both men knew it.

In mid-April, Ferdinand had reported to Lionel from Paris, "Uncle James has been very ailing; he hardly goes to the bureau and sits half the day in his armchair." He was nearly seventy-six and suffered agonizingly from gallstones. Despite failing vision, he oversaw the refurbishing of the offices ("the bureau") of de Rothschild Frères and had his Gobelin tapestries moved there from Ferrières. At long last James also acquired the vineyards of Château Lafite and its *Premier des Premiers Grands Crus*. On October 31, from bed, he dictated a letter to his son Edmond about a loan to Spain. Increasingly jaundiced and having just passed a number of large gallstones, he gave, painfully, on November 3, the last instructions which Alphonse could understand. "With my father in his present state," he reported to London, "it is not possible to talk business with him, and we avoid anything that might upset him."

In the early hours of November 15, 1868, Baron James died. "To the most rare and precious qualities of spirit," Alphonse told his cousins, "he added a gaiety, an affability in every communication, which won over people's hearts and attached them to him for ever." Anthony, Natty, Alfred, and Leo came for the funeral on November 18. Lionel was unable to travel, and Charlotte remained with him. The press of the crowd for official condolences, the makers and shakers of France and diplomatic representatives, was so great that the doors of the rue Laffitte had to be opened at ten in the morning, and Alphonse, with his brothers and his cousins, all received mourners. Ordinary Parisians clustering outside—the merely curious—were astonishingly numerous. To watch the procession, Natty wrote, onlookers in carriages were "lined 5 deep on both sides." At noon an unadorned hearse pulled by a pair of horses drew the simple wooden coffin, followed by dozens of mourning carriages, to the Jewish section of the cemetery of Père Lachaise. First in the cortège were James's three valets; after them came the men of the family, and after them the employees of de Rothschild Frères. Even Parisian revolutions seemed not to have drawn as many people to the streets.

James's gravestone would bear, simply, the letter "R," which, in the grandness of its austerity, suggested to Alfred that it was "more like that of an Emperor than that of a private individual."

James bequeathed his hopes for further "mutual confidence and fraternal accord" among his descendants. "That fraternal union alone, the dying wish of my worthy and revered father, has been our strength and has been our productive shield, [and with] our love of work and practice of probity, has been the source of our prosperity and public reputation."

Long an acknowledged co-equal of his uncle in the Rothschild enterprises, Lionel was now, without question, the senior cousin in the partnership, which increasingly was being managed by the generation of his own sons. In 1870 the British gossip sheet *Period* would certify his status by caricaturing him as "The Modern Croesus," sitting smugly on a throne of cash box, stacks of bonds, shares, mortgages, and loans to Russia, Turkey, Spain, Egypt, and Brazil. On a shelf is a golden calf, and below him in obeisance are such potentates

as Queen Victoria, the Emperor of China, the Pope, the Sultan of
Turkey, and Napoleon III. On November 22, 1868, Lionel would be
sixty. (Charlotte was forty-nine.) He wanted to give more authority
to his own sons, as Anthony and Mayer had none, but only Natty had
shown the requisite enterprise.

Enterprise, nevertheless, was foisted upon Alfred and Leopold.
Alfy's interests lay in the arts. He had acted during his lone year at
Cambridge, had become friends (through Prince Bertie) with such
composers as Arthur Sullivan, and was an art connoisseur in his early
twenties. To involve him in the real world, his uncle Billy arranged to
put him, in 1867, on a City committee "for the Relief of Distress,"
and his mother hoped that "he may, perhaps, become reconciled to
the idea of entering parliament, which, at present, seems so repugnant to his tastes." Yet in 1868, at twenty-six, with no more public
record than that, Alfred became the first professing Jew to be elected
a director of the Bank of England. (Alphonse was already a regent of
the Banque de France.) By the later 1860s the Bank of England
needed a Rothschild on its board—an index of the house's importance. Alfred would serve with diplomatic skill for twenty-two years,
also, more logically, becoming a trustee of the National Gallery.

Although Leo politicked for his less-than-mobile father, he had no
more desire for a seat in the Commons for himself than did Alfy.
When Natty later became a partner in the London house, so did Alfred and Leopold. Although he preferred to speculate on the turf,
Leo began putting in regular, if short, hours at New Court nearly
daily, and he went on missions for the firm. Ironically, it would be his
sons, Lionel and Anthony, still unborn, who would eventually run
the family bank.

As Baron James lay dying, in England Disraeli's minority government eroded. In the first General Election after the new electoral reforms, Gladstone had appealed on divisive religious grounds to the
Evangelical and Catholic constituencies, both now increased in franchise. Before bowing out, Disraeli applied to the Queen for a peerage

for his wife, now a frail seventy-six. Honors bestowed by outgoing governments were traditional. Mary Anne became Countess of Beaconsfield, and her husband, at sixty-four unready to exit political life, went to Windsor on December 1, 1868, to relinquish his seals of office.

To the disappointment, although not the surprise, of Lionel and Charlotte, Lionel lost his seat in the following General Election. He was damaged by accidental association on the ballot with Joseph d'Aguilar Samuda, a convert from Judaism who was a Liberal candidate from Tower Hamlets, and as journalist Richard Simpson wrote to Catholic scholar-politician Sir John Acton, Lionel was also affected by "the desertion of the stricter Jews who are scandalized at his wet[3] Judaism." His time in the wilderness was brief. In a by-election in February 1869 he was again returned.

Baron Lionel remained the obvious member of his religious community to lay the foundation stone of the new Central Synagogue, Great Portland Street, on March 18, 1869. He had to be assisted to the dais by Nathaniel and Alfred, who each held him under an arm. "If the political privileges which we have gained," he told the assemblage to great applause, "could in any way weaken our Jewish sympathies, they would have been purchased at terrible cost and would signally defeat the intentions of those who aided and labored for the movement, and become disadvantages instead of advantages."

Since Lionel was a Liberal M.P. who could possibly defect to Disraeli, Gladstone made it an early order of business from Downing Street to propose a peerage for him, combining the request to Victoria with equivalent rank for two Roman Catholics, one of them John Acton. Gladstone might have tempered his enthusiasm had he known that Lionel wrote to the defeated Disraeli, "[I]n that great parliamentary struggle in which you play so prominent a part, if the tide has turned for a moment, it will only be an opportunity for you

---

3. *Wet:* liberal tendencies as regarded by the right-wing members of one's party.

to display additional powers of eloquence, and talent, and you will allow me to say that we shall always rejoice in your success, and feel personally grateful for the friendly feelings, which on every occasion you have evinced towards us."

Loyalties and friendships were tangled things. To Earl Granville, Gladstone called Lionel "one of the best I know, and if I could get from him a Mem[orandum] of certain services of his father as to money during the [Napoleonic] war I think it wd carry the case over all difficulty. But though I have begged and they have promised for about 4 years, I have never been able to get this." Gladstone would never receive such a paper.

Maintaining her objections to Baron Rothschild (long a baron but not of her making) after renewed arguments from Gladstone, Victoria wrote on August 24, 1869, in her usual third person, "But she *cannot* consent to a Jew being made a Peer—tho' she will not object to a *Jew* baronet—and she is quite certain that it wld do the Govt harm rather than good." Since her interest in propping up a Liberal government was less than minimal, as Gladstone knew, he understood which argument was paramount. When he persisted, the Queen meanly struck out indirectly at her son, the pleasure-loving Prince of Wales, recently a guest at Mayer's Mentmore, in claiming that she could not offer honors to someone enriched by an occupation akin to gambling. "She cannot think," she charged to Gladstone of November 1, "[that] one who owes his great wealth to contracts with Foreign Govts for Loans, or to successful speculations on the Stock Exchange can fairly claim a British Peerage. However high Sr[4] L. Rothschild may stand personally in Public Estimation, this seems to her not the less a species of gambling, because it is on a gigantic scale—& far removed from that legitimate trading wh[ich] she *delights to honour.*" Neither Earl Granville, who had intervened cautiously for Gladstone, nor the Prime Minister himself, dared reply that could she withdraw all the peerages she had made of men who

4. Lionel had no such title although the Queen had created Anthony a baronet.

raced, gambled, speculated in shares, or made money in banking, she would empty the House of Lords.

As Gladstone was failing with the Queen, Lionel was in Paris during the parliamentary recess to consult with James's sons about the future of the "bureau." Immured still in mourning, Charlotte had emerged only once, in May, to accompany Lionel to the Royal Academy annual exhibition at Burlington House, to their east on Piccadilly. Her nerves were on edge. She awaited a visit from Emmy and little Walter, and finishing work on and in Piccadilly House that seemed never to have ended. In an undated letter to Leo, probably that October, she complained that the house that day, as interior finishing continued, was "perfectly odious." The lift was going "incessantly up and down." Ornaments had to be removed from glass cases for safety. Servants were "calling and screaming to each other in the passages, and on the staircase." She had "weekly accounts and bills to settle"; and she had called in their builder "for I fear that something has gone wrong under the library floor, and that colonies of mice, or perhaps rats, are located there." She escaped to Gunnersbury.

Since Charlotte would not go with Lionel to France, Leo was deputed as his escort. On occasion Lionel now walked with some strain, but his wheeled chair, in which he propelled himself vigorously, went with them on the Channel boat. By carriage he even visited several Parisian galleries, and when he heard that a privately owned picture by Jean-Baptiste Greuze—a favorite artist—could be seen and possibly purchased, he was, Leo wrote to Charlotte, "tempted to sally forth." Both Leo and Alfy had become accomplished connoisseurs, and "Alfred will see it with a harsh eye & will let you know more about it."

With a guide they went to the house of an elderly marquis. Leo was taken upstairs into the "red room" while his father waited below:

I wish I had the pen of a great author to describe to you the strange sight. An old man, an invalid seated in a chair, greeted us & in a towering passion asked us what we wanted. When he heard the purpose of our visit his manner changed & he was very polite but I was anything but sorry to leave the stuffy chamber. Poor man, he has not left his bedside for 2 years & I should say that no servant has been allowed to perform any of the somewhat necessary duties. The picture was carried downstairs & you can imagine that I do not exaggerate the state of the little room upstairs when I tell you that dear Papa thought that the picture retains the odour! It is certainly a fine painting & represents a woman praying. The head is beautiful & full of great description but there is an idea that Greuze may have been assisted in the completion by a pupil.

The next day, although Lionel was "much the worse for the exertion," they went off to examine another Greuze, belonging to a Russian countess—"the village priest helping the newly married girl." The countess asked £2,800 for it, but neither Lionel nor Leo considered it "a real gem." In two days they had seen two Greuzes without buying either one, but, Leo told his mother, "Dear Papa was I think pleased to find himself once more *en société.*"

Lionel's visit to Paris was his last glimpse of his brother Nat. Disabled as he was, Nat's mind was sharp, and he had always been a good listening post for the Rothschilds. In February 1869 Nat had passed on the report (there had been many such during the decade) that Napoleon III "will determine upon war, in order to divert public attention from internal affairs," and that the Italian ambassador was attempting a deal for his government in the event of war, with the Austrian-held Tyrol as King Victor Emmanuel's price. Napoleon's hold on France had become increasing shaky. Alternately a revolutionary and a reactionary, his failures in foreign affairs had strengthened the opposition in what he called an imperial democracy. Elections late in 1869 had exposed his diminishing popularity. Lionel listened, but business remained healthy and as long as his contact in Berlin, Bleichröder, remained a disinformation conduit for Bismarck, the Rothschild intelligence network received mixed signals.

On January 5, 1870, Nat's English secretary, John F. Cox, wrote to the Rothschild brothers in London for him, "I have been very poorly and have not been out of my room." A week later he had lost his voice and could barely dictate a line. On February 7 Nat conceded, "I am not much better now," but he remained sufficiently *au courant* to add, "I congratulate you on the great success of the Russian loan." He continued to fade, and on February 19, a Saturday, Cox reported to Lionel from 33 Faubourg St. Honoré, "You will have learnt by telegram this morning the sad news that . . . your brother passed away." At four in the morning Nat had called for a servant to read the English sporting news to him—day or night made no difference to him—and was found dead in his armchair.

Cox telegraphed that the funeral was "fixed for Monday at 11 o'clock as from the state of the body it cannot well be longer delayed." Lionel's sons rushed over for the burial—a far more modest occasion than the obsequies for Nat's father-in-law, James. Alfred spent three hours afterward at the rue St. Florentin home of Jimmy de Rothschild, at twenty-five Nat's "dreadfully cut-up" elder son, and reported to Charlotte and Lionel,

> Uncle Nat thought he had taken a new lease of life and as he had recovered his voice . . . [was] not aware of the great changes that had taken place in himself. . . . On Friday night he talked to Alphonse about American stocks and the Russian loan and had the Mordaunt case[5] read to him. A few seconds before he died he told his servants to bring him a cup of tea as he wished to have the newspapers read. . . .
>
> Jimmy is much obliged for your letter . . . and would like to possess a letter in his father's hand if you can find one at New Court.

---

5. Sir Charles Mordaunt had sued his wife for divorce on the ground of her alleged adultery with several admirers, including the Prince of Wales. The Prince was forced to testify. She was ruled insane—her husband claimed she faked madness—and committed to a private asylum.

In London, Disraeli and Mary Anne arrived at Piccadilly House on a condolence call, and the servants sent them away. They may have been baffled. It was a unique and unfortunate moment in their long and warm friendship and suggested how agitated Lionel and Charlotte were by their cycle of mourning. It seems Charlotte's decision. "We could not make up our minds, dear Papa and I, to receive them," she explained to Leo. "They hardly knew poor uncle Nat, and this is not a day for idle chit-chat." Nat was too "great and noble" for that.

For years Lionel and Charlotte had borne severe family losses, and Lionel's health had continued to decline. Although the Rothschild enterprises were flourishing, both realized that all the money in the world could not replace their loved ones, and Europe's tangled politics continued to complicate their lives.

Laury stubbornly remained optimistic about prospects in France. She wrote to London about Nat's will, which divided his large estate among his wife (Uncle James's daughter) and his children, about market news, and about the Mordaunt trial. "Nobody talks of anything but the Mordaunt case," she deplored, none too persuasively, "which is disgusting." But she followed with a riddle about her royal friend Bertie: "What is the difference between Sir Charles Mordaunt & his wife? Sir C. went to Norway to fish salmon, and Lady M. stayed in town to catch Wales."

To Leonora, insulated from the rue Laffitte, all—at least into May—was "tranquillity." Charlotte had sent her daughter Disraeli's new novel about contemporary—and violent—European politics, *Lothair*, completed after his brief tenure as prime minister. Writing in return, Laury saw troubles only elsewhere—but for a notorious and irrelevant Parisian crime. It was a year, she explained, of external horrors—"massacres in Greece, robberies in England, & at St. Petersburg an assassination." In France only the murder of Monsieur d'Arenberg's twin brother, "garroted and strangled in his bed," relieved the tedium. "I wish I had something lively to relate," she wrote innocently, "but all my news is in that strain."

In London, John Delane observed to Lionel that he didn't believe there would be war between France and Prussia—only "a game of brag." Yet the problem of a successor for the powerless Spanish throne had focused attention on Franco-Prussian rivalries, and the Rothschild family intelligence system was unable to pick up the nuances. The Spanish Cortes had nominated the innocuous young Prince Leopold of Hohenzollern-Sigmaringen, which Napoleon III interpreted as a Prussian attempt to encircle France. On July 5 he summoned Alphonse to St. Cloud and asked him to convey a message to Gladstone through Lionel. Natty received and decoded the telegram that Tuesday and hurried it to his father, who sent him off to Downing Street. He found the Prime Minister departing for an audience at Windsor with the Queen. Natty chatted with him in the carriage en route to Paddington Station just long enough to learn that Gladstone would not intervene in what he considered another country's internal affairs.

Lionel was outraged, but Gladstone had little interest in Europe. Alphonse then urged his father-in-law to intervene directly (but uselessly, given Gladstone's animosity) with Disraeli and the Opposition. Still, in early July, from Berlin, Bleichröder told London that he saw "no cause for disquiet." Indeed, because of French objections, King William of Prussia, while Bismarck remained on summer holiday in Pomerania, had induced young Leopold, through his father, Karl Anton, to withdraw his candidacy. On July 12 Gladstone's foreign minister, Earl Granville (who did, after some delay, send mild notes to Madrid and Berlin), scrawled a note to his chief: "The Rothschilds have recd a telegram. The Prince has given up his candidature. The French are satisfied." Yet, seeking a provocation, Napoleon's bellicose ministers insisted that the Prussian king also disavow any future involvement in the Spanish succession. Since the prospect was humiliating (exactly what the French intended), William refused, very likely with Bismarck's covert absentee backing. France was far less ready for war than Prussia. It was not much of a casus belli, but Bismarck was willing to let the French have it.

In Paris, Alphonse was at first "delighted" by the government's jingostic posture, which appealed to French pride—as long as it was short of war. On July 2, 1870, Mayer Carl spoke with Vincent Benedetti, the French ambassador, who was on his way to take the waters at Wildbad. Despite the succession imbroglio, Benedetti was optimistic. He was, Charlotte's brother informed New Court, "very glad to be able to rest a little after the fatigue of the great Capital. He seems in very good spirits and says that everything is in perfect order and that peace is assured." Again the Rothschild intelligence system was failing in cynicism.

After the Austrian war, as Mayer Carl should have perceived, the Prussians were blooded, experienced, and ready to fight, while the French were belligerent, bombastic, and unready. Napoleon needed an external triumph. Now realizing uneasily what the outcome would be, James's sons Gustave and Alphonse, and Lionel's Natty, all attempted to persuade Gladstone to mediate. Uninterested in Continental disputes, he evaded involvement.

When the withdrawal of the Hohenzollern aspirant, with King William's endorsement, was formally announced on July 12, Gustave wrote to New Court in relief, "Thus peace is made, or rather the war is adjourned." Yet Napoleon, encouraged by his foreign minister, the duc de Gramont, demanded the next day that King William forgo in perpetuity any interest in the Spanish succession. In an insolent response, the French charged that William's refusal was sufficient cause to mobilize. On July 14, symbolically Bastille Day, France declared war. It was a gambler's throw. The Rothschilds found themselves on both sides, and in the middle.

CHAPTER TEN

ENDURING

1870–1874

War seemed imminent as Laury and Alphonse visited family in Frankfurt. Trains were already being stopped by the military. Returning hurriedly, they kept changing trains, each time inching closer to France. At midnight, as it became July 15, they reached Bühl (Bâle), below Baden-Baden, and changed trains again, but at Kehl, opposite Strasbourg, the border station was closed. Desperately, they hired a carriage and rode into the dawn past troop trains full of "screaming and shouting" Prussians going westward—all of them, Laury thought, drunk. Finally, they crossed the frontier into Alsace, soon to become German. "I need not tell you how sad & disgusted we are," Laury wrote from chaotic Paris on July 19 to Charlotte and Lionel, "& in fact all reasonable people must be [disgusted] at the prospect of war. Our mad Empress was I am afraid greatly in favour of it. She sends her son, who is only 14, to see all the butchery with the Emperor. You know how enthusiastic French people are about military glory."

From Frankfurt, Lionel's sister Louise (Mayer Carl's wife) wrote that if the "less-than-great" Napoleon wished to unite all Germany, he could have found no better way. As the Emperor's military adventure began imploding, Alphonse prepared to send Laury and the children to England. He and Gustave rushed telegrams to Lionel about alleged Prussian atrocities, mass French surrenders, and the need for rations for the troops—indeed for everything. French purchases of biscuits and salt pork were underwritten (at a profit) by the London house: Lionel was unwilling to furnish charity to Napoleon III's corrupt and doomed regime, and capital was flowing quickly across the Channel from Paris—an augury of pessimism and panic.

Ferdinand left for Paris as Lionel's emissary and found that French fighting words were unmatched by deeds, while Alphonse entreated his father-in-law to seek English intervention—or, at the least, mediation. Lionel had tried that before, unsuccessfully, but proposed assisting wounded soldiers and their families. Leonora responded that a French committee had been set up for the purpose, with Alphonse as treasurer. "The Empress has given £2000 and of course money will be gratefully received. . . . I am afraid the French will not be satisfied with a drawn battle. But we hope that England will interfere as soon as possible and restore peace. . . . There is a great deal of enthusiasm here & everybody, Legitimists & Orleanists give money and send their sons. . . . On the streets they sing the Marseillaise & other songs of that sort, howling as much as they can! Which you know is a French quality."

As Laury prepared to flee to England, the situation worsened. Anticipating victories to celebrate on large canvases, the publicity-conscious Napoleon had arranged for war artists to accompany his troops, and Jean Meissonier, Auguste Bartholdi, Paul Baudry, Jules Bastien-Lepage, Édouard Detaille, James Tissot, Renoir, Manet, Degas, and Bouguereau went east. Those that made it close to the fighting found they had nothing to record but futile marches followed by retreats, pathetic refugees, villages burning, and peasants burying the dead. They painted *la patrie en danger*. It did not help that the ailing Emperor was a lackluster general. Relaying the attitude of Berlin to Lionel, Mayer Carl wrote (August 27), "The French must be humiliated, which is the only way for us to be preserved from further wars, and I have no doubt that the French must give up Alsace and Lorraine, a great part of their fleet and at least one hundred million sterling as war contribution."

Leonora and her children managed to board a packet to the Isle of Wight, from which they could cross the Solent to Southampton or Portsmouth and take a train to London. From Cowes she wrote to her parents, "I am anxiously expecting news and the definitive results of yesterday's battle. God grant we may soon have peace!" The day before she had seen an aide to the Queen, who told Laury that Victoria was uninterested in the war. She "goes today to Windsor and tomorrow to Scotland. She is certainly most determined never to alter her plans or arrangements for anything or anybody, & I think some of the abuse Mr. Delane so lavishes upon the world, might find its way to her royal person!"

On September 2, 1870, Napoleon surrendered his army and himself at Sedan. September 3 was a Saturday, the Sabbath. Charlotte and Lionel were home in London. Returning to Aston Clinton from Wales, Anthony learned the news, packed the family back into their carriage, and hurried to Piccadilly House. "When we entered the breakfast room," Constance wrote in her diary,

We saw a look of astonishment and partly dismay depicted upon the three faces of Uncle Lionel, Aunt Lionel and Laury. A fourth person, Mr. Bauer, looking gloomy and dark, stood at the table with a telegram in his hand. These were the words of the dispatch: "The Emperor has surrendered himself to the King [of Prussia], and the army of forty thousand men has capitulated." Poor Laury felt humiliated like a French-woman. Then came the fear of revolution. She was dark crimson with excitement, and her voice trembled so that she could hardly speak. After a few moments her children came screaming and shouting into the room. They were allowed to make a fearful noise, as no one seemed to [be] mind[ing] them.

In the midst of their childish voices came the muttered doubts and fears [of their elders] concerning the Empire. In a few moments' time appeared Leopold, then Natty, then Alfred, all with that dumb-founded, bewildered look and gaze. The little dog, Judy, happy in her ignorance, sat begging on her haunches for bread and the children were [now] counting their pence. Thus the great and the trivial seem[ed] to be for ever crossing each other's paths. The day wore on in continued excitement, almost too much to be borne for long.

In Paris, where the news did not arrive until the next day, yet another French republic was proclaimed, and Eugénie, frightened and humiliated, rushed to asylum in England, where the Prince of Wales arranged temporary refuge. The new government resolved to continue the war in hopes of avoiding an abject settlement, but by mid-September the capital was surrounded and besieged. The makeshift command was soon fighting two wars—one against the cannonading Prussians, and another against leftist revolutionaries ready to make a separate peace if the enemy would leave them in control of the wreckage.

In London, Lionel and his brothers turned down any participation in a £10 million loan for which the provisional regime pleaded. It seemed hopeless. On the other side, Mayer Carl offered his brother-in-law five-year Prussian war bonds, their short duration suggesting that likely French reparations would pay them off. In a neutrality that was more anti-Napoleon than anti-Prussian, New Court kept clear of them. Lionel's friend Delane essentially took neither side for *The Times* by thundering first about French aggression, then arguing that England had to do something to prevent Prussian annexation of Alsace and Lorraine.

Alphonse and Gustave remained in Paris, with Ferdinand also at the rue Laffitte acting as observer for New Court. Young Edmond and Nat's son James Edouard served in the Garde Mobile. On September 19, the military triumvirate of King William, General Moltke, and Count Bismarck occupied Ferrières, preceded on the 14th by two lesser generals with heavier hands, who commandeered all the food and wine. Within the week, three thousand Prussian officers and men were bivouacked in the park, and the highest officials billeted in the château. Yet realizing that he would need the cooperation of Baron Alphonse, whose fiscal authority went beyond frontiers, William ordered that all Rothschild antiques and art treasures were to be untouched.

Monsieur Bergmann, the Baron's estate manager, scrupulously catalogued daily Prussian depredations, largely those of Bismarck, who shot as many tame partridges as he could. He was forced to buy a case of Alphonse's wine after officers guzzled hundreds of bottles from the famous cellars. When the royal party left, the King insisted on a written statement from Bergmann that nothing was missing from the château, and left seventy-five soldiers to guard it; but the grounds were already despoiled, and troops would be camped there until August 1871. The ponds were drained and empty of fish; Bismarck himself filched 250 sheep for his farm in Pomerania; and the wine cellars were nearly empty. According to Bergmann, all the livestock were gone, and all the coal. What four-legged game was left by the Prussians was quickly killed by poachers, but the woods survived. "The château," he concluded, "[is] very dirty indeed."

Once troops left, Anthony came from London to survey the damage, finding the mansion little the worse but for the "spoilt" carpets and the empty cellars. "So much for Ferrières," he wrote to Lionel and Mayer on September 1, 1871; "nothing damaged by the war[,] nothing taken by the communists, no person hurt or wounded." He thought their French cousins "ought to thank God that they got off so well."

The aside on the Communists harked back to the months of the siege of Paris, both from without and within. Despite the panic, Alphonse remained in authority and managed to get long letters, much delayed, to New Court, urging English mediation "in not allowing the balance of Europe to be completely overthrown." He was close to the republic's Foreign Minister, Jules Favre, and relayed warnings intended for the Prussians that they would not be able to police all of France, which would be rife with revolutionaries. Before long he was conveying to Lionel, now intermediary for the French with both London and Berlin, what ideas were stirring about how much territorial and fiscal humiliation could be absorbed. Wary of any involvement, Gladstone suspected that Lionel and his brothers were "twisting the words" to suit their own interests. Reporting what he could, Alphonse quoted the government's fighting proclamation "that we are ready to be buried beneath the walls of Paris." It was not, he concluded, an "alluring" prospect.

In London, Rothschild life had changed little. Leo and Alfy were active in French relief efforts, which pleased Charlotte as they were doing something useful. Leonora had visited her parents so often that her extended stay in England with her children was different only because her husband could not join her. At New Court, the house guaranteed payments for supplies contracted for by the new French government and by the Prussians, and in unrelated business raised a loan to consolidate the debt of the government of Argentina.

Charlotte went on her usual "wandering" in the Jewish immigrant quarter of the East End, looking for pockets of "heartrending" poverty requiring urgent assistance. For years she had done it quietly with no air of saintliness. She often chose inclement weather, when she knew other ladies would not be out. This time, since a thick layer of dust coated everything at one house, Charlotte suggested that the woman she visited might improve the air she breathed by some personal effort. "I'm quality," she said, stiffening pridefully, "and don't do any cleaning myself." "I hope I am 'quality' too," said Charlotte, unoffended, "yet I always dust some of my things myself."

On her Tuesday inspections to the Free School, the "good Baroness"—as she was known to the children—examined the progress made by every scholar, finding most "very satisfactory." On one visit she also noted "how much Mrs. Brie has improved the little kitchen girls; what is more wonderful is that she should have got on so comfortably with the surrounding Jews and Jewesses [who were the children's parents]."

From Amsterdam, Lionel received yet another plea for assistance from a chronically importuning Cohen relative (of his mother's family) who wanted £100 for himself, £90 for his sister, and £50 for his brother, "all in the greatest distress." Feeling put upon, the Baron sent nothing. Then he ordered a carriage from Gunnersbury to take him to the nearby lunatic asylum for émigré Indians, Charlotte reported to Leo. "There are 120 sun- and moonstruck men and women at the Elms, and dear Papa wants to exchange a field [with the asylum], as he thinks it would be better to see cows grazing upon it than madmen playing at cricket." Although she put a wry spin on his venture, almost certainly the institution would benefit substantially.

As the siege of Paris continued, citizens became cold and hungry and the city was rife with rumors. Little news came in; communications often left via carrier pigeons and balloons, and those messages that made it to safe territory could be relayed further by telegraph. A balloon shot down contained a letter, relayed to Prussian headquarters, with the line "[Alphonse de] Rothschild told me yesterday that Bismarck was not satisfied with his pheasants at Ferrières, and had threatened to beat his steward, because the pheasants did not fly about filled with truffles." In the capital, sheep and cattle grazed (until slaughtered) in the Bois de Boulogne, and the botanical gardens were pressed into service as burial grounds. Dogs and cats disappeared into cooking pots. *Charivari* published a cartoon of Britannia sneering over France's corpse with the caustic caption, "Prussia hasn't killed her completely. It's not yet time to come to her aid." Minister of the Interior Léon Gambetta escaped in a balloon and set up a government, and army, in the provinces that vowed to fight on, but his troops were green *levées* and proved no match for the Prussians.

On January 18, a glittering ceremony stage-managed by Bismarck in the Hall of Mirrors at Versailles acclaimed William as Emperor of Germany. The subservient south German states clamored to join the new Germany, and their dukes and princes assembled to rubber-stamp their declaration of dependence. An armistice—in effect a surrender of Paris—took effect on January 28, 1871, ending the Franco-Prussian War. The first courier from New Court arrived at the rue Laffitte with a hamper of correspondence on February 3, and soon after came another with food. They "fell like children," Alphonse acknowledged, "on all the excellent things you sent us."

Before the siege, but with defeat inevitable, Alphonse had predicted to Lionel that France would have to relinquish "Alsatia" and the Lorraine ("old German provinces," Charlotte's brother Mayer Carl had characterized them to London) and "one hundred million sterling"—then 2.5 billion francs. Summoning Jules Favre and the veteran statesman Adolphe Thiers to Versailles, Bismarck declared that in addition to territorial cessions, before German troops were withdrawn from France, an indemnity of six billion francs would have to be paid in full. Mayer Carl's earlier forecast had been so staggering that Anselm in Vienna had suggested to Lionel issuing 5 percent rentes with the Rothschild houses arranging the bond issue for a group of banks. The sum actually demanded was even more astonishing.

On patriotic grounds, Alphonse, shaken, insisted upon excluding all German banks from raising reparations for France, even his Rothschild cousins in Vienna and Frankfurt. The Germans in Paris had already demanded two hundred million francs to pay for their own occupation. Now they refused franc banknotes, as they wanted to force the depreciation of the French currency. With Lionel, Alphonse worked out a compromise by which reparations would be raised largely in gold and silver and in short-dated commercial bills on London and Berlin. A syndicate including Barings but managed from New Court arranged the conversion of French notes into English currency, which the Germans would accept, so quickly that Bismarck and his bankers were baffled.

Effacing the reparations bill was one of the great achievements of the London house. The magical name of Rothschild had led to the two-part issue being oversubscribed. Commissions to the banks, which risked none of their own money, were substantial. Although the indemnity schedule was deliberately tight, and labeled "shameful" by Alphonse, the huge sum was delivered efficiently at great interest savings to the French. Repayment, intended by the Germans to be humiliating and ruinous, proved easier than anticipated. The conflict had been so short, and the Second Empire had invested so little in preparing for it, that France had incurred relatively little wartime debt.

At Lionel's suggestion, Natty had applied to Gladstone early in March 1871 to inquire whether the government might guarantee a portion of the loan, as an act of confidence in, and friendship for, France. It was clearly safe. "Not to be entertained," Gladstone wrote curtly in his diary for March 4. It made no difference. For the Rothschilds in London and Paris the processing of the indemnity had been not only a masterly achievement but a boost to battered French pride.

The challenge prompted Lionel to leave for New Court each morning with new zest. Although crippled far more than his clients realized as he pressed forward in his armchair, he was as eager and as attentive as a young clerk striving to be singled out for promotion. The business of the bank in large measure was to have significant sums at its disposal for great operations. Few were greater and more urgent than the French reparations. It was such transactions that attracted the awe of the public and the interest of governments and companies and investors, but the invisible work behind the scenes lay in being prepared for eventualities. From his invalid chair Lionel scrutinized the money markets, the inside politics of nations, and the psychology of policy makers. He also looked for ways to employ funds that should never lie idle, yet never be put at great risk, while remaining available on command. When he pushed a bell for information always accruing, aides rushed in; when he was seen in quiet concentration, his desk became an island. Veteran accountants still remembered Nathan Mayer's hurly-burly. Temperament and disability combined to create Lionel's very different style, as did the increasing complexity of international finance. Lionel unbent only when his carriage brought him home to Charlotte.

While bankers were working out France's economic recovery, a second siege of Paris began, this time of the French by the French. Hasty post-empire elections in February had returned a conservative parliament, in temporary quarters at Versailles. German soldiers were still having themselves photographed on the streets of the capital, while Parisians with brooms and carts were expunging the residue of the war, when radicals—collectively, Communards—unhappy with the results of the balloting, turned on the new government as it was reorganizing. Seizing cannon and hauling them up to the heights around Paris, they turned their barrels on the boulevards. The red flag was again hoisted in the Place de la Bastille.

On March 18, 1871, when Adolphe Thiers ordered the disarming of the increasingly anarchic National Guard, radical bystanders rushed to the guardsmen's assistance and lynched one of their generals, then another. Thiers withdrew what loyal forces he had from Paris to Versailles. Communards demolished his house. On the 26th, Alphonse and Gustave again packed up their families for London and then decamped themselves to Versailles. Recklessly, Alphonse intended to keep his contacts with the rue Laffitte, but on a second return to Versailles he was warned by a trainman that the Commune had ordered rail traffic severed. The city was in the hands of (one could not say controlled by) the Commune. Murder, looting, and arson were commonplace. As in the less sanguinary "Great Terror" of 1793–1794, a new revolutionary calendar was issued, and citizens began denouncing, to whatever authorities there were, friends, foes, neighbors, and people to whom one owed money or fancied a grudge. From New Court, Lionel watched, and waited.

The rue Laffitte survived, but just barely, as Thiers ordered republican forces back into Paris to crush the revolutionaries. Much of the capital was set afire. Corot painted a *Burning of Paris* and Manet a lurid *Civil War 1871*. During "Bloody Week," ending May 28, twenty thousand people died,[1] many of them Communard prisoners ordered lined up and shot. Beneath one wall at, conveniently, the Père Lachaise cemetery, lay the bodies of 147 barefoot Communards.

When Alfred arrived in Paris late in June on an inspection trip for Lionel, and as a member of the Food Subcommittee in the British relief effort, he reported to his parents that Laury's mansion in the rue St. Florentin had survived the Communards with only a corner of the ceiling in one room knocked out. The "ruffians" intending to "petrolize" the house had failed. Visiting on another mission for Lionel in August, Ferdinand was shocked at the "painfully green and yellow" complexions of Alphonse and Gustave, and he found them secretive about their personal experiences. The stress had been difficult to bear.

Still, their financial house had survived, and following the indemnity coup arranged with Lionel, the Parisians had the advantage of that solidly continuing relationship. "Our opinion, I have no doubt," Alphonse wrote to him, will have a very great influence over the decisions which [Augustin Pouyer-Quertier,] the [Finance] Minister is in the process of taking and our attitude must necessarily be very influenced by yours." He expected that for some time to come, the London house would be central to French financial recovery. War had further fractured the already tenuous connections between the German-language houses—Frankfurt and Vienna—and both London and Paris. With Germany forcibly united, financial power in *Mitteleuropa* would gravitate inexorably to Berlin, and the Rothschild houses in Vienna and Frankfurt would fade. For a while, however,

1. In 1793–1794 only 2,596 Parisians perished in the Terror.

Charlotte's brother expected to gain with the victors, writing smugly to Lionel about a profitable new rail line from Cologne to Minden in which New Court apparently had a share, "I am sure you will be *more* than satisfied, & think that *old* Charly is not so stupid as he looks."

With the war finally over and reparations settled, Charlotte and Lionel could relax again, even celebrate. At the height of the partying season, early in June, they had the Prince of Wales and Alexandra to dinner atop a huge guest list at Piccadilly House. The royal presence may have been a concession to their sons. Bertie was close to Alfy and Leo, less so now to Natty, but Charlotte was skeptical that such social success was real achievement. She found the future king "most enchantingly agreeable," with "manners . . . not to be surpassed," but it was "to be deplored that he does not give a portion of his time to serious pursuits, nor any of his friendship or society to distinguished men in politics, art, science or literature."

Although Gladstone remained prime minister, there was no chance he would have been invited. His relationship to Lionel and Charlotte was increasingly remote, for they were too close to Disraeli to be regarded with anything but suspicion. Lionel had not even been duly grateful for the failed recommendation for a peerage. According to Gladstone's 1871 diaries, Disraeli allegedly made "much and varied mischief" and, as "the wizard of Hughenden Manor," was always "behind the scenes." He continued to be a frequent guest of Lionel and Charlotte's. Where Gladstone was dour, Disraeli sparkled. He invited both Rothschilds to a harvest home at Hughenden, realizing that only Charlotte was likely to come. Then he warned her off, joking that there would be too many bishops present, and suggested a private visit on a working day for Lionel. His affection for her was as unconcealed as her amused admiration of "the illustrious Caucasian." For companions in her carriage en route she had only *The Times* and *Telegraph*. Writing to Leopold on September 15, 1871, she noted Dizzy's new look—"a suit of pearl grey, a soft hat, a new set of teeth and a new collection of curls." Nearly sixty-seven, he "had done all in his power to keep the double headed monster—if I may so express myself—time, . . . and personal old age at bay." Nearly eighty, the Viscountess was "in youthful muslins, profusely decorated with blue and yellow ribbons"—Rothschild racing colors—in honor of a victory of Hannah's (in effect, Mayer's) horse. The late summer weather was "wonderfully brilliant," Disraeli's beeches "magnificent," and the flower beds "dazzling." He "ought always to be seen at Hughenden," she concluded, "where he is neither politically severe and spiteful as becomes a party leader, nor grandly mysterious." Where he wanted to be, however, was back in Downing Street.

As Mary Anne aged, she concealed her years as best she could under wigs and extravagant dress, but by 1872 her emaciation from cancer left her wheelchair-bound in London. Her last appearance was at a reception given by the Countess of Loudon on July 17. Mary Anne had to be carried out, and home. Until the parliamentary session ended, Disraeli would write affectionate notes to her from the Commons and send Monty Corry to check on her. On July 25 one note closed that Natty Rothschild "was very affectionate about you, and wanted me to come home and dine with him . . . but I told him that you were the only person, now, whom I could dine with, and [I] only relinquished you tonight for my country." From Piccadilly House came dishes for Mary Anne, about which her agonized husband wrote to Corry, "the feats of Lionel's *chef*" went untouched. Her delusions from brain cancer in some cases could hardly be separated from her earlier eccentricities. A visiting clergyman, she explained to Corry, "told me to turn my thoughts to Jesus Christ but I couldn't. You know Dizzy is my Jesus Christ." She died at eighty on December 15, 1872.

Disraeli responded to a message of condolence from Mayer's wife, Juliana, that Mary Anne "often said that the intimate relations with your family formed one of the greatest sources of her happiness." The Rothschilds were indulgent about her absurdities. Charlotte recognized them as an element of her warmheartedness, unlike many of the rigid Tory ladies on the periphery of her husband's party. And they were as close to "family" as Mary Anne had.

Mourning and seclusion were difficult for a political animal like Disraeli. Since he possessed 2 Grosvenor Gate only during his wife's lifetime, he was suddenly homeless in the city. He took rooms temporarily at Edwards's Hotel in George Street, Hanover Square, describing it as "a cave of despair." When he sought company at dinner or tea, he often went, unannounced, to 148 Piccadilly. If Charlotte was alone, he could unbend. Lionel thrived on political talk, as Disraeli described to Monty Corry on February 10, 1873. "At Lionel's where I was asked to a family circle I found, to my annoyance, not merely Charles Villiers and [Bernal] Osborne, whom I look on as family, but Lords Cork and Houghton.[2] The political excitement was great."

Newly widowed and newly homeless, yet with the top of what he had called the greasy pole again in reach, Disraeli was often agitated and cranky. More than ever, he needed the Rothschilds. "Today," he minuted Corry on April 4, "I went by appointment to New Court, expecting to do business: nothing done. Lionel there, but not well: a terrible luncheon of oysters and turtle prepared, and after that nothing settled. This was disgusting." He was expecting Lionel to help solve his financial problems in the wake of the loss of his wife's income and property, but Lionel knew better than to have New Court (with three of its executives M.P.'s) overtly finance a highly visible politician—even if "family."

It was not that Lionel could not have made Disraeli very comfortable. In 1872 he had proposed that each of the four houses withdraw £700,000 from capital, the surplus to be shared by the partners. The partnership had become so prosperous that it could afford to deduct £2.8 million for personal use. All the cousins agreed. Although Lionel and Charlotte could afford the expenditure without the added

2. Baron Houghton was the former Richard Monckton Milnes.

funds, this was an excuse to purchase the estate of Tring Park in Hertfordshire for Natty and Emma. Built in 1670 by Sir Christopher Wren and added to since, Lionel acquired it on May 20, 1872, for £250,000 and then poured much more into refurbishing it inside and out. To Charlotte, Emma praised "this beautiful house and its perfect arrangements." She could not believe she was actually living there. After Lionel and Charlotte had passed from the scene, and Natty became the first in the family in England to receive a peerage, he would style himself Lord Rothschild of Tring.

From Tring, Emma wrote Charlotte gossipy letters much in her mother-in-law's own style—about Alfred's cook, now that Alfy, too, had his own residence (the Prince of Wales called the chef "by far the best in London"); about fasting on Yom Kippur; about a speech by Dizzy at Halton; a ball at Mentmore; schoolchildren singing; Uncle Mayer's horses; Uncle James's wine—and the doings of little Walter. And Emmy was again expecting. The first child to be born at the reconstituted Tring, on April 3, 1873, would be named Charlotte Louise Adela Evelina.

The death of Evelina continued to obsess Charlotte. In 1873 she published, anonymously, with the prestigious house of Longmans, Green, *From January to December: A Book for Children*.[3] Few beyond the pupils and tutors at the school in Spitalfields may have recognized the author's identity, although Charlotte's cousin Emma Montefiore wrote to her that the book had been her "companion" during a journey. Much of the miscellany had been tried out on the Bell Lane children—poems, stories, translations from French and German, and natural history, from birds to the aurora borealis. She even imagined a child's hospitalization, to prepare pupils for such an eventuality. Other segments visited the zoo and Kew Gardens, and described the picturesqueness of gypsies and the devotion of dogs. For

---

3. Felix Mendelssohn's sister Fanny, whom Charlotte had known, had composed a piano cycle of the months, *Das Jahr*, which she played at her Sunday salon-concerts in the mid-1830s.

February she wrote about tree frogs; larks came in April, swallows in June, and bees in August. For October, pheasants furnished an opportunity to decry shooting as "a pastime and a pleasure," and in November she continued to deplore the cruelty of hunting, hoping for a time "when man will cease to hunt and snare, and kill wild animals . . . for the sake of amusement."

A poem in April about a "loving fairy" now "far away" in heaven openly identified the "cherished" one as Charlotte's mother, but her December fable, "The Precious Jewel," concealed its origin in her loss of Evelina. A queen forgets to invite the household fairies to a party for her infant princess. In retaliation, the fairies curse the child with a litany of unattractive features—even poor complexion. Her fairy godmother cannot undo the threats but secretly gives to the girl she names "Nonbella" a mysterious, unseen amulet embedded in her heart. As the child of mixed blessings grows up, she evidences a love for languages and for music, sets free trapped birds, releases fish from the hooks of anglers, rescues a baby from a stream, and persuades her mother the queen to endow schools. Within the royal circle Prince Carissimo mocks such good deeds, but Nonbella persists. At her birthday ball at eighteen she painfully realizes her plainness compared with the charms of the lovely young guests, but the amulet reflects only her radiance of soul. Prince Carissimo is finally smitten. He proposes, explaining to Nonbella that she possesses a beautiful jewel—her heart.

The story is Charlotte's retelling of the brief life of Evelina, the ugly duckling to her beautiful sister Leonora, and Evy's courtship by the sophisticated Ferdinand. And it is placed in December, the month of Evelina's death. However much the pages from January through November reveal aspects of Charlotte, it is December which seems the reason for the book. "The Precious Jewel" was her gentle act of exorcism.

Both Charlotte and Anthony's Louisa had long hoped that Natty would choose Constance or Annie as bride. That had not happened, and as both girls were drawn into a wider society, Annie fell in love with Eliot Yorke, a younger son of the 4th Earl of Hardwicke. The Hardwickes, of Wimpole Hall, near Cambridge, had long been close to Sir Anthony, and it was on a visit to Aston Clinton in 1867 for a shooting party that the Earl's second son, Victor, at twenty-seven, had collapsed and died. It created a link of shared family tragedies. Eliot, the third son, was equerry to Prince Alfred, Duke of Edinburgh, captain of the *Galatea*, which had just returned from the Far East. By the autumn of 1872 Annie had been ready (as Connie put it) "to force a consent." Acknowledging other marriages of Rothschild women not only out of the *mischpocheh*—family—but out of the faith, Anthony and Louisa yielded. Lionel and Mayer opposed the betrothal, but in her household Charlotte and her sons were persuasive. Soon Alfred wrote to his Aunt Louisa to assure her of the support of "everyone at Gunnersbury," and Charlotte added her good wishes.

In November 1872, from Balmoral, the Queen sent her felicitations via a lady-in-waiting, and George Samuel, a friend of Sir Anthony's, observed with satisfaction, "You have broken a barrier unfitted for our times." A civil wedding in a registry office in February 1873 was followed by a service in the Hardwickes' family chapel at Wimpole, and the couple moved into a house in Curzon Street, Mayfair—a wedding gift from the bride's parents. When Eliot's father died the next year, and Eliot's high-living brother Charles succeeded to the earldom, Eliot reluctantly took his brother's seat as an M.P. for Cambridgeshire. He preferred sailing his steam yacht *Garland*. At an open-air political rally in 1878—he despised such public meetings—he caught a cold which developed into pneumonia, and he died that December. Neither of the Aston Clinton girls—Connie married an effete socialite, Cyril Flower, who became an M.P. and minor peer—would have any children.

Also in Charlotte's orbit in the early 1870s, Disraeli at sixty-eight was discovering, not entirely comfortably, the allure to widows of a major politician bereft of a wife. Several ladies (at least one an aggressive harridan) offered him inheritances as well as themselves, but he became captivated by a witty and attractive married lady, Selina, wife of the 4th Earl of Bradford, who accepted his attentions with more patience than ardor. Disraeli even considered marrying her widowed elder sister, Lady Chesterfield, to remain close to Lady Bradford. He still adored Charlotte, but she had never been available to be wooed, and he explained his constancy at Piccadilly House and at Gunnersbury to the Earl of Bradford, who was more interested in his racing stud than his racy (but loyal) spouse, in terms not of Charlotte but of access to her husband: "Baron Rothschild . . . is a Liberal," but he "knows everything." Yet was that the reason Dizzy wrote to Charlotte in July to ask for a gift? He wanted a portrait of Lionel, he claimed, whose short beard and wiry hair had now turned white. "My lost, or my absent friends," he wrote, referring to the pictures in his study, "are assembling about me in my solitude, and it pains me that the countenance of one of my dearest should be wanting." At her insistence no contemporary likeness of Charlotte existed.

Awaiting, still, a General Election, he spent the early weeks of the parliamentary recess in September 1873 at Hughenden. With the exception of an emissary from the Queen, he wrote to Charlotte, "I have neither seen, nor spoken, to a human being." After a stay in Brighton for the sea air, as in earlier days with Mary Anne, he spent the late autumn and early winter at the country seats of friends, including Gunnersbury. "[P]ray consent to spend some time under this roof," Charlotte urged on September 11, 1873. "The sooner you come and the later you stay after the 1st of October which is our great fast & day of atonement, the better we shall all be pleased and the more grateful we shall feel."

Everywhere Disraeli went but for Gunnersbury and Piccadilly House, where he could be himself, he was greeted as the future prime minister, but Gladstone had not yet made his decision to hold a General Election that would pre-empt the opening of Parliament. Disraeli learned about it only when he opened his *Times* at Edwards's

Hotel on Saturday morning, January 24, 1874. (*The Times* still published only classified advertisements on its first pages.)

Readers early the next year, when Anthony Trollope published his harsh and sweeping political novel *The Way We Live Now*, would recall that its rogue financier of uncertain origins, Augustus Melmotte, hints "to certain political friends that at the next general election he should try the City." But the City suggests (although Trollope does not spell this out) a banker of impeccable reputation, Lionel de Rothschild. Having second thoughts, the uncouth Melmotte, a perverse caricature of a Rothschild who speculates in high-flying railway stock and with his gauche wife, allegedly from Bohemia (perhaps a twisted Charlotte), gives grand political dinners in ostentatiously bad taste, connives a candidacy instead from Westminster. Trollope had sometimes ridden with the Rothschild hounds, but his ambiguities left much to the imagination.

The actual campaign opened a fissure between the Rothschilds and Gladstonian Liberalism, as Lionel preferred pragmatism to party rigidity. Although politicking was difficult for him, as he had little use of his legs, he participated in a large election meeting, reported by *The Times*, in which he contended that Gladstone's proposal to abolish the income tax, intended to be popular with voters, "would deprive the country of £9,000,000 a year." To replace the lost revenue "there must be more new taxes." When the partisan audience shouted "No!" and "Economy!" Lionel warned that no government economies could match the deficit. "Baron Rothschild's opinion was that new taxes must be imposed, and that they must be imposed upon property. He [also] suggested license duties, such as are paid . . . in Austria." He was one of the few rich men who could make such a proposal without being suspected of evading what was properly due from him. No one better represented probity.

Disraeli's Conservatives turned Gladstone out, and substitute taxes became unnecessary. But cut by his own Liberals in the City for his fiscal reality, Lionel lost his seat. He would not try to regain it and may have felt, with Charlotte, a sense of relief. He knew that he had made history by having been there. Although his elective career was over, he would no longer need to access the House of Commons by backstairs and wheelchair. And he would have his evenings with Charlotte back. With Dizzy in office, Lionel would be more power-ful than ever.

CHAPTER ELEVEN

SUEZ AND AFTER

1874–1879

Although Lionel's health continued to decline, after morning tea with Charlotte he took his carriage implacably to New Court every working day. Charlotte concealed her anxieties beneath a façade that her circle saw as unchanged. She could be counted upon for grand gestures and quiet ones. For Disraeli's luncheon celebrating his new Tory government, in the Foreign Office's reception rooms, she had sent from Gunnersbury to supplement Gunter's of Piccadilly, the leading caterer in London, "six large baskets of English strawberries, 200 heads of gigantic asperges, and the largest and finest Strasburg foie gras that was ever seen. All agreed that the change of nationality had not deprived Alsace of its skill." Lionel could not attend.

The Baron was largely restricted now to his own table. As he usually blossomed when interesting people dined with them, Charlotte tried to assure stimulating company for him even when she preferred privacy. Disraeli joined them every Sunday he could. Following one dinner, alone with his greatest friend, although he scrupulously addressed him as "Baron" (while Lionel used "Ben"), Disraeli observed to Lionel that as prime minister he had to sacrifice pleasure to business while Parliament sat. When Lionel later mentioned that to Charlotte, she wondered whether such sacrifice included "the hours and hours at the feet at Lady B[radford]," who had captured his "septuagenarian heart." Disraeli's seventieth birthday was not until December 21, but the feline remark may have suggested some jealousy. His long and warm relationship with Charlotte and Lionel had to be delicately balanced. Often "Dis" was their only guest, explaining, "Solitude has charm in the country, but not in the city."

On one occasion he invited himself midweek, arriving just after Lionel had returned from his doctor. It made no difference, Lionel wrote to Laury. "As we are quite alone, if he likes to come we shall be glad to see him and hear all his news." It was not only Lionel who received the news. Out of politics, he continued to be a source of reliable political information. Learning of the fall of the latest revolving-door French Cabinet from a telegram delivered to Lionel at dinner, Disraeli complained afterwards to his foreign minister about their Paris embassy's inefficiency.

Following a visit in January 1875 *en famille*—he often stayed overnight—Disraeli wrote to Lady Bradford that he had "found the great Baron much broken and greatly complaining, and I think his family are very anxious about him. This would be a great death, for his brains are as large as his fortune and he does everything." Charlotte worried about Lionel far more than did the Prime Minister, but she kept her concerns to herself. Lionel, a stoic about his handicaps, must have been extremely unwell to have suffered aloud.

Much more ill than Lionel was the head of the Vienna house, Anselm—cousin to both Charlotte and Lionel, and father of Ferdinand. Anselm had received, in 1861, the Austrian political equivalent of an English peerage, a seat in the Reichsrat, a sham legislature. When Baron Anselm died on July 27, 1874, his three sons inherited huge sums. Ferdy's share enabled him to buy the Buckinghamshire hilltop upon which he built Waddesdon. His younger brother Salomon Albert ("Salbert"), continued the banking firm. (The eldest, another Nathaniel Mayer, was disinclined to business.) Salbert also would become chairman of the largely Rothschild-financed Nordbahn. In 1876 he married his cousin Bettina, Laury and Alphonse's eldest daughter. Her grandmother Betty, Anselm's sister, was "sad and mournful," Leopold reported to his parents from Paris about the reading of the will, "but when she heard that her name had not been mentioned in her brother's testament, either as legatee or with a word of affection—the tears were dried up & the old grievances recalled."

Lionel's generation was falling away. His genial brother Mayer, once "Tup," had long been softened by his lifestyle into "Muffy." (Not long before his death, Anthony's Louise had written to Charlotte of "the great Baron's bountiful measurements.") Mayer died of a heart ailment on February 6, 1874. He was only fifty-five. The funeral took place on February 10 at his town house, once his mother Hannah's, at 107 Piccadilly, and he was buried at semi-rural Willesden Cemetery, to the west of Regents Park, opened only the year before. There, after Rabbi Benjamin Ascher read the service, the mourners replied in Hebrew, "May he come to his appointed place in peace," and cast the traditional handfuls of earth on the oak coffin. Lionel was physically unable to be present, but his sons, and James's sons from Paris, attended.

Although Mayer was M.P. from Hythe to the end, and an efficient banker when called upon, the stock he had most valued had four legs. His cattle won prizes and his horses won races. His vast, museumlike Mentmore housed striking art treasures, and invitations to his country seat were coveted by sultans and princes. His nephew Ferdy wrote to Lord Rosebery in response to a condolence letter that the "youthful and kindly" Mayer had been "the centre of all our amusement which can never be replaced." Juliana would survive him only three years, leaving their only child, Hannah, twenty-two at Mayer's death, sole mistress of Mentmore and his millions.

With Lionel still ailing, Charlotte was unable, despite torrid summer weather, to enjoy her luxuriant gardens at Gunnersbury until mid-August. Although Lionel insisted upon daily attendance, however painful, at New Court, she would not, she told Leonora, "even upon charitable errands," take her carriage "about the streets of London . . . in the glow of day." With the expected supplicants calling, daily, upon her, charity began at home. One was a young Roman Catholic priest from Brentford who told her that he could not rebuild his school as the funds of St. George's Parish covered only half the cost. "Of course," she wrote, "I shall help a little." Charlotte's "little" was always substantial.

When finally at Gunnersbury, she could not "walk much" in the "oppressive" heat. "The older I grow," she confessed, "the more bat-like I become, and able to flit about only in the evening, but it is sinful to complain." She envied Leo's holiday venue in the highlands of the Swiss Engadine, where the air was like "the external application of iced champagne." An unexpected diversion was the visit of the Swedish prima donna Christine Nilsson, the operatic Violetta, Martha, Cherubino, and Donna Elvira, then thirty-one, whom Alfred brought with members of her company to "warble" through the evening. Professionals under Charlotte's roof were rare. She had once financed the training of young musicians and, to launch them, had had them perform for guests at Gunnersbury or at Piccadilly House. Such entertainments had ended with Evy's death.

Gunnersbury otherwise remained quiet, but for the cooing of doves, the buzzing of bees, and the faint rumble from their four neighboring rail lines. Charlotte loved all the familiar sounds. "I really do believe that human beings possess the double attributes of . . . cats and dogs, the fidelity and devotion of the latter, and the attachment to houses and places of the former."

When Lionel resumed his daily routine at New Court, she urged him to curtail his hours and return by six-thirty to drive with her about the London she had never seen although she had lived there for thirty-eight years. She knew little of such locales as the South

Bank. "I should like to see Lambeth Palace . . . and the old quaint houses around it. I have seen them only [from] across the river." It was nearly seven one evening when Lionel returned, but summer light lingered. "London even when more or less foggy or smoky is never uninteresting," she contended, but her exploration to the Archbishop of Canterbury's residence and its environs proved a disappointment. Lambeth Palace was only "curious," and the back of venerable St. Thomas's Hospital was "finer than the front." There was "positively nothing to be admired."

After Mayer's death the family became anxious about Anthony, still "Billy" to his elder brother. Much more of a financier than Mayer had been, Anthony was self-effacing at New Court, where Lionel was dominant, yet a tough negotiator and a tireless traveler and art connoisseur. (Lionel once remarked to Leo, "Billy is returning from Nuremberg, which will make Colnaghi [& Co., the art dealers] happy.") Where Lionel in earlier years had often handled sticky money matters for Prince Albert, and the Prince of Wales might dine with Lionel and shoot with Mayer, he would borrow only from Anthony—who quietly arranged a £160,000 New Court mortgage on the Sandringham estate to stave off Bertie's creditors. In August 1874 the Queen learned of it and was helplessly indignant.

Like Mayer, Anthony bred livestock and kept a stud, but his passion away from the firm was to assemble shooting parties at Aston Clinton to massacre clouds of pheasants. The good life had not been good for his heart, however, and he was seriously ill through 1875.

Although Lionel himself could do little walking unaided, and felt cold summer and winter, Dr. Chepmell was satisfied with his condition. At home Lionel "objected to air," Charlotte wrote in May 1875, "and continues to have a fire night and morning in his dressing room." At work again as usual, he often saw powerful people not listed on his calendar, and some slipped into Piccadilly House after hours. After bargaining with Russian diplomats about cooling off rivalries in combustible Afghanistan, Disraeli "paid a flying visit to your father," Charlotte wrote to Leo on May 14, 1875, "and told him of his immense success in negotiating for the maintenance of peace on the [Asian] continent." Although the "Great Game" would continue unabated in Central Asia, Dizzy had needed someone to whom to boast, or with whom he could consult confidentially.

Lionel's gradual withdrawal from public life only enhanced his reputation as a mysterious, unseen figure able to influence events and pluck profits from them. In a letter to Sidney Colvin that June, which Robert Louis Stevenson claimed was only "mild, babbling, sunny idiocy" but was actually darker than that, the young Scottish writer, twenty-five and still unsuccessful, confessed, "I want coin badly. . . . I would like . . . as much money as my friend the Baron Rothschild can spare." And he fantasized,

> I used to look across to Rothschild of a morning when we were brushing our hair, and say—(This is quite true: only we were on the opposite side of the street; and though I used to look over, I cannot say I ever detected the bugger; he feared to meet my eagle eye, and lurked shamefully behind the walls of his Pallis.)—Well, I used to say to him, "Rothschild, old man, lend us five hundred francs"; and it is characteristic of Rothy's dry humour, that he used never to reply when it was a question of money. He was a very humorous dog, indeed was Rothy.

That fantasy, on a grander scale, became a reality to the public a few months later. In November 1869, in the presence of Empress Eugénie and with the benediction of slippery Monsignor Bauer, the Suez Canal had opened to shipping, much of it involving the British Indian trade. For his granting a concession to a French company to build it, the Khedive of Egypt, Sa'id Pasha, received shares and then bought the unsubscribed shares. His successor, Isma'il Pasha, spending lavishly and unable to live within his large income, became quickly in debt, at ruinous interest, to European financiers. When in mid-November 1875 he had little left to bargain with, he began trying to raise money on his Suez holdings. The editor of the *Pall Mall Gazette*, Frederick Greenwood, learned about the Khedive's anxiety to sell his 177,000 shares (of 400,000 outstanding), apparently to a French syndicate, from Henry Oppenheim, formerly a former Frankfurt investor, recently settled in London. Later, Oppenheim claimed that because he had become proprietor of the *Daily News*, it was improper for him to communicate directly with the government. Instead he informed Greenwood and Baron Lionel, an old friend. Greenwood immediately told young Lord Derby, the foreign minister; Disraeli learned of it from Lionel.

On November 20, Disraeli had written to Lady Bradford that he was living "quite alone" and was not even going to the Rothschilds'— where "there is ever something to learn, and somebody distinguished to meet." He appeared to be concealing his sources of information from the gossipy Selina, for he and Derby were at odds over Suez. Derby telegraphed suspiciously to the Consul General in Cairo, General Stanton, and to his ambassador in Paris, concluding that the purchase "would be a bad one financially" and create "disagreeable" tensions with the Sultan of Turkey and with prideful France. Disraeli was hastening in the opposite direction. Having assured himself of Lionel's financing, he summoned his Cabinet the same day, and between the 18th and 24th held five more meetings to bring anxious colleagues into line.

After the first discussion, almost a debate, Disraeli claimed excitedly to the Queen, "I was so decided and absolute with Lord Derby . . . that he ultimately adopted my views." But the Khedive, he added, was desperate: "[He] now says, that it is absolutely necessary that he should have between three & four millions sterling by the 30th of this month! . . . Scarcely breathing time! But the thing must be done."

The year before, when Ferdinand de Lesseps, who built and operated the Canal, had raised passage fees in defiance of an international commission examining charges, Disraeli had approached Lionel to use his influence to have the Canal internationally administered, so that no government, nor the Suez Canal Company itself, could close it to shipping. Lionel had sent Natty secretly to Paris to ask, also, whether de Lesseps would sell the company to the British government, but he had refused. Still, Lionel had been prepared to back a purchase before the new emergency arose.

Myths about how the Rothschild involvement occurred, and how the transaction was accomplished, include Monty Corry's hurrying from Downing Street to St. Swithin's Lane, where the Baron was supposedly interrupted while eating muscatel grapes and, as he agreed to extend millions to Disraeli, was said to have calmly spit out the pips. The pips were fiction. As Parliament was in recess, Lionel had already promised Disraeli the funds, an enormous sum in contemporary buying power, but subject to Cabinet approval. That came on November 24, 1875, after which the Prime Minister rushed to New Court. Lionel wrote afterwards to Leo, "Dizzy has just left; he has the difficulty of [explaining] our putting ourselves at the head of a large financial operation . . ." Since Disraeli did not want to be "attacked by the opposition," his potential difficulties required "a first-rate performer to get over."

As Lionel was writing to his son, Disraeli was informing Victoria. "It is just settled: you have it, Madam," he wrote. He claimed that the French had been "outgeneraled." But four millions sterling had to be made available—almost immediately: "There was only one firm that c[oul]d do it—the Rothschilds. They behaved admirably; advanced the money at a low rate, and the entire interest of the Khedive is now yours." Four million pounds in 1875 terms was the equivalent of 8.3 percent of the annual British budget. Such an outlay was bound to raise questions in Parliament. And public misunderstanding of the coup, which Disraeli encouraged, was that the entire ownership of the Canal had been purchased. Although the millions secured a powerful, effectively controlling, interest in the Canal, the Khedive had owned somewhat less that half the shares. Also, he had not confided that, in previous need, he had pawned his share coupons through

1894. The Khedive would have to pay interest on that. Yet for Britain the purchase was a diplomatic as well as a practical triumph.

Lionel anticipated problems in the aftermath. He had to await payment, which was not guaranteed. He had to prevent the huge sum from affecting international markets or the price of money. And, having kept the deal a secret, he had to prevent outrage among his Paris cousins and a breakdown of their crucial relationship. As Disraeli argued to the irate Prince of Wales, who found out about the transaction from *The Times of India* while touring the subcontinent,

> Our friends, the Rothschilds, distinguished themselves. They alone cd. have accomplished what we wanted, & they had only 4 & 20 hours to make up their minds, whether they wd., or could, incur an immediate liability of 4 millions. One of their difficulties was, that they cd. not appeal to their strongest ally, their own family in Paris, for Alphonse is *si francesse* that he wd. have betrayed the whole scheme instantly.

Following the transaction, Lionel recognized the need for some cousinly sensitivity and invited the rue Laffitte to take part. The strategy worked: Alphonse put his resources at the call of New Court. "We have the pleasure of receiving your good letters," he wrote, "in which you have told us of the operation you have concluded . . . We accept with pleasure your offer of participation and will keep the money ready at the times you indicate. The news . . . has produced a very strong reaction here."

First to publish the news, thanks to Lionel, was Delane, in *The Times*. Although Charlotte was finding him increasingly cranky and difficult, the editor still dined regularly at Piccadilly House. He was glad, he wrote wryly to the Rothschilds, that Disraeli "had set right that little scene with Pharaoh which has so long been owing."

Encouraged by Gladstone, Liberals in the Commons attacked Lionel's charging 5 percent interest and a 2.5 percent commission, cagily annualizing the interest to inflate the numbers, although costs ended after four months once Parliament authorized payment. Ferdy wrote to Lionel that he was reading the speeches from both sides, deplored former Chancellor of the Exchequer Sir Robert Lowe's "coarse" remarks, and thought that the family had emerged very creditably. The firm had risked paying out pounds that, in a volatile market, might have been repaid in cheaper money. It was part of the merchant banking business to take such risks with secrecy and with speed—and to take the profits when stratagems worked. To Monty Corry, Lionel also observed that the Bank of England could not have been *"compelled"* to furnish the funds and "could not have found the required sum without grave disturbance of the money market."

One potentially damaging accusation remained to be dismissed. In the Commons on February 28, 1876, Natty's participation, as a Member of Parliament, was questioned, as the Act on Privilege precluded conflicts of interest. Natty then rose to point out that he was not a partner in N. M. Rothschild & Sons, and made no decisions. His father was, but no longer sat in the Commons. (Anthony, a partner, now very ill, did not participate.) Since there was nothing else to question, Parliament approved payment of £4,075,996 13s. 7d. in reimbursement and commission for New Court. The shares became the government's, and the market price proved the success of the deal. Shares purchased at £19 had already risen to £34, and at their maximum in 1935 would be valued at £528. Disraeli emerged with enhanced prestige, as did the Rothschilds, who earned nearly £100,000 (£53,000 of it in interest) by exploiting an enormous international opportunity.

Ironically, although Gladstone was bitter at Lionel's fait accompli, and it was clear to him that Natty, closer than ever to Disraeli, was drifting away from the Liberal Party, Charlotte dismissed factionalism from her drawing room. "What do you say to the visitor who is now with dear Ma, whilst I am writing this?" Lionel wrote to Laury and Alphonse in Paris from New Court before the final parliamentary division on Suez payments took place. "I have just heard that the famous Mr. Gladstone is with her drinking tea and eating bread and butter. I doubt whether he will come and see me." But he would visit Charlotte, and they safely discussed theology.

As the Suez affair unfolded, Anthony's heart was failing. Following medical advice that sea air might be salubrious, a yacht had been chartered for him in Southampton Water. As early as July 18, 1875, when Disraeli had called upon his neighbor at Grosvenor Place, he was too ill to see anyone. "I am sorry—very—for Sir Anthony," Dizzy wrote to Lady Bradford: "a thoro[ugh]ly good fellow, the most genial being I ever knew, the most kind-hearted and most generous."

Once Anthony was conveyed to Southampton early in September, Lionel and Charlotte would not see him again. Louise reported that Anthony "enjoys the sea air and varying panorama of ships and boats, giving him constantly something new to look at whilst on deck." His condition remained hopeless. He died aboard ship on January 4, 1876.

The obituarist in *The Times* (commissioned by Delane) observed that Sir Anthony's life was "not eventful and he was less known, probably, to the public than either of his two brothers"—the writer forgetting the late, expatriate Nat. It noted his having been president of the United Synagogue and his many benefactions, which helped maintain a "voluntary Poor Law"[1] for the Jewish community. Anthony was buried in a plain oak coffin at Willesden on Sunday, January 9. Police stood at all street corners from Grosvenor Place to his last resting place, assisting one of the largest processions of the kind in decades, the mourning carriages including the Russian and Austrian ambassadors, the Lord Mayor, and the Governor of the Bank of England. "According to invariable custom," *The Times* reported, "no ladies were present at the ceremonial," where aged Chief Rabbi N. M. Adler quoted the words of King David on the death of

---

1. The Poor Laws were early nineteenth-century welfare legislation, more mean-spirited than their surface intention and lacking in humanity what they made up in economy. Jewish community welfare attempted to keep needy Jews off the demeaning public rolls.

Abner, Saul's general: "Know you not that a great Prince and a great man hath fallen in Israel." Again, Lionel was not able to be present, nor was he at the memorial service with Charlotte and Laury at the Bell Lane school, where two thousand pupils crowded into the assembly hall. There, Rabbi A. L. Green of the Great Portland Street Synagogue eulogized Anthony "for the great claims which he had upon the affections of everyone." N. M. Rothschild & Sons was down to its last son.

Circumstances now made it essential that Leopold become his father's legs and that Natty, who was now Sir Nathaniel, his uncle's baronetcy having devolved upon him, become more involved in the firm. Lionel went almost daily to his desk at New Court, and to the hushed Partners' Room, moving about restlessly in his wheelchair. When he was home, agents and clients came to Piccadilly House, sometimes while he was still at breakfast with Charlotte. She, too, was now ailing, with a cyst on an eyelid affecting her diminishing sight and chest "spasms" that caused Dr. Cameron to look in. Neither was able to travel to Paris for the wedding of their eldest granddaughter, Bettina, eighteen, Laury's firstborn, to "Salbert" of Vienna on March 22, 1876—yet another match within the cousinhood, and nearly the last.

Remembering her own embarrassment, now forty years before, Charlotte was anxious about Bettina's wedding night, and Lionel wrote for her to Leo, in Paris, remarking, too, "So many good ladies find themselves as well the day after as the day before." He also wanted to know, perhaps hopefully for Charlotte, who knew that bridesmaids often became brides, "How do the princesses of Israel look? Has anyone made an impression on anyone?"

At Piccadilly House, Charlotte and Lionel marked the occasion quietly by having the servants—who invited forty guests—celebrate, and they danced through the night while the bride's grandparents dined early and alone. When Lionel was away at New Court, Charlotte often now lunched with Nelly, her current favorite spaniel, at the Baroness's feet with her own bowl. She still called for her carriage, though with less frequency than in more energetic years, to visit the most wretched districts in the East End to determine what assistance might be useful to embody self-help rather than passive bounty.

A decade later, "East-Ending" became a modish pastime for society grandes dames seeking to adopt causes. In Mary Augusta (Mrs. Humphry) Ward's immensely popular novel *Robert Elsmere* (1888), Lady Charlotte is advised to wear "a dowdy dress and veil" for venturing into the tenement district, and promises to borrow an outfit from her housekeeper. When Elsmere, the reformist minister, seeks out the bad but beautiful Madame de Netteville, he is told, "She is East-Ending for a change. We all do it nowadays." Was Lady Charlotte a sly borrowing from the Baroness?

At the burgeoning Jews' Free School in Spitalfields, Charlotte still examined both teachers and students. She still maintained at her own expense a kitchen for the sick poor at Sandys Row, Bishopsgate, where prepared meals were distributed, and the Home for Aged Incurables she had founded in 1859 in Bedford Square, Commercial Road. With all her ongoing benefactions she was in effect head of a large, informal charitable enterprise and had to employ almoners to oversee them all.

Lionel remained "fidgety" in the aftermath of the "Egypt business" as government debts there had not been pared down by the Canal shares purchase, which only bailed out the Khedive. Lord Derby sent Stephen Cave, the Paymaster-General, to Cairo to investigate, and Lionel sent Natty to consult with Alphonse as to whether Rothschild assistance in consolidating the Egyptian debt was too great a risk. Only in 1878 would the London and Paris houses combine to float an £8,500,000 loan, arranged after a new European crisis intervened.

Lionel had written to the empire-minded Disraeli on May 26, 1876, "I hope very soon to be able to congratulate you on the conclusion of an arrangement, which will ensure peace for a good many years owing to an energetic and determined policy." Peace would not be easy to manage, as so many conflicting interests and ambitions were involved. Turkey, mismanaged and falling apart, wanted to cling to Balkan dependencies, where the Christian inhabitants were in revolt. Russia wanted to move into the agitated territories and open its way into the eastern Mediterranean. Austria, a hodgepodge of nationalities, felt threatened by ethnic divisiveness. France and Germany were seeking aggrandizements abroad. Britain was at odds with Russia about its expansion into areas perceived as London's spheres of influence. Also, almost every nation, seeing popular appeal in the gesture, deplored how badly the holy places in Jerusalem were overseen from Constantinople.

For the Paris and London Rothschilds, bond deals with Russia between 1870 and 1875 worth £62 million were in possible jeopardy if war came, as were £5.5 million in loans to Turkey. If they backed Russia out of self-interest, how would that conflict with their propping up Turkey? While in pseudo-retirement, Gladstone had been manipulating his Liberal puppets in Parliament, but now he saw opportunities to combine religion and politics to oust Disraeli. He would campaign against his political nemesis, but ostensibly against Turkey (and implicitly for Russia), allegedly to protect Balkan Christians and Palestinian holy sites.

Now past seventy and in poor health, Disraeli could no longer preside over what he and the Queen considered Britain's interests while retaining what she called his "cumbersome burden" as day-to-day political leader of the House of Commons. Victoria proposed elevating him to the less strenuous House of Lords as Earl of Beaconsfield. On August 11, 1876, still using black-bordered paper in memory of Mary Anne, Dizzy wrote, employing, for him, a rare salutation,

> My dear Lionel,
> You are such a dear friend, & have proved yourself so true a one, that I should be annoyed if you hear of any important change in my life from any other quarter, except myself. . . . I

have yielded to the Queen's strong wish that I should conduct Her Majesty's affairs in the other house of Parliament. . . . I hope, when you have heard my reasons for it, I may have your approval.

That Friday, responding to a Liberal attack in the Commons on government inaction about Turkish atrocities against Christians in Bulgaria, Disraeli closed with a characteristic note, "What our duty is at this critical moment is to maintain the Empire of England." He left the lobby leaning on Monty Corry's arm, never to return to the Commons. The next morning his earldom was announced. The elevation altered nothing in his relationship with Lionel and Charlotte, which remained as affectionate as ever, although all three were ailing in different degrees and he was no longer up to sending Charlotte handwritten spur-of-the-moment notes from Parliament before visiting, inquiring whether she was alone. He merely came.

A month later, Louise wrote to Charlotte, also on mourning paper, from Deeside in Scotland. She could not observe the new year Holy Days, she confessed, as before, and had to get away. They were too full of "painful recollections." For decades the Rothschilds had gathered for a Passover seder in the spring at 148 Piccadilly, and for the autumn High Holy Days at a seaside locale like Brighton, or at Gunnersbury. The family was now fractured by marriages and by deaths.

Disraeli's elevation meant a by-election to fill his Buckinghamshire seat. Since Natty was M.P. for Aylesbury, Liberal political managers assumed that out of party loyalty he would employ his regional influence to get the tenantry out to vote, and to help finance a win. Yet Sir Nathaniel cautiously did nothing, for him the safest course while he remained technically a Liberal. He had not (at least yet) become a Conservative—only a Disraelian. Earl Granville complained to Gladstone, "The Rothschilds are behaving abominably."

They continued behaving abominably, for Gladstone's "Eastern question" campaign across Britain exploited a naked religious appeal that likened the expulsion of the Turks from the Balkans, and the Holy Land, to a new crusade. He and some of his allies employed anti-Semitic rhetoric in seeing Disraeli's Turkish leanings and Russophobia as a reflection of his Jewish background. Writing to Dizzy in March 1877, Lionel called his policies "patriotic and just," and Disraeli told the Queen that he was acquiring confidential information on Eastern affairs through Rothschild connections in France, Germany, and Austria. Yet Disraeli's own foreign minister, Lord Derby, was being swayed in the opposite direction by his pro-Russian wife. The Russian ambassador, Count Peter Shuvalov, complained to Lady Derby in December 1877 (as her husband wrote sourly in his diary) that the Rothschilds "are in daily communications with the Premier, hear all that passes, & use it for their own purposes. I am certain that the leakage of cabinet secrets . . . is mainly in that quarter. . . . [T]he Rothschilds no doubt get their news directly from himself." Derby remained peeved that Lionel's complex and informal multinational intelligence network had picked up a report as early as January 1877 that Russia was preparing to invade the Turkish Balkans in April—and that the Baron had passed the information to Disraeli. Derby's own sources found out six weeks later. His sympathies were rather Gladstonian in foreign affairs—for less involvement, rather than more. Ultimately, events would force Disraeli to replace Derby with Lord Salisbury, then Secretary for India. To Salisbury, national prestige was "a precious thing to have"—and Disraeli intended to have it and not relinquish it.

On occasion Lionel asked, in effect, for some reciprocity, requesting from Disraeli, on January 10, 1877, his formal representations on behalf of Romanian Jews under Russian control, "who are being tormented in the usual way." Apparently, since they were not Christian victims, the subject had not engaged the interest of Gladstone.

Despite divisions in his Cabinet, Disraeli retained his mastery of Parliament, and on May 18, 1877, Leopold wrote to Lionel and Charlotte, "[T]he Government must be enchanted at their wonderful majority & I hope now that Gladstone will remain quiet for a short time." It was the last cheerful letter he wrote to both parents. His next surviving letter, undated, was to "Papa":

> Il Dottore will give you the latest accounts of dear Mamma & will tell you that it was an excellent night.
>
> This morning Mamma is very quiet & has not talked any nonsense of consequence. I hope Laury arrived quite comfortably.
>
> > Your son,
> > Leo

The next note, also undated and from Gunnersbury, apparently sent by messenger to Piccadilly House for Lionel, reported, "Mamma had a good dinner & was asleep the minute she was in bed about 9 o'c & has not moved since then—so I think she will have an excellent night."

Many letters and documents were later burned by Natty, apparently to conceal such family delicacies. Charlotte's friends and relatives seem to have avoided writing about it to each other. There is nearly nothing in the surviving record about her apparent stroke. She had been having what seemed minor medical problems, including headaches; she had lived for years with Lionel's increasing disability, with which he had coped, seemingly, better than Charlotte had; and she had never recovered from the shock of Evelina's sudden death. Leo's few surviving letters to her suggest that her recovery was slow, that she remained at Gunnersbury during her convalescence, and that with her mind still unclear she was at the least a semi-invalid into 1878.

Although this was a crushing blow, Lionel would not concede New Court to Natty and sit at Charlotte's bedside: At first she did not even know him, and such a vigil seemed useless. Grimly, he continued his routine. Like Sherlock Holmes's brother, Mycroft (an auditor of government accounts), who would sit at the window of his London club and seem to know, or infer, everything beyond, the eldest Rothschild, bound to his chair, gleaned intelligence from his agents and continued working.

With the Balkans in crisis, and Gladstone taking Russia's side, Lionel left it to Natty in December 1877 to inform the Liberal leadership, unyieldingly hostile to Disraeli, that the Prime Minister "had no intention or wish for war." No one doubted that the Rothschilds were privy to confidential information from the Tory side, and also from European informants.

In June 1878, soon after the defeat of Turkey by Russia, and the humiliating Treaty of San Stefano by which large Balkan tracts were ceded to the Tsar, Disraeli and Bismarck forced Russia into a conference in Berlin to review the concessions. Although the Queen thought that Disraeli—Lord Beaconsfield—was too ill to travel, he went anyway, with Lord Salisbury to manage the details, in a posh special train furnished at Calais by Baron Alphonse. Lionel's sources assisted the Prime Minister in playing his rather weak hand. Gerson Bleichröder[2] even reported to Lionel from Bismarck's camp. Somehow the wily Disraeli emerged, just short of an asthmatic collapse, with concessions from Russia which deprived it, through its Bulgarian satellite, of an outlet on the Aegean—and thus the Mediterranean. Turkey would survive a little longer.

Always conspiracy-minded, Disraeli told Lionel that he had been "the subject of espionage" in Berlin; "& those who make up my bags had actually been asked whether I were in regular communication with you. I decided to disappoint their malignity, which has only occasioned you the loss [here] of some agreeable gossip." (He assumed that his letters to Lionel were being surreptitiously opened and read.) Disraeli returned in triumph, and Lord Barrington of the British delegation wrote to Constance Rothschild Flower (now married to Leo's Cambridge crony), "Lord Beaconsfield . . . has been a great lion here, the *Lion of Judah!*"

---

2. The Berlin banker received a supply of Château Lafite from Alphonse for the delegates.

A note from Lionel to Disraeli dated July 18, 1878, congratulates him on what appeared to be his Berlin coup. And the head of the London firm was still keeping his eye on other things. Perhaps in part as therapy for Charlotte, he made, sight unseen, the most substantial art purchase en bloc for which he had ever negotiated, the Jonkheer Willem van Loon collection in Amsterdam. It comprised eighty-two Dutch and Flemish paintings left by his widow at her death in 1877. Both Lionel and Charlotte shared a love for the art of the Low Countries.

As Charlotte slowly recovered, remaining at Gunnersbury, Lionel and the children were at a loss as to how to restore her equilibrium. They eschewed reporting anything that might upset her. It is unclear whether she was told of the marriage, on March 20, 1878, of Mayer and Juliana's only child, Hannah, twenty-six, to the Earl of Rosebery, in Christ Church, Mayfair. Hannah had inherited upwards of two million pounds and Mentmore, with its treasures. Had Charlotte been reading the *Jewish Chronicle*, she would have found the editors expressing "the most poignant grief" that Hannah was marrying outside her people, but Mayer was dead, and beyond objection, and it fell to Disraeli to give away the bride. A letter from him to Charlotte a month later (April 22) establishes that she was again up to receiving mail. Another, from Lady Emily Peel dated October 21, 1878, is among the few that survive from those difficult months.

Leopold even talked to his mother blandly about horses. He had acquired Mayer's stud, including Corisande, the filly named after a heroine in Disraeli's *Lothair*. He also was managing Lionel's stables. From Newmarket on October 22, 1878, he began a letter, "My dearest Mamma, I know that you do not care to hear about racing, but still . . ." And he boasted of new turf successes. On December 2, 1878, from Ascott, his home near Leighton Buzzard (and Mentmore) acquired from his uncle Mayer, he told her of Laury's trying his favorite horse, Claro. "I hope you will have some pleasant visitors & that you will feel more comfortable," he closed.

The very fact of visitors she could host implied significant recovery, as did her reading, again, the *Revue des deux mondes*, which she had often shared with Lionel. Even more so did a Disraeli letter, opening with "Dearest Baroness," and dated January 13, 1879. Its tone suggests a delicacy in writing to someone perhaps still unready for the mixture as before. But she had already written to him. "I was very much pleased at receiving your letter," he began, "which reminded me of [the] old days, when we were often correspondents. I hope we shall continue so." His poor health, he explained, accounted for his not responding with more alacrity to her "wondrous gifts"—elegant baskets of fruit from the Gunnersbury greenhouses. When he gave his parliamentary dinner, he promised, "I intend your marvellous corbeille, & its enchanted purses, full of Alladin-like gems & jewels, shall be carried round the great table, in the Foreign Office, in procession." It was apparent that they had not seen each other since her illness, for he closed, "I hope we shall soon meet, ever dearest Baroness, Yr faithful & affectionate Beaconsfield."

Although Leo, less reluctantly than had Alfy, now assisted his father at New Court, Leopold's obsession remained horses, and a letter to Lionel on March 10, 1879, elaborated on the prospects for their stud. But he added, prudently, "I am glad to learn that the prices of Egyptian securities are better. Hoping I find you in every way perfectly satisfied . . ." His father had never relinquished his own racing stable, but because of Charlotte's dislike of racing and betting, he continued to send his horses out as "Mr. Acton," and the press in his interest kept up the fiction. It was as "Mr. Acton" that Lionel raced Sir Bevys in the 1879 Derby under his familiar colors of blue and gold. As Leopold was his legs, for years Lionel had not been at Epsom Downs for the great event, so much the social apex of the calendar that Parliament adjourned for a fortnight, on May 27, for the 100th Derby. *The Times* reported that "Mr. Acton's brown colt" had "not run this year, but . . . is bred to stay."

At the Chantilly Races, the French Derby, on May 25, Baron Alphonse's Commandant had come in second. On the 28th, after a day of persistent rain had softened the turf and altered the odds, the

Derby at Epsom was run. *"Sir Bevys,"* reported *The Times*, "had all the cut of a useful horse, sound-looking and with short legs, and such propelling power that he looked like galloping the Derby course [would be easy]." Winning was another matter, but his jockey, "who had been patiently biding his time, now brought up Sir Bevys with a well-timed rush, and having the best of Lord Rosebery's colt in the middle of the stand, drew away and won with something to spare." With a time of 3 minutes, 2 seconds, "Mr. Acton" had won his first Derby.

Lionel never ceased working—and not only for New Court. One of his letters that week was to the Chief Rabbi of Vaslui in eastern Romania, where Jews had been expelled from their homes and were starving. (Lionel had long attempted to help the Jewish communities there both politically and financially.) He told Natty that New Court could get along without him if he and Emma wanted to visit family in France, and on June 1, a Sunday, they crossed the Channel. Late that afternoon, after spending the weekend with Charlotte at Gunnersbury, where the gardens were in full flower, Lionel returned to Piccadilly House.

Although Monday, June 2, was a bank holiday, he expected to be driven on schedule to New Court, but before his usual departure hour he complained of feeling unwell and appeared to be confused. Sir William Gull and Dr. Chepmell were sent for in carriages. It seemed useless, and even upsetting, to inform Charlotte, and no one did. Alfy and Leo were found, and a telegram went to Nathaniel in Paris, urging his return.[3] With Emma and Leonora he rushed back to London—but not in time.

About midday Lionel suffered an apparent second, more severe,

---

3. A story which seems an invention is that "the day before he died, [Baron Lionel] summoned the broker Edward Wagg to his bedside at 148 Piccadilly to tell him: 'I have been looking at my fortnightly account and you have made a mistake in the addition.'" He could not have summoned anyone to his bedside, let alone troubled himself with an accounting detail.

stroke, and never recovered consciousness. Alfred and Leopold sat at their father's silent bedside through the afternoon and into the night, until he was pronounced dead at 6:30 on Tuesday morning. Immobility and years of strain from his wheelchair had taken their toll. He was seventy.

Natty—Sir Nathaniel, and never to adopt his father's baronial title—arrived early on Tuesday afternoon. Learning on Monday that Lionel had suffered a seizure and was dying, John Delane, soon to retire on grounds of poor health, rushed a message to the Rev. Henry Wace, later Dean of Canterbury, that he urgently needed an obituary of Baron de Rothschild. (Wace, who had been writing for *The Times* since 1863, was also co-editor of the ongoing *Dictionary of Christian Biography*.) Delane's cool instructions entirely belied the long intimacy he had enjoyed with Lionel and Charlotte:

> Though it cannot be said that the Jews have added much to Parliament, the removal of their exclusion was no doubt very necessary to its character, for it could not be considered the representation of the whole nation so long as one influential body was excluded. What I am most anxious to avoid is anything like adulation of wealth, and as your article will be much read and criticised abroad, where the family is much more powerful than here, I think it might be worth stating that great as its accumulations are, they are probably inferior in amount to the inherited fortunes of some of our great families.

Disraeli was gossiping happily in a letter to Lady Chesterfield early on June 3 when he interjected, "I cannot write any more. I have just received a tel. announcing the death of Baron Rothschild, one of my greatest friends, and one of the ablest men I ever knew. I am greatly shocked. Very sudden and short the illness." To Montagu Corry he referred to "this great death, which will affect much." To the Rothschild sons, Disraeli wrote, "My Dearest Children, I am overwhelmed—and cannot trust myself to say more." In such days of fast and frequent post Alfred responded for himself and Leo the same day, "My dear Lord Beaconsfield, It is only just like your usual kindness to have conveyed to us so promptly your message of sympathy. . . . Leo and I are most deeply touched. We are quite overwhelmed with grief, which is not diminished by the fact that our dear mother, whom we have just seen at Gunnersbury, seemed to share it. I ventured to send you a telegram this morning, because my dear father looked upon you as his 'dearest friend.' Pray extend your generous friendship to his children."

That Charlotte "seemed to share" her children's grief suggests the ups and downs of her recovery. Not only her sons were overwhelmed.

Bernal Osborne subdued his usual wit to write Natty sorrowfully about "my best friend your father." Gerson Bleichröder's son Hans happened to be in London when the news broke, and reported to his father in Berlin with utter incomprehension (or bias) that "few people genuinely mourned because Lionel did not know how to make himself liked and did next to nothing for the poor."

Henry Wace's obituary in *The Times* was little like what the cranky Delane, ill himself, had ordered. Writing about Rothschild's rather modest manner, given his wealth and his impact upon "the political and social world," Wace observed that the exception to the Baron's "judicious" lifestyle was "in his charitable expenditure, to which there was no apparent limit." Yet unaware of Lionel's long and stoic accommodation to pain and disability, Wace concluded, "He had, indeed, suffered so severely from illness for many years that for his own sake there is nothing to lament in his release."

On Friday, June 7, Lionel followed his brothers Mayer and Anthony to Willesden Cemetery. No invitations had been issued, as the family wanted a funeral as simple and as private as was possible, given the Baron's fame, but the press had reported that last respects might be paid at Piccadilly House beginning at nine o'clock. The unornamented oak coffin, covered with a black cloth on which were flowers from Gunnersbury and Ferrières, rested in an anteroom off the en-

trance hall. So many carriages were expected to flood Piccadilly that
the Queen's cousin, the Duke of Cambridge, among whose titles was
Ranger of Hyde Park, issued a permit enabling the procession to
Willesden to muster in the park, close to 148 Piccadilly.

The first mourners were Charlotte, her daughter, and her three
sons, followed by others of the family, ambassadors, the Prime Minister, and the Lord Mayor; then came a queue of dignitaries, male
and female, that suggested the columns of the *Court Guide* for London. Among the many financiers from abroad were (despite his son
Hans) Gerson Bleichröder of Berlin and Siegmund Warburg of
Antwerp. At nine-thirty, the Baron's servants, clerks from New
Court, and tenants on his farms filed past the coffin with authentic
grief etched on their faces.

Taking forty minutes to pass, the lengthy cortège proceeded
slowly through Park Lane, Edgware Road, Kilburn, and Willesden
Lane, past houses where blinds were drawn, and shops where shut-
ters were down, as marks of respect. At Willesden the procession to
the gravesite was led by children from the Jews' Hospital and Or-
phan Asylum; the Westminster Free School; the Jews' Free School;
the Stepney School; the Bayswater School; the "Gates of Hope"
Schools; the Villareal and Infant Schools of the Spanish and Portuguese Congregation; and the Borough Jewish Schools. Members
of the Baron's synagogue carried the coffin to the gravesite, past the
resting places of Mayer and Juliana, and Anthony, whose graves were
already covered by thick ivy. Halting the procession midway, Rabbi
Ascher, overcome with emotion and bringing the throng to tears, offered a eulogy on a line from Isaiah. Although the Baron worked successfully to vindicate the rights of his brethren "as true and loyal
British subjects," sat high "in the councils of merchant princes," and
saw his "advice . . . sought for by statesmen," the Rabbi, in more
florid rhetoric, emphasized something more:

He worked quietly and unostentatiously for the amelioration of
our social, domestic, education and political welfare, but his uni-

versal benevolence ran noiselessly through the channels of society . . . like an irrigating and fertilising rivulet, spreading comfort
and diffusing light and cheerfulness into the abodes of darkness,
misery and wretchedness. Justly may we apply to him, "Thy righteousness shall precede thee, the glory of the Eternal shall be thy
rear-guard."

The first three spadefuls of earth were placed upon the lowered
coffin by Lionel's sons, and other mourners followed somberly. At
the mortuary hall, the ceremony was open only to men, where Natty,
Alfy, and Leo said the traditional *Kaddish* prayer.

The next day, a Saturday and the Sabbath, Rabbi A. L. Green at
the Central Synagogue called on Sir Nathaniel to raise the Torah
scroll in the sight of the worshipers and repeat the *Kaddish*. Then he
took as his sermon text about Lionel the words spoken to Abraham,
"Thou shalt be a blessing."

In the pragmatic secular world, perhaps the most concisely appropriate appraisal came from *The Economist*, which observed that "the
Baron for thirty years"—it was more like forty—"guided transactions
so delicate, so large, and so likely to inspire nervousness, with great
general success, and deserves to be recorded as one of the greatest, if
not the greatest, of his kind. . . . In four great capitals, the classes
which possess nothing wish well to a firm which, of all others, most
distinctly represents capital. That is a very great proof of consummate ability in management."

In his diary the venerable Sir Moses Montefiore wrote of the great
loss he had sustained in Lionel's death: "I have known him from his
earliest youth, and ever entertained the highest esteem and regard
for him." Montefiore, Lionel's uncle, was ninety-five. It remains impossible to know how the loss of Lionel affected Charlotte, whose
mind still wavered in and out of reality. But there would be no more
weekends sitting with him in Gunnersbury's lush gardens. Loneliness
for her would take on a new dimension.

The Baron's will, on two ordinary sheets of letter paper, written in his own hand in 1865 and never altered, was probated on June 21, 1879. "God almighty," he wrote in a better day, "has been more than kind to me and I have to be thankful for many years of great happiness." After minor bequests he left his millions to be divided among his sons, with £100,000 to Charlotte as well as their homes (and their upkeep) for her lifetime and an annual £25,000. He also bequeathed £100,000 each to Leonora—and Evelina.

EPILOGUE

DUET FOR ONE

1879–1884

Charlotte returned quietly to Gunnersbury after Lionel's funeral. The documentary record of her post-Lionel years is very limited. Her children may have been too attentive to family reputation. To preserve the former Charlotte, they may have effaced much related to her life after her long illness and discouraged potentially gossip-prone visitors. Much the fullest portrait of Charlotte, replete with nostalgia for the vanished past, was the evocative autobiographical novel that Disraeli had been writing as Charlotte lay ill. Monty Corry recalled watching the Prime Minister putting the unfinished manuscript away in the strong room at Hughenden on October 15, 1878. On one level it was an imaginative spin on Disraeli's young manhood. On another it was an extraordinary love letter to the now-inaccessible Charlotte.

When Lionel died, Disraeli had not yet recovered his draft. So distraught that he misdated his letter by a month, on the day before

Lionel's funeral he wrote emotionally to "My dearest Nattie" on black-bordered mourning paper,

> Tomorrow is a sacred day, & I had wished not to have written to you a line until the solemn obsequies of one of the best & dearest of men had been fulfilled. Indeed, it is a subject on which I cannot get sufficiently command of myself to write. The world[1] seems to have done some justice to the kindness of his heart, the sweetness of his disposition, his justice & generosity: hardly enough to his commanding intelligence & the munificent magnanimity of his spirit.
>
> But I must stop. I was with him as late as Friday afternoon, almost evening—speaking of many affairs of gravity & weight. . . .
>
> Adieu! Adieu! My dearest friend!
>
> B.

Disraeli, it seemed, had been the last person in public life to have talked with Lionel. Now Natty, who hero-worshiped Disraeli, had replaced his own father in the Prime Minister's pantheon.

As Sir Nathaniel de Rothschild, Natty issued an announcement in the name of Messrs. N. M. Rothschild & Sons that the business of the firm would henceforth be continued by him with Alfred and Leopold. Unlike Lionel's burden just as he married, now there was no formidable widow in the wings empowered to intrude into the family enterprise. Charlotte, who had once been privy to great affairs, was only a shadow of her earlier self. The disinclination of Natty's brothers for business changed nothing. By Lionel's will they were co-equals, although Natty—like his father—would manage affairs.

Charlotte had long expected the family summons to come, whatever the reluctance of her younger sons, and had urged Leo on May 14, 1875, when the lure of the stables was far greater than that of

---

1. Obituaries in the press.

bonds and shares, "[F]ind an hour or two in the course of the day to write English exercises . . . [as] it would enable you, even in the practical routine of New Court life, to draw up contracts, make statements upon important financial transactions, and furnish those great papers, which should not really be drawn up by clerks." The younger brothers would involve themselves as called upon, Leopold more than Alfred, as Alfy was also a director of the Bank of England.

After Lionel's death a conclave of cousins rearranged relationships to establish twelve partners, some of them less active than others, in the four houses. Ferdinand von Rothschild—though seldom in Austria and soon to be an English M.P.—became a partner in the Vienna house with his eldest brother, another Nathaniel, and the more active youngest brother, Salbert. (When, in 1885, Natty became Lord Rothschild of Tring and vacated his seat in the Commons from Aylesbury, Ferdinand was elected in his place.) Other cousins were also confirmed as partners but with little role. All were personally wealthier than ever, as in the September 1879 agreement they shared £4.7 million withdrawn from surplus capital, such reductions made intermittently in periods of prosperity.

All three of Lionel's sons would see much of Disraeli, who, when out of office after the General Election in early 1880, would again be homeless in London. Transferring the lost filial connection to Dizzy, Natty would write in a New Year's greeting, "You know my Lord Beaconsfield the great affection my brothers and myself have always entertained for you. That feeling has been greatly strengthened by the very great kindness we have received from you during the past year, a year in which we had the misfortune to lose a beloved father." After relinquishing 10 Downing Street once more to Gladstone late in April 1880, the homeless Disraeli was offered a suite of guest rooms in Alfred's art-filled mansion at 1 Seamore Place. He would remain there contentedly until a cash advance on his new (and last) novel enabled him to purchase the lease of a town house nearby on Curzon Street in Mayfair.

Endymion had been begun in the days following Mary Anne's death when Disraeli, alone in London, spent many of his afternoons and evenings with Charlotte and Lionel. Because of Charlotte's long illness and isolation, both were now lost to him. As his loneliness led to looking back, the novel became a nostalgic fantasy about his early political life and his attraction to the world of Gunnersbury and Piccadilly House. Public affairs and poor health forced him to put the manuscript away. He even jotted notes for Monty Corry on how the plot was to be worked out in case Corry had to finish it. Soon after Lionel's death and during Charlotte's long convalescence, with Disraeli out of office and living under congenial if very different Rothschild hospitality, the draft of *Endymion* was retrieved and completed.

Through Corry, now Lord Rowton, Disraeli was offered £10,000 for all rights by Thomas Longman, who had not read a page of it. The bid was more than Dickens or anyone else in England had ever received for a novel. Few readers would realize its secret. Only in the disguises of fiction can a writer powerfully suggest, more discreetly as well as more profoundly than through indelicate fact, realities of character otherwise untellable. The ailing old conjurer would evoke Charlotte more sensitively and profoundly than Lionel might have appreciated.

Young Endymion Ferrars, an idealized and more diffident Disraeli, grows up in the era of George IV and William IV, and matures in the political world of the new queen. To disguise real-life parallels, Disraeli has Endymion enter politics somewhat earlier than he did, but like him sponsored by attractive and well-connected older women who create opportunities he can exploit. The novel's Metternich figure observes for him that "Semites now exercise a vast influence over affairs through their smallest though most peculiar family, the Jews. There is no race gifted with so much tenacity, and such skill in organization. These qualities have given them an unprecedented hold over property and illimitable credit." Predicting, in effect, Lionel's seating in Parliament, he adds, "In another quarter century they will claim their share of open government."

Adrian Neuchatel, senior member of a banking family from

Switzerland (a thin veil), is recognizable as Baron Lionel, but unburdened by a faith awkward to the plot. He is elected "at the head of the poll." Hainault, Neuchatel's country seat, is much like the Gunnersbury of the Rothschilds, although east rather than west of London, "not an hour's drive from Whitechapel." Like Lionel's "Mr. Acton," Adrian is also "passionately fond of horses, and even in his father's lifetime had run some at Newmarket in another name." As at Gunnersbury, "It seemed there was nothing that Hainault could not produce," including tropical fruits and flowers: "The conservatories and forcing-houses looked, in the distance, like a city of glass." On Sundays the gardens were crowded with grand invitees—Right Honourables and members of the Stock Exchange, and their ladies.

Neuchatel himself becomes young Endymion's informal university. Among other things he recommends careful reading of foreign newspapers. "The most successful man in life," he contends, "is the man who has the best information." In business as in politics, he cautions, a confident pose is crucial. "Nobody should look anxious, except those who have no anxiety." If there are echoes of Lionel in such genial shrewdness, there is affectionate yet sharp reminiscence in the portrait of Neuchatel's lovely wife, Emily, who so resembles Charlotte that the portrait suggests her private confidences. Her husband, Disraeli writes,

> had married, when [she was] very young, a lady selected by his father. . . . She was the daughter of a most eminent banker and . . . was a woman of abilities, highly cultivated. Nothing had ever been spared that she should possess every possible accomplishment, and acquire every . . . grace that it was desirable to attain. She was a linguist, a fine musician, no mean artist; and she threw out, if she willed it, the treasures of her well-stored and not unimaginative mind with ease and sometimes eloquence.

Seldom able to rein in excess, Disraeli also has his fictional Charlotte surround herself with "all the literary journals and choice publications" in a variety of languages, "and there was scarcely a branch of science and learning with which she was not sufficiently familiar to be able to comprehend the stir and progress of the European mind." Perhaps to concede that his prototype is a mature woman and not a maiden, he stops short of utter perfection, making her "interesting" yet not "absolutely beautiful," with "a degree of fascination in her brown velvet eyes." And he reveals a degree of deep inner sadness and disillusion in her that overwhelming wealth cannot suppress and which it may have influenced, for—as with Charlotte—her bounty was a mixed blessing:

> Mrs. Neuchatel was not a contented spirit; and though she appreciated the great qualities of her husband and viewed him even with reverence as well as affection, she scarcely contributed to his happiness as much as became her. . . . [As] the consequence of having been born and bred, and [having] lived for ever, in a society in which wealth was the prime object of existence, and practically the test of excellence, Mrs. Neuchatel had imbibed not merely a contempt for money, but absolutely a hatred for it. . . . But Adrian, though kind, generous and indulgent, was so absorbed by his own great affairs, was a man at the same time of so serene a temper and so supreme a will, that the over-refined fantasies of his wife produced not the slightest effect on the course of his life.

Warm and witty, Emily is a tireless news gatherer and correspondent. (As Charlotte put it to her children in 1874, "We Rothschilds are inveterate scribblers, and cannot live without letter writing and letter receiving.") "Her feelings were her facts, and her ingenious observations of art and nature were her news." She is so uninterested in dazzling jewels, as was Charlotte, that Neuchatel tells his nephew, a young M.P. like Natty, "Your aunt must feel that I give her diamonds from love and not from vanity, as she never lets me have the pleasure of seeing them." Much like Charlotte, Emily is also such a tireless benefactor to "her schools" that her husband remarks to a visiting prince about a recently purchased Gainsborough picture, "I won't tell you what I gave for it, because perhaps you would tell my wife and she would be very angry. She would want the money for an infant school. But I think she has schools enough."

Also like Charlotte, Emily is also a zealot for solitude, which she can embrace only rarely. There seem always to be guests about; and she is indifferent to, but willing to employ, "like a princely prisoner of state," elegant cuisine and elaborate ceremony. "She had contrived to get rid of the chief cook by sending him off on a visit to Paris," Disraeli writes, "so she could, without cavil, dine off a cutlet and seltzer-water in her boudoir."

Despite her inner melancholy arising from the satiety of fortune, she is a gracious hostess for her husband to ambassadors, aristocrats, and Cabinet ministers; bankers, merchants, and men of the cloth. And of course such of their wives "who were socially strong enough to venture on such a step." (In the novel, Emily's elite guests, as Lord Macaulay recalled with wonder after dining on ortolans at Kingston House, are served "delicate dishes . . . looked at with wonder, and tasted with timidity.") "In a very short time," Disraeli writes of Neuchatel hospitality, "it was not merely the wives of ambassadors and ministers of state that were found at the garden fêtes of Hainault, or the balls, and banquets, and concerts, of Portland Place,[2] but the fitful and capricious realm of fashion [also] surrendered like a fair country conquered as it were by surprise. To visit the Neuchatels became the mode; all solicited to be their guests, and some solicited in vain." Lord Roehampton explains, "I like the family—all of them. . . . I like his house and style of living. You always meet nice people there, and hear the last thing that has been said or done all over the world."

Lady Dorothy Nevill, a lively Disraeli neighbor at Grosvenor Gate, and Charlotte's close friend, pored over *Endymion*, she told critic Edmund Gosse, almost as personal history. "What a charm," she gushed, "after the beef and mutton of ordinary novels." She had

2. Obviously Piccadilly House.

often been a guest in Charlotte's homes and may have known more of the originals of Disraeli's characters than anyone but the author himself. Among the presentation copies he inscribed was one "from her friend Beaconsfield" to Emma, Natty's wife. If Charlotte herself, remote in Gunnersbury, read the autumnal novel that was in part Disraeli's farewell to her, no intimation of that exists.

The author of *Endymion* did not long survive its publication. On the last day of 1880 he returned to Alfy's mansion at Seamore Place. Disraeli's Curzon Street house was not yet ready for occupancy. The Rothschild brothers were so involved with politics on both sides of the aisle that once when Gladstone was scheduled to visit Alfred, Natty came and hurried Dizzy off to dine with him. Although ill with nephritis and asthma, Disraeli stubbornly managed to get himself to the marriage of his host's brother, Leopold.

Although Charlotte and Lionel had queried Leopold hopefully about eligible "princesses of Israel" at a wedding in Paris, he discovered the one he wanted later in London. He had vowed not to marry until he found a bride "as beautiful and accomplished" as Louise Sassoon, of a notable Austrian-Italian Jewish family. Arthur Sassoon introduced him to his pretty young sister-in-law, Marie Perugia, eighteen to Leo's thirty-six. Prudently, she began taking riding lessons. "I have always been of opinion," Disraeli had congratulated him from Hughenden on December 11, 1880, "that there cannot be enough Rothschilds."

On January 19, 1881, a wind-whipped snowstorm kept Dizzy from the ceremony at Central Synagogue, Great Portland Street, but he managed to get a carriage to take him to the reception at Arthur Sassoon's town house at 2 Albert Gate. He was just in time for the cutting of the enormous wedding cake, adorned with authentic orange blossoms. In the first residence he had ever visited illuminated by what he called "magical" electricity, Disraeli raised a glass of champagne, which his doctor would not let him drink, and toasted the Prince of Wales, who in turn toasted the bride and groom. Not permitting the Prince the last word, Leopold responded unaffectedly, "I believe it is unusual to talk of oneself. But on an occasion like this one may be permitted to say a few words. I have enjoyed till now a happy life. I have had the kindest of fathers, the best of mothers, the dearest brothers and sisters. I will only hope that I shall make my dear wife as happy as I have been. I am sure, Sir, you will excuse me if I do not say more. Every word I have said was from my heart."

Four days earlier, Disraeli had moved into the house which income from *Endymion* had made possible. Almost entirely bedridden thereafter, he died on April 19, 1881. He had made his wishes known that he wanted neither a clergyman at the close, nor a show funeral. His executors were Sir Philip Rose (his lawyer) and Sir Nathaniel, who complied with Disraeli's wishes for a quiet interment at Hughenden. It was not yet one in the morning on Sunday, April 24, when, with the crowds that had gathered respectfully each day in Curzon Street gone, Alfred arrived at the darkened house and gazed upon his old friend's face for the last time. With Disraeli's valet, Baum, he saw the coffin placed on a special train from Paddington. At Wycombe, Nathaniel received the body. The funeral at Hughenden took place on the 26th, a Tuesday, with Natty handling the arrangements. The Rothschilds had been with their dearest friend outside the family to the end.

Charlotte had been warmly referred to, with Lionel, at Leo's wedding, but had not attended. She was not up to crowds. Recovering slowly, she wintered at Gunnersbury. Although her family wanted her to be discreetly away from London, almost certainly the decision became her own. Since her marriage at seventeen, she and Lionel had been a duo—seldom apart for long. Piccadilly House was Lionel's dream. She had always preferred the country, and solitude which she could breach at will with her pen. Charlotte was again up to that, yet Ferdinand's chatty letter to her dated March 11, 1880, the year before, sent from Jerusalem, where he was visiting the Rothschild Hospital and the Evelina School, is one of the few surviving of the very many she received and sent during her fading years.

In 1881 she was at least briefly at Piccadilly House, where August

Belmont's wife, Caroline, arriving from New York, visited her. Charlotte's hair, she reported to her husband, "has grown quite gray." She looked well, and she "asked me as usual a world of questions. She sat in her little salon on the lower floor, where we were always received, embroidering; and she had her books, etc., about her. I should never have known that she was out of her mind [earlier], and indeed from all accounts she is much better. They say that she used to imagine herself a grain of sand."[3]

Although there is no record of it in the more elderly Gladstone's diaries of the early 1880s, he apparently continued to call on Charlotte at Gunnersbury to chat, especially to discuss theology. She had long been sending him scriptural commentaries by Jewish scholars— "Baroness L. Rothschild (conversation on the state of belief)" as he had put it in his diary for March 6, 1875. Such visits were "almost the last pleasure my dear mother enjoyed," Natty told Gladstone.

Leopold remained a faithful correspondent and a regular caller. He kept her apprised of the "troublesome teeth" of infant Lionel Nathan, born January 25, 1882, and other family news; reported on his horses and cattle, shooting parties and balls. One letter describes the dress rehearsal of Gilbert and Sullivan's Savoy opera *Princess Ida*, and others are filled with social comings and goings. Leo also updated her on such delicious gossip as the charges of adultery brought by the beautiful Lady Colin Campbell and in return by her estranged husband. On a sunny day in May 1882, Charlotte's nieces Constance Flower and Annie Yorke, scheduled to visit Gunnersbury, came anyway, although shocked by the news they had just heard of the mur-

---

3. There are so many references in the Bible, from Genesis on, to the people of Israel as grains of sand that Charlotte's temporarily confused mind may have been affected by them. Or she could well have been recalling, however disordered her brain then, William Blake's

> To see a world in a grain of sand
> And a heaven in a wild flower,
> Hold infinity in the palm of your hand
> And eternity in an hour.

der, in Dublin, of Lord Frederick Cavendish by a Fenian gunman. They were relieved not to have to discuss the "dreadful subject" with Charlotte. It was not "mentioned by the Gunnersbury patient—though she knew it," Constance wrote in surprise. "With the exception of that one extraordinary reticence, as to every [other] sad or horrible topic she seemed perfectly well."

Constance's reaction (that the "patient" appeared "perfectly well") seems something out of melodramatic Victorian fiction—arising from decades of unhappy Victorian fact. The madwoman in the attic, hidden away out of potential family embarrassment, existed not just in *Jane Eyre* but in actual families, where a person no longer sound in mind was warehoused not in a dread asylum but under watchful sequestration at home, kept unseen and hopefully forgotten—often pretended to have been forgotten—by family and friends. After her stroke, Charlotte evidenced symptoms of mental dysfunction, from incoherence to aphasia, from paralysis to coma. But she had come through, and some of her old self remained. Leo even referred to her "vivid description of your lovely visitors." But he also worried that some of her guests—covert schnorrers, perhaps—might take advantage of her, as he put it, without explaining what he was certain she would understand. In one case of a person persistently seeking to visit, he advised, late in 1883, that Charlotte should "conveniently forget her existence."

That October she wrote to Sir Moses Montefiore to congratulate her venerable uncle on his one-hundredth birthday. He responded on October 31, 1883 (except for his feeble signature, he dictated), that none of the many letters he received had "afforded me so much pleasure. For the flattering terms in which you refer to my labours in the cause of humanity I am greatly indebted to you. I cannot tell you how pleased I am to know that you are in good health."

Other letters acknowledged Charlotte's "charming" and "delightful" responses, and there is no doubt that they were exactly that. Her children visited—Natty and Emma, Leo and Marie, and Alfy. Her grandchildren visited, and she was especially delighted, as Leo put it, by "our little Lionel." Charlotte learned what commodities from Berlin, Bologna, Alsatia, Trieste, and Genoa the house was importing, and she even began receiving such businesslike messages as "The markets are all very firm." She was now well past her most serious infirmities, yet she was treated still as if she were very fragile.

The last letter from her surviving in the family archives is to Alfred, who was planning a grand ball and weekend of entertainment at his Buckinghamshire estate, Halton, on January 17, 1884. The Prince of Wales was expected, as well as his current mistress, the beautiful and possessive Lady Brooke. A special train from Euston Station chartered by Alfred was to bring many of the elite party.

Charlotte's crowded and knowledgeable letter was so typical of her as to echo decades past. One would never guess that the recipient was a sophisticated forty and a director of the Bank of England:

Monday morning

My dearest Alfred,

You will probably have seen in the "Morning Post" that the marriage of Lady Hermione Duncombe [to Lord Kildare] is to be solemnised on the 17th of January, the day fixed for your ball. Now it strikes me, indeed I feel sure, that some of your expected guests will deem it their duty to be present at the wedding, and I subjoin the following list to which some other names might perhaps be added. The Duke of Sutherland, Lord Kildare being the son of His Grace's only surviving sister. Lord and Lady Granville, also nearly related to the bridegroom. Mr. Chaplin, a cousin of his marriage with poor Lady Florence, and Lord Hartington, a real cousin of the Duchess of Leinster (Lord Kildare's mother).

Don't you think that, when sending an invitation "to remind" your expected guests, you might express the hope to retain them under your roof until Friday afternoon as H. R. Highness has promised to stay on till then. The reply of the ladies and gentlemen would then enable you to replace the possibly, nay probably, departing guests, by others. This is a mere hint; forgive me if I am troublesome, and if you can find a better solution.

Laury is quite well, and in high good humour; we both [erred], you and I, in trying to laugh at your dear sister's fancy for sending telegrams, and no woman likes being called "old" before she is [a] wrinkled great-grandmother,[4] whom the relentless scythe of time has deprived of every charm and grace, replacing the departed attractions by deep lines and furrows, and ugly crows' feet.

Excuse me if I bore you, and let me embrace you in thought with fondest love, and wishing you all blessings.

In haste

C L de R

The festivities were a great success although a foggy morning kept the shooting party's bag of tame pheasants to four hundred. Apart from the ball and the bag, the many guests played whist and poker, gossiped and gawked, toured the park and examined Alfred's art treasures, ingested and imbibed the best food and drink in England, and rendezvoused through bedroom hallways in the darkness.

Leopold's little Lionel Nathan was two on January 25, 1884. Charlotte showered him with gifts, his father writing in thanks, "You are a fairy Granny." She was still keeping her fabled greenhouses at Gunnersbury going, and on February 10 Leo explained from Ascott that the press of business at New Court made him feel that in the country he was only a "Sunday proprietor." His "chief and important news was the cutting of the Gunnersbury pineapple. It was pronounced excellent." That encomium would have gratified, too, the shade of his grandmother Hannah.

No later letters to or from Charlotte seem to survive. After an-

---

4. Laury was already, via Bettina (and "Salbert"), three times a grandmother, with Georg (1877), Alphonse (1878), and Louis (1882). Thus Charlotte was satirizing herself as indeed an aging great-grandmother.

other apparent stroke, she died at Gunnersbury early on March 13, 1884. That June she would have been sixty-five.

Charlotte's sons were with her. Constance Flower rushed there to be with the family when she heard the news. "Aunt Lionel has passed away," she wrote in her diary. "I felt stunned. Went down to Gunnersbury and found that Mamma [Louise] had just arrived. It was sad to see them one and all, prostrate under the blow. Saw dear Aunt Charlotte lying like a beautiful marble statue on her bed, her mouth in sculptured repose, her broad, high brow in all the dignity of rest. I was deeply affected."

"Her last years," the *Times* obituarist wrote the next day, "were spent in complete retirement among flowers and pictures"—a vision of decline rather than of a remarkable return almost to her former self. It went on to praise her former philanthropic industry and energy, and her "courtly hospitality" in behalf of the late Baron Lionel. In her will she asked her sons to continue her benefactions as in her lifetime and scrupulously itemized tens of thousands of pounds in bequests to schools and hospitals and relief organizations she had funded in her active years.

The funeral, on the morning of March 16, 1884, took place from Piccadilly House. Drivers of omnibuses on nearby West End routes bore crêpe rosettes on their whips. Just before the coffin was removed, the Baroness's female servants entered for a farewell to their late mistress.

Charlotte was buried quietly at Willesden, next to Lionel. In turn Natty and Leo,[5] then others, followed tradition and symbolically cast earth into the grave atop her beloved Gunnersbury blossoms. Thousands of mourners visited the grave that afternoon and all the next day.

Her husband had left a legend, and a formidable enterprise to confront the generations after him. Beyond her tireless benefactions and her role as Lionel's chatelaine, Charlotte's bounty was unique.

5. Alfred was ill and absent.

Not just as the most memorable women in three Disraeli novels, but in her sparkling letters and her family legacy, Charlotte still lives. With Lionel, she embodied one of Victorian England's most re-markable and unfading love stories. A marriage arranged by ambi-tious mothers between cousins who hardly knew each other and came from different countries, it endured and was even enriched by adversity and challenge. As Charlotte had said, wealth was not enough. Love abides.

SOURCES

The key source for Rothschild family papers is the Rothschild Archive, now housed in the Rothschild Bank on St. Swithin's Lane. Many books on the Rothschilds, or referring to them, have appeared over the last two centuries. Despite the plethora, the only essential study is Niall Ferguson's *The World's Banker: The History of the House of Rothschild* (London: Weidenfeld & Nicolson, 1998), based upon the archive, which begins at the beginning and concludes in the 1990s. Also valuable, but largely for background to my biography, is *The Life and Times of N. M. Rothschild, 1777–1836*, ed. Victor Gray and Melanie Aspey (London: N. M. Rothschild & Sons, 1998), the catalogue-history of Nathan Mayer Rothschild and his bank based upon the exhibition at the Museum of the City of London in 1998. Its reproduction of documents and memorabilia, some of which, again, are dispersed, makes this publication a crucial contribution; however, it necessarily concludes in the year of the marriage of Charlotte and Lionel. Much general Rothschild history is drawn from these books even when otherwise found in earlier publications, as these, based upon archival sources, can be considered authoritative. Many sources are also imbedded in the narrative.

FOREWORD

The gravestone story is from *A Treasury of Jewish Folklore*, ed. Nathan Ausubel (New York: Crown, 1948). N. M.'s encounter with the bootblack, probably apocryphal, is from Frederic Morton, *The Rothschilds* (New York:

Atheneum, 1962). Earl Spencer's vicious remark about Leonora's "accidental beauty" is quoted from Spencer's diaries by Anthony Allfrey in his *Edward VII and His Jewish Court* (London: Weidenfeld & Nicolson, 1991). The Gilbert and Sullivan light opera using "Rothschild" as metaphor is *Utopia, Limited*. Victoria's excuses for refusing a peerage to Lionel are in *The Political Correspondence of Mr. Gladstone and Lord Granville*, ed. Agatha Ramm (London: Oxford University Press, 1952). For the Rothschild loan to the impecunious Prince Oettingen-Wallerstein cosigned by Albert, see S. Weintraub, *Albert: Uncrowned King* (London: John Murray/New York: The Free Press, 1997). Charlotte's German diary is in the Rothschild Archives. For Charlotte's anonymously published book, see Chapter 10.

CHAPTER ONE   *Investing in a Bride, 1808–1836*

Lionel's letters to his mother, Hannah, and his father, N. M., Hannah's letters to Charlotte, and the letters of Lionel and Charlotte to each other are in the Rothschild Archives (hereafter "R Fam C"). C's letter to her cousin Charlotte Montefiore, in Berlin, Sept. 16, 1835, on her engagement, is also in R Fam C. A detailed biography of Hannah by Melanie Aspey, "Mrs. Rothschild," is in *The Life and Times of N. M. Rothschild* (noted above). For background on Nathan Mayer Rothschild, I have also consulted Lord [Victor] Rothschild's valuable "The Shadow of a Great Man," in his *Random Variables* (London: Collins, 1984). A persuasive explanation for N. M.'s rejection of the Austrian peerage, and his second thoughts, is in Ferguson. Extracts from *Diaries of Sir Moses and Lady Montefiore*, ed. Louis Loewe (London: Jewish Historical Society of England, 1890), are from the facsimile edition (London: 1983). N. M.'s "take two chairs!" remark is from the obituary of Lionel in the *Jewish Chronicle*, June 6, 1879, as is the story of "walking on gold" stored in the New Court living quarters. The obituary is also the source of Lionel's seeking admission into the London and Westminster Light Horse Volunteers in 1828. The allegation that a conclave of Rothschild brothers in 1836 determined on a policy of arranging marriages within the family is in a lengthy and scurrilous family history, "The Knights of the Red Shield," by Junius Henri Browne, in *Harper's New Monthly Maga-*

zine, December, 1873. A summary of the railway incidents musicalized by Rossini in "Un petit train de plaisir" is in Herbert Weinstock's *Rossini* (London: Knopf, 1968), which also quotes the composer's letters.

CHAPTER TWO *A Wedding in the Cousinhood, 1836*

Felix Mendelssohn's letters are from Herbert Kupferberg, *The Mendelssohns* (New York: Scribner's, 1972.). Letters between Lionel and his brothers, and Hannah (for N. M.), are in R Fam C. Greenwich outings by the new railway are described in R. H. G. Thomas, *London's First Railway: The London and Greenwich* (London: Batsford, 1972). Biographical data about Dr. Chelius were furnished by Professor Jürgen Miethke, University of Heidelberg. Biographical data about the painter Moritz Daniel Oppenheim are from the Jewish Museum (New York) catalogue, *The Emergence of Jewish Painters in Nineteenth Century Europe*, ed. Susan Turmarkin Goodman (New York: Merrell, 2002), which includes the wedding portraits of Lionel and Charlotte. The marriage certificate dated June 14, 1836, with Rossini's bold signature is R Fam C 000/89. Wedding ritual likely to have been followed, where not described in family letters, is drawn from *The Jewish Ritual: Or the Religious Customs and Ceremonies of the Jews, Used in their Publick Worship and Private Devotions* (London: M. Cooper, 1773). Baron James's letter to Anthony, June 18, 1836, about the unconsummated marriage is in R Fam C, as are other family letters quoted or referred to. Various memorabilia regarding N. M.'s death are illustrated in *Life and Times*, as is the August 9, 1836, announcement by his sons of the firm's continuity.

CHAPTER THREE *Charlotte in Exile, 1836–1839*

Charlotte's diary references about her early years in England are from R Fam PD. Beginning with the birth of her first child, she kept separate R Fam volumes recording their development, illnesses, medical reports, etc. They will be referred to until the youngest children are teenagers. Moses Montefiore's diary entries here and in the next chapter on the Damascus affair are from the Loewe edition. Eva Besso is described in Disraeli's *Tancred* (London: Colburn, 1847). Sydney Smirke's architectural work at Gunnersbury and elsewhere is detailed by J. Mordaunt Crook in *Seven Victorian Architects*, ed. Jane Fawcett (University Park, PA: Penn State Press, 1977). Descriptions and maps are in Ann and James Collett-White, *Gunnersbury Park and the Rothschilds* (Hounslow, England: Heritage, 1993). Sallie Stevenson's letter to her sister on a garden party at Gunnersbury is from Edward Boykin, *Victoria, Albert, and Mrs. Stevenson* (New York: Rinehart, 1957). Disraeli's letter to his sister on Charlotte's appearance at a concert is dated by the editors as February 15, 1838, in *Benjamin Disraeli: Letters, 1838–1841*, ed. M. G. Wiebe, et al. (Toronto: University of Toronto Press, 1987). The de Dreux painting of Lionel in a gig is owned by an English Rothschild who declined permission to reproduce it although it has been published before. The comment by a Mr. Haas to Lionel commiserating on the birth of a daughter is from Ferguson. Pugin's letter to Lord Shrewsbury is quoted by Rosemary Hill in "Of Shopping and Sacramentalism," *Tiimes Literary Supplement*, July 13, 2001.

CHAPTER FOUR   *The World Intrudes, 1839–1846*

Charlotte's letters to Lionel when he was away on business are from R Fam C 000/848. Lionel's in return are from R Fam C 4. Hannah's to Charlotte and to Leonora (when a child) are from R Fam C 1. For Hannah Mayer's troubled life, see Robert Henrey, *A Century Between* (London: Heinemann, 1937). The report in *The Times* of her marriage was described as taken from the *Swabian Mercury*. Barnum's description of Tom Thumb and himself at Charlotte's home is from his *Struggles and Triumphs: Or, Forty Years' Recollection of P. T. Barnum* (New York: Penguin, 1969). Letters in *The Letters of the King of Hanover to Viscount Strangford*, ed. E. M. Cox and Charles Whibley (London: Williams and Norgate, 1925), are replete with King Ernest's anti-Semitism. For Lady Palmerston's letters, see Tresham Lever, ed., *The Letters of Lady Palmerston* (London: John Murray, 1957). Charlotte's and Lionel's relationships with Lord Lyndhurst and his second wife are detailed in his niece Martha Babcock Amory's *The Domestic and Artistic Life of John Singleton Cop-*

ley, R.A. . . . and Reminiscences of His Son, Lord Lyndhurst, Lord High Chancellor of Great Britain (Boston: Houghton Mifflin, 1882). Disraeli's Sidonia character first appears in *Coningsby* (London, 1844); his *Sybil, or The Two Nations* followed the next year. Disraeli's further letters are from the Wiebe edition. For his attempts at extracting investment advice from Lionel, see also S. Weintraub, *Disraeli* (New York: Dutton; London: Hamish Hamilton, 1993). Lucy Cohen's *Lady Rothschild and Her Daughters, 1821–1931* (London: John Murray, 1935) quotes in full Charlotte's letter to Louisa on Mary Anne Disraeli's breathless visit with her will, and family references to Leopold (as a result of Mary Anne's overenthusiastic encomium) as the "Little Messiah."

CHAPTER FIVE   *"The Jew Bill," 1846–1850*

For *Times* editor Delane and extracts from his letters and diaries, see Arthur Dasent, *John Thadeus Delane* (New York: Scribner's, 1908). Letters from Lionel and his brothers on the baronetcy offer are from R Fam C, as are Hannah's and James's to Lionel. Albert quoted Lionel's "You have nothing higher to offer me?" (on the rejected baronetcy) to his confidant, Baron Stockmar, on December 3, 1846 (Royal Archives, Windsor, Y-148/6). Russell's letter of February 13, 1849, chastising Lionel, is in the Rothschild Archive as XI/109/70/2. The note on behalf of Prince von Oettingen-Wallerstein cosigned by Albert on June 1, 1847, is also in the Rothschild Archive. The entire history of the loan is in S. Weintraub, *Uncrowned King: The Life of Prince Albert* (New York: Free Press, 1997). Nicholas Cummins is quoted on the Irish famine in Cecil Woodham-Smith, *The Great Hunger* (New York: Harper & Row, 1962), where the Rothschild role is also described. Disraeli's letter to Lionel on the famine is in Wiebe, IV. A description of the meeting on famine relief at New Court is in a letter to Delane at *The Times* by J. Standish. For Charlotte and Mary Anne Disraeli, see S. Weintraub, *Disraeli* (New York: Dutton; London: Hamish Hamilton, 1993). Lionel's political relations with (and encouragement by) Lord John Russell from 1847 through 1857 are seen through Russell's perspective in his letters to Lionel in the Rothschild Archive. Louisa's diary is MS. 97 in the Hartley Library, Univ. of Southampton; a copy is in the Rothschild Archive; extracts appear also in Lucy Cohen, ed., *Lady de Rothschild and Her Daughters: 1821–1931* (London: John Murray, 1935). Charlotte's letters to Louisa are in R Fam C. Her descriptions of a phrenologist's interpretation of family "bumps" and the texts of his reports are in R Fam PD.

Monckton Milnes's letter from his father is quoted in James Pope-Hennessy's *Monckton Milnes: The Years of Promise* (London: Constable, 1949). Carlyle's cranky letter on the "Jew Bill" to Milnes, December 30, 1847, is from *The Collected Letters of Thomas and Jane Welsh Carlyle*, vol. 13 (Durham, NC: Duke University Press, 1987), ed. C. de L. Ryals, et al. Elizabeth Davis Bancroft is quoted from her *Letters from England: 1846–1849* (New York: Charles Scribner's Sons, 1904). Charlotte's snappish note to Lionel about having to do "what others want" is quoted in Richard Davis, *The English Rothschilds* (Chapel Hill: University of North Carolina Press, 1983).

For Lionel's letter to constituents thanking them for support, July 20, 1849, see R Fam C 14-442. The King of Hanover's letters to Lord Strangford are in the Cox and Whibley edition (see Chapter 4, above). Accounts of Charlotte and Louisa at the parliamentary debates are from Louisa's diaries. Lord John Manners's letter to Lionel is in the Rothschild Archive as 000/948. Charlotte's undated draft of her letter to "My Lord" signed "A Jewess" is R Fam C/ 21R.38. Her letters to Louisa on family matters, including the visits to Frankfurt and Wildbad, are also in R Fam C/ 21. For Lionel's role in the early financing of the Crystal Palace exhibition, see S. Weintraub, *Uncrowned King: The Life of Prince Albert.*

CHAPTER SIX   *Oaths and Elections, 1850–1858*

Charlotte's evaluations of her children's progress and activities are the R Fam PD accounts she kept in separate volumes for each child. Louisa's diary describes the visit of the two ladies to the Great Exhibition. Her other references to Charlotte are also from the diary. Thackeray's appearances and writing are identified in the text but for Charlotte's description of the sleeping writer, which is from a letter to Louisa, quoted by Constance as Lady Battersea in her *Reminiscences* (London: Macmillan, 1922). The children's visit to the convent is also recounted by Constance. Disraeli's letters are from Wiebe, V and VI. The original of Macaulay's letter to John Russell, June 19, 1853, is in the Rothschild Archives as 000/848. Banking affairs are drawn from Ferguson. Parliamentary affairs relating to Jewish emancipation are from *Hansard* and the daily press, and the Montefiore diary. The "peculiar animal" aspersion on Lionel as a Jew by Robert Cecil as a hostile M.P. is quoted by David Steele in *Lord Salisbury: A Political Biography* (London: UCL Press, 1999).

Charlotte's escorting of Leonora to be presented to Queen Victoria is from the Royal Archives. Leonora's wedding was widely covered by the London press. Thackeray's account was as usual unsigned. Laury's wedding concludes Charlotte's accounts of her in R Fam PD. Charlotte's letters to Lionel and to her sons are in R Fam.

CHAPTER SEVEN *Kingston House, 1858–1863*

Delane's letters are from Dasent. Charlotte's and Lionel's letters to each other are in R Fam, as are Charlotte's now-burgeoning letters to her sons, especially to Leopold. Constance's *Reminiscences* contains much on her three male cousins. Macaulay's letter on dining at Kingston House is July 10, 1859, in Thomas Pinney, ed., *The Letters of Thomas Babington Macaulay* (Cambridge and London: Cambridge University Press, 1981). Princess Vicky's letter to the Queen on using Rothschild couriers is March 15, 1858, in her multivolume correspondence with her mother. Louise's letters to Charlotte are in R Fam. For Baron James and his vintages, see Anka Muhlstein, *Baron James* (London: Collins, 1983). The visit of Napoleon III to Ferrières at the close of the chapter is drawn from Muhlstein, Ferguson, and the children's letters to their parents in R Fam. For Natty's relations with the Prince of Wales, see S. Weintraub, *Edward the Caresser* (New York: Free Press, 2001); some of the material is drawn from R Fam. Anthony Allfrey in *Edward VII and His Jewish Court* (London: Weidenfeld & Nicolson, 1991) quotes Earl Spencer's vicious remark to the Queen about Laury's "accidental beauty." Laury's and Evy's letters to their parents are in R Fam FP.

Charlotte's practical benefactions to the Jewish Board of Guardians are described by Harold Pollins in *Economic History of the Jews in England* (London: Associated University Presses, 1982). Dickens quotes Carlyle's aspersions about Lionel and Piccadilly House to W. C. Macready on June 11, 1861, in *The Letters of Charles Dickens*, vol. 9 (1859–1861), ed. Graham Storey, et al. (Oxford: Oxford University Press, 1997). The anonymous New Hampshireman's encounter with Lionel is told in the first person in "A Morning with the Rothschilds," *Portsmouth Journal*, August 25, 1866. His identity remains unknown. Plans of Piccadilly House are in the architectural journal *The Builder* as "Baron Rothschild's New Mansion in Piccadilly," November 1, 1862. Lionel's dinner for the workmen is described in *The Builder* on March 22, 1863. *The Illustrated London News* published a view of the Piccadilly façade on September 6, 1862. The grand staircase was pictured in the Sotheby auction catalogue on April 19, 1937, when the contents were offered for sale by Victor Rothschild.

August Belmont's letters to Lionel on the American Civil War are in the Rothschild Archives. Monsignor Bauer is described by Julian Osgood Field in his anonymously published *Uncensored Recollections* (Philadelphia: Lippincott, 1924). An entry by C. Laplatte in the *Dictionnaire de Biographie Française*, vol. 5, adds corroborating details about the womanizing *abbé*, who was born in Pest in 1829 and died in Paris in 1903, four years after, at seventy, marrying *"une ancienne ballerine,"* presumably for her money. Laplatte also refers to the "procession of fashionable women [who] went to him craving his advice and consolation."

The description of the refurbished bank at New Court and its business customs is from Ronald Palin, *Rothschild Relish* (London: Cassell, 1970); other accounts about contemporary practices in similar banks in the City are from Roger Fulford, *Glyn's, 1753–1953: Six Generations in Lombard Street* (London: Macmillan, 1953); T. E. Gregory, *Hoare's Bank: A Record, 1672–1955* (London: Milford, 1955); and Francis Sheppard, *London, 1808–1870: The Infernal Wen* (London: Secker and Warburg, 1971).

CHAPTER EIGHT   *Piccadilly House, 1863–1866*

Family letters are in R Fam files, including Lionel's comments to Leo about the Heenan-Sayers fight. Other details about the bout are from Alan Lloyd,

The Great Prize Fight (New York: Coward, McCann, 1977). Matthew Arnold's January 1863 letter to his mother is from Arnold's *Letters*, vol. 2, ed. Cecil Y. Lang (Charlottesville, VA: Univ. of Virginia Press, 1996), while his October 1863 letter to his mother is quoted in Israel Feinstein, *Anglo-Jewry in Changing Times* (London: Vallentine, Mitchell, 1999). Delane's letters are from Dasent, Disraeli's from C/2 in the Rothschild Archives. For further details on the Disraeli–Brydges Willyams relationship, see S. Weintraub, *Disraeli*.

Boyle's Court Guide (London: Boyle's, 1863) for Piccadilly West lists the Rothschild neighbors. The marriage that forced the Rothschilds out of Kingston House early in May 1864 is reported in *The Morning Post* on April 30, 1864. Mayer's letters to his brothers are in R Fam C. Evy's marriage was widely reported in the London and Paris press. Her long honeymoon and return were described by her in many letters to her parents in R Fam.

CHAPTER NINE   *Losses, 1866–1870*

Constance's diary has been referred to earlier. Family letters are from R Fam. Lord Stanley's diary is published as *Disraeli, Derby, and the Conservative Party* (New York: Barnes & Noble, 1978), ed. John Vincent. (He would be 15th Earl of Derby, succeeding his father, Disraeli's precursor as prime minister.) Disraeli's letters to Charlotte and Lionel (and Mary Anne's to Charlotte) are in the Rothschild Archive as R Fam C. The remark about the rarity of Rothschilds in Russia is from *A Treasury of Jewish Folklore* (see above). Richard Simpson's letter to Sir John Acton, November 21, 1868, is from *The Correspondence of Lord Acton and Richard Simpson*, vol. 3, ed. Josef L. Altholz et al. (Cambridge, England: Cambridge University Press, 1975). Lionel's letter to Disraeli and Victoria's exchanges with Gladstone over a peerage for Lionel are quoted in Davis, ed., *The English Rothschilds* (see above). Matthew Arnold's correspondence with Charlotte is from his *Letters*, vol. 3. The letters of Nat's secretary, John F. Cox, to Nat's brothers are in the Rothschild Archive as XI/ 109. Earl Granville's exchanges with Gladstone about Napoleon III's involvement in creating a Spanish succession crisis are in David Wetzel's *A Duel of Giants: Bismarck, Napoleon III, and the*

Origins of the Franco-Prussian War (Madison: University of Wisconsin Press, 2001).

CHAPTER TEN   *Enduring, 1870–1874*

Family correspondence is again from the R. Archive. Constance's diary entries are as above. The Rothschilds during the siege of Paris is from Muhlstein and Ferguson as well as from John Milner's *Art, War, and Revolution in France, 1870–1871* (New Haven: Yale University Press, 2001) and from family letters in the R. Archive. The grateful letter to Charlotte, November 23, 1871, from the Reverend William Rogers is 000/924/6 in the R. Archive. C. P. Villiers's letters to Charlotte are also in the R. Archive.

Charlotte's anonymous *From January to December: A Book for Children* (1873) was printed by Wertheimer, Lea and Co. for publishers Longmans, Green in an edition, without preface, of 343 pages. Presumably, it was quietly subsidized for use in the Bell Lane school as well as made available for the trade. Disraeli's letters are in the R. Archive. Gladstone's diary entries are from the multivolume *The Gladstone Diaries*, ed. H. G. C. Mathew (Oxford and London: Oxford University Press, 1994). For the closing years of Mary Anne Disraeli and her husband's widowerhood, see S. Weintraub, *Disraeli*. Trollope's *The Way We Live Now* (London, 1875) was first published in monthly parts between February 1874 and September 1875. Lionel's campaign message about replacing taxes lost by reforms is from Ferguson.

CHAPTER ELEVEN   *Suez and After, 1874–1879*

Disraeli's letters to Lady Bradford and her sister are in *The Letters of Disraeli to Lady Bradford and Lady Chesterfield*, ed. the Marquis of Zetland (London: Benn, 1929). The funerals of the Rothschild brothers were reported in detail in the *Jewish Chronicle* as well as the daily London press. Charlotte described her daily life in lengthy letters (RA Fam C) to her children, notably to Leopold, to whom she wrote almost daily. Lionel also wrote often to Leopold, who was at Cambridge or traveling. R. L. Stevenson's letter to Sidney Colvin, June 7, 1875, is in *The Letters of Robert Louis Stevenson*, vol. 2, eds. Bradford A. Booth and Ernest Mehew (New Haven: Yale University Press, 1994).

The most authoritative account of the Suez shares loan and purchase is by Lord [Victor] Rothschild, *"You Have It, Madam": The Purchase, in 1875, of Suez Canal Shares by Disraeli and Baron Lionel de Rothschild* (London: W&J Mackay, 1980), repr. in his *Random Variables* (London: Collins, 1984). Lionel reported the transaction to Leopold on November 24, 1875, in R Fam C 4/443. John Delane's reaction is in Dasent. That Nathaniel was not yet a legal partner at New Court is made apparent by his being cleared of charges of parliamentary conflict of interest in that he was acting for the sole surviving partner, his father. The market future of the shares is analyzed in Ferguson. The decline and death of Anthony is reported by Louisa in her letters and diary (see above). For the Russo-Turkish war and the Berlin Congress, see David Steele's *Lord Salisbury: A Political Biography* and S. Weintraub, *Disraeli*.

News of Charlotte's illness first appears in Leo's undated letters to his father, R Fam/5. Post-Berlin correspondence between Disraeli and Lionel, and also to Charlotte, is also in the R. Archive. Disraeli's nostalgic letter to Charlotte, January 13, 1879, is quoted from a copy in the Disraeli Project files (see below). Further post-Berlin details are in Fritz Stern, *Gold and Iron: Bismarck, Bleichröder, and the Building of the German Empire* (New York: Knopf, 1977). The espionage allegation to Lionel (by Disraeli) is transcribed from the Monypenny papers by M. G. Wiebe and in the Disraeli Project files (Queen's Univ., Kingston, Ontario).

Lionel's purchase sight unseen of the vast van Loon collection is detailed by Michael Hall in *The Rothschilds: Essays on the History of a European Family*, ed. Georg Heuberger (Sigmaringen, Germany: Thorbecke, 1994). The collection is now dispersed. Leo's letters to his father (R Fam) on Charlotte's illness are undated. Lady Emily Peel's note to the convalescing Charlotte, October 21, 1878, is in the R. Archive in Box 6, Letters from Friends and Family to Charlotte. Leopold's letters to his mother are in R Fam. Lionel's May 19, 1879, letter to Leo is his last on record to his children.

Letters to Natty on his father's death from Disraeli and from Bernal Osborne are in the R. Archive. Delane's commissioning an obituary even before Lionel was actually dead is in Dasent. The response to Disraeli from

Alfred and Leopold, on Alfred's letterhead, June 3, 1879, is printed in full in a Maggs auction catalogue on file in the Disraeli Project, furnished by M. G. Wiebe. A copy of Lionel's will is in the R. Archive.

EPILOGUE   *Duet for One, 1879–1884*

Disraeli's obviously misdated letter to "Nattie" is 000/848 in the R. Archive. The document between the representatives of the family houses drawn up to admit Nathaniel, Alfred, and Leopold to full partnerships on the death of their father was signed in Paris, Frankfurt, London, and Vienna between September 24, 1879, and October 3, 1879, presumably conveyed by courier for signatures. A copy is in the R. Archive. For further background on *Endymion*, see S. Weintraub, *Disraeli*, where the involvement of the Rothschild sons in Disraeli's burial is also described. Leopold's wedding to Marie Perugia was most fully reported in the *Jewish Chronicle* and the *Illustrated London News*. Caroline Belmont's visit to Charlotte, with her report to her husband quoted, is in David Black, *The King of Fifth Avenue: The Fortunes of August Belmont* (New York: Dial Press, 1981). Family letters, including Charlotte's late letters, are in R Fam C. Constance Battersea's visit to Charlotte's deathbed is described from her diary in Cohen (above). The obsequies for Charlotte were most fully reported in the *Jewish Chronicle*, but were also covered by the general London press.

ACKNOWLEDGMENTS

Many individuals on both sides of the Atlantic have assisted me in my research over two decades. My gratitude goes especially to Lucy Addington, Melanie Aspey, Daniel Bernstein, Jonathan Brown, Pamela Clark, Anthony Curtis, Sarah Curtis, Richard Davis, Melanie Doebler, Phyllis Dolich, Beate Engel-Doyle, Oliver Everett, Niall Ferguson, Christopher Gayer, Victor Gray, Helen Gummer, Alan Hanley-Browne, Eileen Hanley-Browne, Jürgen Kamm, Sylvia Kelly, Rolf Lessenich, Grant McIntyre, George Mauner, Marianne Mauner, Jürgen Miethke, Bruce Nichols, Jenny O'Keefe, Susan Reighard, Jacob Lord Rothschild, Barbara Ryan, Willa Silverman, Sandra Stelts, Gerhard Strasser, Stefan Tertünte, Daniel Walden, Rodelle Weintraub, M. G. Wiebe, Richard E. Winslow III, Katharine Young, Vickie Ziegler, and Peter Zimmerman.

INDEX

ABOUT THE AUTHOR

STANLEY WEINTRAUB is Evan Pugh Professor Emeritus of Arts and Humanities at the Pennsylvania State University and the author of numerous histories and biographies, including *Victoria, Uncrowned King: The Life of Prince Albert, Edward the Caresser,* and *Silent Night: The Story of the World War I Christmas Truce*. Weintraub is a book reviewer for *The New York Times, The Wall Street Journal,* and *The Washington Post*. He lives in Boalsburg, Pennsylvania.